THE NEW NEAPOLITAN CINEMA

THE NEW
NEAPOLITAN CINEMA

Alex Marlow-Mann

EDINBURGH UNIVERSITY PRESS

© Alex Marlow-Mann, 2011, 2012

Edinburgh University Press Ltd
22 George Square, Edinburgh EH8 9LF

First published in hardback by Edinburgh University Press 2011

www.euppublishing.com

Typeset in 10/12.5 Adobe Sabon
by Servis Filmsetting Ltd, Stockport, Cheshire, and
printed and bound in Great Britain by
CPI Group (UK) Ltd, Croydon, CR0 4YY

A CIP record for this book is available from the British Library

ISBN 978 0 7486 4066 9 (hardback)
ISBN 978 0 7486 6877 9 (paperback)

The right of Alex Marlow-Mann
to be identified as author of this work
has been asserted in accordance with
the Copyright, Designs and Patents Act 1988.

CONTENTS

ILLUSTRATIONS

ACKNOWLEDGEMENTS

I would like to thank all those involved in Neapolitan cinema who took time out to meet with me and discuss their work: Antonio Capuano, Antonietta De Lillo, Vincenzo Di Marino (Artimagiche), Giogiò Franchini, Roberto Gambacorta, Nicola Giuliano (Indigo Film), Stefano Incerti, Giorgio Magliulo, Pasquale Marrazzo, Enzo Moscato, Rino Piccolo (former President of the Campania Film Commission) and Romolo Sticchi. Thanks also go to Antonietta De Lillo and Giogiò Franchini for allowing me to visit the post-production of *Il resto di niente* and to Mario Martone and Giorgio Magliulo for allowing me on to the set of *L'odore del sangue*.

For their help in obtaining commercially unavailable films I would like to thank Artimagiche, A.S.P., Antonietta De Lillo, Giogiò Franchini, Julian Grainger, Stefano Incerti, Kubla Khan, Pasquale Marrazzo, Vincenzo Terracciano, Christopher Wagstaff and Mary Wood. I would also like to acknowledge the assistance and advice in a variety of capacities of Francesco Napolitano and Francesco Tartaglia of the Mediateca Santa Sofia in Naples, Sean Delaney and the staff of the BFI National Library, Teatri Uniti, Paola Accampa of the Premio Massimo Troisi, Daniela La Penna (University of Reading), Pasquale Iaccio (Università degli Studi di Napoli Federico II), Dario Minutolo (Associazione Italiana per le Ricerche di Storia del Cinema), Richard Dyer (King's College London), Sergio Angelini, Sergio Rigoletto and Alberto Castellano. Thanks for assistance with the maps go to Emma Butler and for their hospitality in Naples to Claire Jenkins and Giorgio D'Agostino.

This book is based on a PhD thesis conducted with a grant from the Arts and

Humanities Research Council, to whom I would like to express my gratitude. Thanks also to my colleagues at the University of Reading Italian department and above all to my supervisor, Christopher Wagstaff, for his encouragement and ever-insightful comments. A final word of thanks to my parents for their support – both moral and financial – throughout this project.

NOTE

When subject to detailed discussion, films of the New Neapolitan Cinema are referred to by the original Italian title, together with date of production, director and the most common English title (or a literal translation in square brackets where no such title exists). Elsewhere they are referred to solely by the original Italian title and the reader is invited to refer to the filmography on pp. 217–20 for further information. The first reference to any other film includes date of production, director and the most common English-language title, if one exists. All subsequent references are then under the original title.

All translations of Italian quotations are by the author.

GLOSSARY

Basso: One-room ground floor apartments that open on to the street, which are typical of the historic centre of Naples.

Camorra: The Neapolitan Mafia.

Camorrista: A member of the *camorra*.

Delitto d'onore: Often rendered as 'crime of passion', this expression literally translates as 'crime of honour'. It is an action that, due to an antiquated article in Italian law, was treated with considerable leniency by the Italian courts. The relative social acceptability of such an action in Southern Italian society is parodied in *Divorzio all'italiana/Divorce, Italian Style* (1961, Pietro Germi).

Figlio di nessuno: An orphan.

Guappo: A 'man of honour' and the hero of the *sceneggiata* (see p. 43).

Isso, Essa e 'o malamente: Literally 'Him, Her and the Bad-guy', this phrase indicates the romantic triangle underpinning the classic narrative of the *sceneggiata* (see p. 43).

Malafemmena: An immoral or promiscuous woman.

Muschillo: Young child employed by the *camorra* as a drug dealer or assassin because of the relative impunity of minors.

Napoletanità: 'Neapolitanness'.

Sceneggiata: A peculiarly Neapolitan form of popular musical theatre (see pp. 43–4).

Scugnizzo: Street-urchin.

TRADITIONS IN WORLD CINEMA

General editors: **Linda Badley and R. Barton Palmer**
Founding editor: **Steven Jay Schneider**

Traditions in World Cinema is a series of textbooks and monographs devoted to the analysis of currently popular and previously underexamined or under-valued film movements from around the globe. Also intended for general inter-est readers, the textbooks in this series offer undergraduate- and graduate-level film students accessible and comprehensive introductions to diverse traditions in world cinema. The monographs open up for advanced academic study more specialised groups of films, including those that require theoretically oriented approaches. Both textbooks and monographs provide thorough examinations of the industrial, cultural, and socio-historical conditions of production and reception.

The flagship textbook for the series includes chapters by noted scholars on traditions of acknowledged importance (the French New Wave, German Expressionism), recent and emergent traditions (New Iranian, post-Cinema Novo), and those whose rightful claim to recognition has yet to be established (the Israeli persecution film, global found footage cinema). Other volumes concentrate on individual national, regional or global cinema traditions. As the introductory chapter to each volume makes clear, the films under discussion form a coherent group on the basis of substantive and relatively transparent, if not always obvious, commonalities. These commonalities may be formal, sty-listic or thematic, and the groupings may, although they need not, be popularly identified as genres, cycles or movements (Japanese horror, Chinese martial arts cinema, Italian Neorealism). Indeed, in cases in which a group of films is not already commonly identified as a tradition, one purpose of the volume is to establish its claim to importance and make it visible (East Central European Magical Realist cinema, Palestinian cinema).

Textbooks and monographs include:

- an introduction that clarifies the rationale for the grouping of films under examination
- a concise history of the regional, national or transnational cinema in question
- a summary of previous published work on the tradition
- contextual analysis of industrial, cultural and socio-historical conditions of production and reception
- textual analysis of specific and notable films, with clear and judicious application of relevant film theoretical approaches
- bibliography(-ies)/filmography(-ies).

Monographs may additionally include:

- discussion of the dynamics of cross-cultural exchange in light of current research and thinking about cultural imperialism and globalisation, as well as issues of regional/national cinema or political/aesthetic movements (such as new waves, postmodernism or identity politics)
- interview(s) with key filmmakers working within the tradition.

INTRODUCTION

In the early 1990s three Neapolitans made their directorial debut in quick succession. Antonio Capuano's *Vito e gli altri* (1991), a highly stylised account of a street-kid's initiation into a life of crime, was closely followed by Mario Martone's *Morte di un matematico napoletano* (1992), an account of the last seven days in the life of Neapolitan mathematician Renato Caccioppoli, and Pappi Corsicato's *Libera* (1993), a comic anthology revolving around issues of gender and sexuality. All three films were independently produced, were set in Naples and differed greatly in both subject matter and style from the Neapolitan films of previous decades, whether it be the musical-melodramas starring Mario Merola and Nino D'Angelo (late examples of the 'Neapolitan Formula'), the comic plays on cultural stereotypes directed by Lina Wertmüller and Nanni Loy, or the sentimental comedies of Massimo Troisi. Critics immediately began to talk about the emergence of a new Neapolitan 'school' of filmmaking, which they soon associated with the so-called 'Neapolitan renaissance' initiated by the election of a left-wing city council under Mayor Antonio Bassolino in 1993. In 1997 these three filmmakers collaborated with two other recent Neapolitan debutants, Stefano Incerti and Antonietta De Lillo, on a five-part portmanteau film, *I vesuviani*, whose concept and title appeared to consolidate the idea of an emerging Neapolitan school. These filmmakers were subsequently joined by a steadily growing number of first-time Neapolitan directors, many of whom had worked on the earlier films in some capacity: Nina Di Majo, Vincenzo Marra, Paolo Sorrentino, Nicola De Rinaldo, Vincenzo Terracciano, Maurizio Fiume, Valia Santella, Giuseppe Gaudino, Laura Angiulli, Carla Apuzzo, Sandro Dionisio, Pasquale Marrazzo, Francesco Patierno, Giuseppe Rocca and Nino Russo. The group was also joined by a number of non-Neapolitan directors based in Rome who, given the renewed prominence of Naples on the cinematic screen, decided to set films there: Fabio Conversi, Pablo Dammicco, Tonino De Bernardi, Matteo Garrone, Aurelio Grimaldi, Wilma Labate, Paolo Genovese and Luca Miniero. This proliferation of filmmaking in the city of Naples was partly the result of the creation of new production companies such as Megaris, established in Naples in 1992 by Antonietta De Lillo and Giorgio Magliulo (who would go on to produce *I vesuviani*) in order to take advantage of Government incentives favouring the development of industry in the South. Megaris was one of the first companies in Italy to equip with Avid technology and soon became a significant base for post-production in the city. Even more important was Teatri Uniti, the theatrical collective Martone had co-founded in 1987. When Teatri Uniti diversified into film production in 1992, it brought with it a ready-made network of established Neapolitan actors and technicians who would go on to work on most of the films made in the city.

The proliferation of Neapolitan films since 1990 has meant that the idea of a 'New Neapolitan Cinema' (hereafter abbreviated to NNC) has become an increasingly widely used concept in writings on Italian cinema.[1] Furthermore, earlier Neapolitan cinema, which had for so long been neglected or denigrated by film critics, historians and scholars, was reappraised through a series of retrospectives and book-length studies. However, following the critical failure of *I vesuviani* at the Venice Film Festival, several critics began to question the validity of the idea of a new Neapolitan 'school' of filmmaking, beginning with Alberto Castellano's provocative essay in the festival catalogue, which asks whether the idea of a 'Neapolitan new wave' is merely the product of a 'new rhetoric' introduced by the Bassolino-led Neapolitan renaissance (Castellano 1997a). Many of the filmmakers involved also tried to distance themselves from the concept and instead emphasise their authorial individuality.

> Corsicato: It's a lazy definition, applied by others. I don't feel like I belong to a school. I am bound by my respect for these people, but there is no such thing as a school. (Addonizio et al. 1997: 39)
> Capuano: It's a definition that doesn't concern me, or Martone, or Corsicato, but only whoever said it. Are their common traits between our films? In short, yes and no. (Armiero 1996: 34)
> De Lillo: Our ability to work together stems from our diversity. Each of us has an individual and instantly recognisable gaze and way of making films. (Addonizio et al. 1997: 60)

Incerti: This label of 'Neapolitan director' persists as if it were a licence . . . and ultimately it is restrictive because it lumps together individuals who are very different from one another. (Author's interview, Rome, 17 June 2003)

Martone: We weren't able to convey the idea that Naples is the city in which we work and that's all . . . For the media, Naples is the theme of our work . . . It is all too easy to label us and get away with a comment about the new Naples when discussing our work. (Martone 2004: 130)

Despite their objections to the idea of a Neapolitan 'school', the directors also repeatedly mention their personal and working relationships, the common pool of actors and technicians, and the shared production context. Moreover, several have also emphasised the original depiction of the city of Naples common to their films:

Corsicato: We have in common the fact that we all make a freer cinema, away from Rome, which refuses the commonplaces on Naples. (Addonizio et al. 1997: 39)

Incerti: I realise that from the outside it is easy to identify points in common, such as our autonomy, the use of a common troupe of technicians, art directors and cinematographers, and a fairly original vision of the city. (Author's interview, Rome, 17 June 2003)

Capuano: It was a Naples never seen before; a Naples seen with a new eye. This was the novelty of our films . . . and it was this new gaze that created this idea, this label, which is useful to critics who feel the need to categorise. (Author's interview, Naples, 14 June 2003)

Despite a discomfort with the notion of a Neapolitan school, which can probably be attributed to an understandable desire to assert their individuality and artistic autonomy, these statements suggest that there may still be something distinctive and new about recent Neapolitan cinema and therefore that it may be fertile ground for further investigation. The persistence of critical debate about the validity of the concept arguably stems from the failure to answer a series of fundamental questions. For example, what does one mean when one describes a film as 'Neapolitan' and is the term really applicable to all the films to which it has been attached? In what ways can recent Neapolitan films be considered 'new' and what is their relationship to earlier filmmaking in the city? What do these filmmakers really have in common beyond merely producing and setting their films in Naples? What constitutes this 'new gaze' of which Capuano speaks? Providing an answer to these questions, and thus resolving whether or not it is legitimate to talk about a New Neapolitan Cinema, will be the primary goal of this book.

THE CONCEPT OF REGIONAL CINEMA

Let us begin to address these questions by considering what it means to talk about a regional cinema and by making reference to the more established and theoretically grounded concept of national cinema. National cinema must be understood as both an industrial and a critical-historical concept, and it first became relevant in the mid-1910s when it was used as a tool to differentiate films from Hollywood product, which was rapidly becoming dominant in international film markets. However, since the Second World War, European cinema in particular has, under pressure from Hollywood competition, frequently relied on international co-productions in order to spread the cost of financing and guarantee wider international distribution, and this has complicated the definition of national cinema. Should, for example, *The Last Emperor* (1987, Bernardo Bertolucci) be considered a British film (on account of its producer and language), an Italian film (on account of its director and many of its key creative personnel) or a Chinese film (on account of its setting and themes)? To deal with this problem the film industry has developed complex but clearly defined laws governing the assignation of nationality since in many countries (including Italy) tax breaks, financial incentives and exhibition quotas operate to protect domestic films from the economic dominance of Hollywood product. Several factors are taken into account when assigning nationality to a film:

1. Production context: what is the origin of the production company (or companies) and finance behind the film's production?
2. Personnel: what proportion of the actors and crew belong to a given nationality?
3. Location: where was the film shot?
4. Language: what language is the film in?

On the basis of these criteria, the industry assigns nationality to a film. In the case of co-productions, the origin of the company that has the greatest financial input is generally taken to be the primary country of origin.[2] While this definition may be adequate for legal matters, it is hardly sufficient for a historical-critical analysis that seeks to identify a body of films that share particular characteristics and can be interpreted as an expression of national culture. Such studies take into account a film's content: the location where it is set (as opposed to shot), the nationality of its characters, and the presence of themes, iconography and cultural references specific to the nation in question. Peter Bondanella's *Italian Cinema from Neorealism to the Present* is one example of such a cultural approach to national cinema; it interprets individual films defined as Italian in relation both to other films similarly defined and to wider issues related to Italian national identity, society, culture, politics and history. This approach is as problematic as the industrial one, given that no nation can be considered culturally and socially homogenous; thus any study of national cinema must take into account internal divisions within that nation such as class, gender, race and region. For example, 'Canadian cinema' encompasses both Anglophone films, produced primarily in Ontario, and Francophone ones from Québec, despite the fact that their concerns and aesthetic are arguably very different. Similarly, assigning nationality to *Yadon ilaheyya/Divine Intervention* (2002, Elia Suleiman), which deals with Palestinians living within the State of Israel and is shot largely in Arabic, becomes a politically fraught question.[3] *Mean Streets* (1973, Martin Scorsese) focuses on a group of first-generation Italian-Americans in New York, whose lifestyle and culture is characterised as much by their Sicilian origins as by the American environment in which they now live. Thus while films like *The Last Emperor* stretch the notion of national cinema because their scope is so broad, these films stretch it because they are so specific.

Although the concept of transnational cinema has gained increasing prominence in academic circles in recent years in response to these problems,[4] the notion of regional cinema, which could prove equally useful, has not yet received the same attention. Like national cinema, regional cinema would need to be defined in both industrial and cultural terms. For example, New York is frequently seen as an alternative centre of film production to Hollywood and there is a historical reason for this, given that Hollywood emerged in the 1910s in opposition to New York, over which it soon became dominant. Since then, filmmaking in New York has usually taken place independently, far from the control of the major studios. In terms of a cultural analysis, films from New York are often perceived as thematically and stylistically distinct from Hollywood cinema. Take, for example, the work of John Cassavetes, Martin Scorsese and Abel Ferrara; although these are all highly individual directors with a strong auteur sensibility, the presence of thematic and stylistic parallels between their New York-based work clearly distinguishes them from products of the Hollywood studio system. Thus commonly used terms like 'New York indie' identify a body of films as distinct in terms of both their mode of production and their textual strategies.

The case of regional cinema is even more complex than that of national cinema, however: firstly, because all cinema is, in a sense, regional, in that all films have to be made somewhere. Nevertheless most countries have one area in which the majority of film production takes place and which comes to be associated with national cinema output (Los Angeles in the case of America; Rome in the case of Italy). A regional cinema would therefore have to be understood as filmmaking taking place beyond the 'cinematic capital'. Secondly, while national cinema is usually defined in opposition to an other (typically a dominant other such as Hollywood), regional cinema must be defined primarily in opposition not to other regional cinemas but to the national cinema of which it is itself also a part. This not only makes definition more difficult, but also means that it is not always and automatically useful to consider a film made outside the capital as an expression of regional, rather than national cinema. I would propose that there are three criteria that can help to establish the applicability and utility of the notion of regional cinema:

1. The national culture is, for historical, cultural or political reasons, particularly fragmented, making it difficult to identify universal national traits.
2. Alternatively, markedly different regional traditions contrast with a distinct and dominant national culture.
3. The national cinema is inextricably associated with filmmaking in one place, but film production also regularly takes place in other locations in a largely autonomous fashion.

On the basis of these criteria, Naples constitutes a particularly interesting case study for an investigation of regional cinema:

1. Italy remains a particularly fragmented country, both culturally and politically, because it was not unified until the Risorgimento in the latter part of the nineteenth century and because the act of unification failed to eradicate internal differences within the country; in fact, it exacerbated them, giving rise to the '*questione meridionale*', or 'Southern Question'. Language also differs greatly from region to region, and these differences have only recently begun to be eroded by more widespread education and the advent of mass communication – in particular, television. If one examines the stereotypes associated with Italian national identity, one finds that many of them are actually regional traits, and thus the creation of a national identity becomes problematic. Italians tend to identify themselves first and foremost as Neapolitan, Roman, Florentine or whatever, and only subsequently as Italian.
2. Before the Risorgimento, Naples was a centre of political and economic power, the capital of the Kingdom of the Two Sicilies and home to a monarchy. Since Unification, its significance has declined, although it remains the most important urban centre of the South. Naples has a long artistic tradition, particularly in theatre and music, which differs markedly from equivalent national forms. Tourism has always been important to Naples and has been largely responsible for maintaining a strong and readily identifiable Neapolitan identity at both national and international level.

3. Filmmaking began in Italy at regional level (in particular in Turin, Naples, Milan and Rome) but, after the advent of Fascism and the conversion to sound, the majority of the industry's resources and production capabilities were centralised at Cinecittà in Rome in imitation of the German model. Since the Second World War, production has primarily been concentrated in Rome, but has also emerged at various times in other parts of the country, most notably in Naples.

It is now necessary to define more systematically what we mean by 'Neapolitan cinema'. Firstly, and most simply, we need to define what we mean by Naples in geographic terms. Naples is a city that has expanded enormously over the past century and the Province of Naples now covers a far wider area than the city's limits. Furthermore, because it is the regional capital, much of Campania is often closely identified with Naples. In terms of the cinema, most of the film production in the area tends to be concentrated in the city of Naples, although the surrounding area (in particular Pompeii, the Amalfi coast and the islands of Capri, Ischia and Procida) has frequently been used for location shooting by Neapolitan, national and international productions. For this reason this study will focus on filmmaking within the Province of Naples as a whole, and not simply the city itself.[5] Secondly, we need to define carefully what we mean by a 'Neapolitan cinema'. Neapolitan cinema should, like national cinema, be seen as a construction on the part of the film industry, filmmakers and audiences, as well as the critical and discursive practices surrounding the films. Broadly speaking, it can be defined as the point of intersection between the output of a local film industry and the representation of regional identity in film. As a workable solution I therefore propose using a two-tier definition of Neapolitan cinema:

1. films made by Neapolitan production companies and/or utilising a predominantly Neapolitan cast and crew
2. films set primarily in Naples and/or dealing primarily with Naples and Neapolitans.

Criterion 1 alone is not sufficient; otherwise the spaghetti western *Ringo, il volto della vendetta/Ringo: Face of Vengeance* (1966, Mario Caiano) would constitute an example of Neapolitan cinema, while a film as crucial to the cinematic image of Naples as *L'oro di Napoli/The Gold of Naples* (1954, Vittorio De Sica) would not. Equally, relying solely on criterion 2 would mean including titles like the Hollywood-produced *It Started in Naples* (1960, Melvin Shavelson). Instead, this analysis will concern itself with films that fulfil both of these criteria and will pay close attention to the shifting construction of a Neapolitan cinema over time.

THE FUNCTION OF REGIONAL CINEMA

A number of industrial factors help explain why filmmaking may take place beyond the cinematic capital. The production of a film brings numerous benefits to the region in which it is shot; it generates business for local firms, brings wealth to the economy, provides jobs and raises the region's profile, thus favouring future investment and tourism. For this reason film commissions have been set up in many countries (including Italy, in all the major regions), with the aim of attracting film production to individual regions. Filmmakers themselves may decide to produce their films independently at regional level rather than through the more established channels of the national film industry. This can be the result of a conscious choice (gaining freedom from the restraints imposed by the industry or working in the more familiar and congenial environment in which they live) or of a necessity (a lack of opportunities within the national industry). The recent development of cheaper, higher-quality, domestic and professional video equipment and digital post-production has obviously facilitated such a process. A third explanation lies in the distribution and exhibition sector. In addition to national film distributors, there are also a number of sub-distributors, often referred to as regional independents, which exploit their closer ties with local exhibitors to release films that would never find space in national cinema chains in one or two local cinemas. Such companies deal solely with low-budget or minority films, whose rights inevitably cost less, and often favour films that appeal particularly to local audiences. The reasons behind the existence of a regional cinema must, therefore, be sought in a combination of these factors.

In order to understand fully the function served by regional cinema, it is also important to consider its relationship to the national cinema. Steve McIntyre describes this relationship in terms of a 'core' and 'peripheral' industry (McIntyre 1985). Similarly, Carole Sklan adopts Foucault's idea of the Panopticon to explain the way in which regional cultures are defined and co-opted by the national cinema. She argues that:

1. The centre defines what is 'excellent', 'innovative', 'competent', 'relevant', 'commercially appealing' etc.
2. Its power requires the internalization of these beliefs by those in the peripheries, who seek to ape these values and preferences.
3. The centre then under-develops the peripheries by siphoning off the 'productive' possibilities that emerge there, claiming them as their own, as evidence of their correctness. They can then point to what has been denied, excluded, devalued and suppressed in the periphery and say 'They are just not good enough, they haven't got what it takes' (Sklan 1996: 237).

Sklan's ideas are only partially applicable to Neapolitan cinema. In later chapters I will suggest that, rather than 'internalising the beliefs' and 'aping the values and preferences' of the centre, Neapolitan cinema has developed in opposition to those beliefs, values and preferences. Nevertheless it is undoubtedly true that in the past the centre has defined what is 'excellent, innovative, competent, relevant, and commercially appealing' and has also 'siphoned off the productive possibilities of Neapolitan cinema'.[6] Despite the useful ideas proposed by these two writers, I nevertheless think it is also possible to offer a more positive interpretation of the way in which regional cinema functions in relation to national cinema. Andrew Higson notes that, 'to identify a national cinema is first of all to specify a coherence and a unity' (Higson 1989: 37). However, regional cinema operates in opposition to this process of homogenisation by representing and addressing a part of the population that is, or feels itself to be, excluded from the national cinema. There is a clear parallel here with those cinemas that address minority social groups traditionally excluded from mainstream film culture such as black or gay/lesbian cinema. Such a function undoubtedly becomes crucial for regions that have a distinct sense of cultural identity and which are under-represented or misrepresented by the national cinema. This is unquestionably the case with Neapolitan cinema in the silent era and immediate post-war period and, arguably, also of the NNC.

At this point it is worth making a further distinction between regional films aimed solely or primarily at local audiences and regional films addressed to national or international audiences. In this regard we should recall that post-war Neapolitan cinema developed in parallel with Neorealism, a product of the Rome-based industry that also made use of location shooting and re-engaged with the complex geographical realities of Italian society that had been suppressed under Fascism. Giovanni Scarfò discusses the way in which this process constituted a drive towards the creation of a 'national-popular cinema' in the Gramscian sense of the term (see Scarfò 1999: especially 35–42). However, while De Sica's *L'oro di Napoli* was a big-budget national production aimed at national and international cinema audiences, Armando Fizzarotti's *Malaspina* (1947) was a low-budget, locally produced film aimed at the second- and third-run cinemas of Naples and the South. The two films differ greatly in subject matter, narrative technique and style, and this fact betrays not only the different production context from which they emerge but also the extent to which they set their sights on fundamentally different markets. One could thus hypothesise that a Neapolitan film aimed predominantly at a Neapolitan or Southern Italian audience would be likely to establish a different kind of address with its spectators than one aimed at a national or international audience; while the former would be exclusive in its address, the latter would be inclusive. Thus one might expect to find more esoteric, deeply rooted cultural traits in the former and a greater reliance on stereotype and the superficial trappings of Neapolitan culture in the latter. Whereas locally distributed regional cinema speaks to a minority audience of their own concerns, regional cinema distributed nationally or internationally can serve the function of promoting that culture, of educating people from elsewhere about the region. Certainly Neapolitan cinema has also served this latter function, particularly in the early 1950s when Neapolitan cinema first achieved greater popularity at national level, and this can, perhaps, also be related to the promotion of Naples as a tourist destination that was so crucial to the policies of Mayor Achille Lauro during the period.[7] However, the dilution of cultural specificity that often characterises those films addressed to a wider audience frequently entails a reliance on simplistic, inaccurate or stereotypical representations of the culture, characteristics to which regional films directed solely at local audiences can be seen as a response.[8]

Regionalism constitutes a third dimension to the dichotomy of the national and the international, which has been the source of great tension throughout the history of cinema. If cinema was initially conceived of as an international art form, it very soon became problematically so; the rise of Hollywood in the mid-1910s and the problems of comprehension caused by the development of synchronised sound in the late 1920s introduced issues that still affect cinema today. While there is much debate in Europe about the need to produce an internationally viable cinema (given the limited size of the potential domestic audience in most countries), equally pressing is the need to create a cinema that is successful at home (given the dominance of Hollywood over national cinema in most European countries). Drawing on the specificity offered by films with a strong emphasis on regional culture has been one strategy to achieve this, usually by combining universal themes that might appeal to a national audience with specific local trappings (for example, in the films of Italian regional comics of the 1990s like Leonardo Pieraccioni). Furthermore, even those films that have achieved international success often have strong regional ties in order to exploit the kind of cultural exoticism favoured by the arthouse circuit (for example, *Nuovo Cinema Paradiso*, 1988, Giuseppe Tornatore; *Il postino*, 1994, Michael Radford; or *Respiro*, 2002, Emanuele Crialese).

Clearly this strategy is very different from that of regional cinema directed primarily at local audiences, which gives voice to and addresses a minority group that would not otherwise be addressed by the national film culture. Such a process constitutes both a cultural and a political act; it fractures the image of unity sought by national cinema, creates a more complex, less unilateral image of national traits, and engenders a pluralistic culture. Thus McIntyre argues that within the context of nationalist political agendas, 'peripheral film cultures have an urgent and inescapable role to play in the construction and circulation of progressive and relevant discourses of national identity'

(McIntyre 1985: 66). This process assumes even greater significance when viewed from the perspective of current debates about globalisation. If globalisation is to be seen as a process of cultural homogenisation and the erosion of national or local identity, then regional cinema offers a significant corrective to this process. In this light, the renewed emphasis on regionalism in films like *Tano da morire* (1997, Roberta Torre) or *Sangue vivo* (2000, Edoardo Winspeare) can be seen as a reaction to the lack of cultural specificity in films like *La leggenda del pianista sull'oceano/The Legend of 1900* (1998, Giuseppe Tornatore) or *Io ballo da sola/Stealing Beauty* (1996, Bernardo Bertolucci).[9] A useful way of understanding this process is through the term 'glocalisation', coined by the sociologist Roland Robertson (Robertson 1995). Whereas earlier theories of globalisation stressed the way in which local traditions were being destroyed – as in the classic idea of 'the McDonaldisation of society' (Ritzer 2000) – according to Robertson, a renewed emphasis on the local is actually a key part of globalisation. On the one hand multinational companies market their products differently to specific local markets, while on the other locally produced goods are marketed globally (for example, the ethnic jewellery, clothes and ornaments sold in 'alternative' shops throughout the Western world).

METHODOLOGY

This book will seek to establish whether or not a 'new Neapolitan cinema' exists. It will propose answers to the following questions: is there a local production industry in Naples? Do the Neapolitan films produced in recent years have thematic and stylistic commonalities? Are these films distinct from traditional Neapolitan cinema? The principle subject of this book, then, will be the construction of a 'Neapolitan cinema' and the ways in which the characteristics of this construction have changed since 1990.[10] Chapter 1 will place Neapolitan cinema in its industrial context and consider how economic and institutional changes have influenced the evolution of Neapolitan cinema. This chapter is concerned with the 'industrial' approach to the subject of Neapolitan cinema, while later chapters adopt the 'cultural' approach. Using the definition of Neapolitan cinema provided above, Chapter 2 will argue that at certain key moments a distinct body of Neapolitan films with a shared generic identity and common thematic and stylistic traits emerged, and that these films have come to be identified as a distinct 'genre' of Neapolitan filmmaking. It is possible to object that the ensuing focus on the 'Neapolitan Formula' results in a partial account of Neapolitan cinema that ignores the films of crucial figures like Totò, Eduardo De Filippo and Francesco Rosi. However, it is important to bear in mind that, in terms of their production context, the work of these filmmakers is primarily a product of the national film industry rather than of the Neapolitan one. Moreover, each of these filmmakers constitutes an anomalous and exceptional case, whereas what is at stake here is the construction of a regional cinematic culture *per se*. If, as will be suggested, the Neapolitan Formula (hereafter abbreviated to NF) constitutes the primary cinematic expression of Neapolitan culture throughout much of the twentieth century, then it provides an important point of reference against which one can measure the NNC of the 1990s – and this will form the subject of the rest of this book. Broadly speaking, Chapter 3 will consider the shift in the representation of Neapolitan identity (or *napoletanità* – 'Neapolitanness') within the films of the NNC; Chapter 4 will examine the change in the narrative and stylistic models employed; and Chapter 5 will consider the politics of the NNC and its relationship to the Neapolitan renaissance of which, it is often claimed, it is one of the principal expressions. Finally, the conclusion will summarise the changes brought about by the NNC, explore its relationship to the evolving debates around 'Meridionalismo', and consider its legacy and impact on national film production.

NOTES

1. A wide variety of labels have been proposed to describe this concept (see Dario Minutolo's comments in Zagarrio 2000: 326). I would argue that the more neutral term 'New Neapolitan Cinema' is preferable to 'New Neapolitan School', which suggests a programmatic intent lacking from the work of these filmmakers, or more cumbersome neologisms like 'Partheneon Laboratory' (Pellegrini et al. 1996).
2. Current legislation governing the assignation of Italian nationality can be found in article 5 of the New Cinema Law (Law 153, 1 March 1994), a copy of which is available at www.anica.it.
3. It was disqualified from consideration for the 2003 Oscar for best film in a foreign language because the Academy refused to recognise the existence of the State of Palestine, its stated nationality. Under an industrial definition, the film is actually a French-German-Moroccan-Dutch-American co-production, but this fact clearly does not reflect the film's cultural origins.
4. See, for example, the recent journal from Intellect Press, *Transnational Cinemas*.
5. See the maps in Appendices 6 and 7 for a clearer idea of the area under consideration here.
6. The relationship between Neapolitan cinema and Italian national cinema has actually changed markedly in recent years and this constitutes one of the most significant differences between the NNC and earlier Neapolitan filmmaking, as will become clear in the chapters to come.
7. On the relationship between Lauro's policies and the Neapolitan cinema of the period, see Fusco 2006.
8. See, for example the films of Lina Wertmüller (*Pasqualino Settebellezze/Seven Beauties*, 1975 and *Io speriamo che me la cavo*, 1992) and Nanni Loy (*Mi manda Picone*, 1983 and *Pacco, doppio pacco e contropaccotto*, 1992).
9. Carole Sklan calls such films 'hybrid cinema' (Sklan 1996: 245). A more widely used moniker is 'Europuddings'.
10. This periodisation is convenient, but not completely arbitrary. The year 1990 marked the return to Naples of Antonietta De Lillo and Giorgio Magliulo (two

figures who would come to be inextricably associated with the NNC), and this was closely followed by the three debuts described at the start of this introduction. Two other factors which contributed to the expansion of the NNC followed soon after: the election of Bassolino in 1993 and the passing of the New Cinema Law in 1994.

1. NEAPOLITAN CINEMA AND THE ITALIAN FILM INDUSTRY

Films are not merely works of art or cultural artefacts, but commercial commodities produced within an industrial system ruled by Government legislation, financial constraints and market forces. Institutional and industrial factors dictate what kinds of film are made and what kinds of film are seen, so before we can begin to analyse Neapolitan films in stylistic or thematic terms, it is necessary to examine their place within the Italian film industry. This chapter has three basic aims. Firstly, it will contextualise the NNC within the broader history of Neapolitan production and examine some of the factors that have favoured filmmaking at regional level. Secondly, it will examine the mode of production employed by Neapolitan films in the 1990s and the role played by Government intervention and legislation. Thirdly, it will consider how Neapolitan films have been distributed and exhibited, paying particular attention to any regional disparities. In this way, this chapter will help establish whether or not it is legitimate to talk about a 'Neapolitan cinema'. Such a concept presupposes the existence of both a distinct film 'industry' in the region and/or a body of films aimed exclusively or primarily at Neapolitan audiences. This chapter will establish the validity of such claims.

THE HISTORY OF FILM PRODUCTION IN NAPLES

Conventional histories of Italian cinema describe an increase in film production from the beginning of the sound era until the early 1970s, followed by a sharp decline. They also describe a centralisation of production during the 1930s, in response to Fascist policy, which sought to create a national film industry based around Cinecittà, followed by a partial decentralisation during the Neorealist period when the studios were temporarily closed and the national industry was plunged into crisis as a consequence of the Second World War. Both of these trends are borne out by Appendix 1, which shows the locations of production companies in Italy over time. The decrease in regional production over the subsequent two and a half decades evident in Appendix 1 probably results from the increased standardisation of the production process, when studios like Cinecittà became a veritable factory line of film production. The last two decades reverse this trend, probably because once again the industrial crisis drove producers to set up companies wherever and however they could. Another cause might be the development of new technologies, which freed many filmmakers from the need to follow the traditional route of a course at the Centro Sperimentale di Cinematografia (CSC) or an apprenticeship as an assistant director and instead allowed them to begin production independently. In short, there are two moments when regional production became more significant, constituting over 20% of the total number of companies operating in Italy: the late 1940s/early 1950s and post-1990. The statistics for Naples more or less follow the same trends as regional production in general, with few companies operating during the Fascist era and a sudden resurgence after the war. The early 1950s register the highest number of companies in the city (11), and this is followed by a decades-long fluctuation of between 5 and 10 companies.[1] Let us now take a more detailed look at the evolution of production in the city and the reasons for these trends.

Film production began in Naples as early as (and arguably earlier than) the rest of Italy. The first fiction film was produced in 1905 by Roberto Troncone and over the next 20 years more than 50 production companies developed in the city, several of which also constructed their own film studios, producing in excess of 350 films.[2] Many of these companies were family-run operations, the best-known example being Dora Film,[3] but they nevertheless constituted a conspicuous presence within the Italian industry throughout the silent era. By the end of the 1920s the crisis affecting the national film industry worsened and production fell to its lowest ever levels. Although Neapolitan production continued right up until the beginning of the new decade, the number of films produced fell steadily from 37 films in 1920 to just four in 1929. None of the Neapolitan producers re-equipped for the transition to sound and by 1930 Neapolitan production had ceased and did not recommence until after the Second World War. The economic crisis besetting the industry as a whole and the transition to sound, with its inevitable problems for a dialect-based cinema, were not the primary cause of the collapse of the Neapolitan film industry, however. From its very inception the Fascist Government took a dim view of Neapolitan cinema, for its transgressive subject matter, the unflattering portrait it painted of Italian society and its use of dialect at a time when the regime was trying to construct a unified national culture. In the mid-1920s, Neapolitan cinema was subject to increasing censorship both in the removal of violent and sexual content and the Italianisation of intertitles. This tendency was formalised in 1928 by the following Government directive:

> Some films are unworthy of the natural beauty with which the city of Naples has been blessed. Scenes of certain Neapolitan environments which, even if they have not totally disappeared, are no longer character-istic of Neapolitan life only serve to offend the city's dignity. Therefore, in recognition of the new regime's opposition to regional autonomy and to the use of dialect, the censorship board hereby informs interested parties that such films will be denied a seal of approval and thus the possibility of release. We will no longer tolerate films featuring itinerant musicians, tramps, *scugnizzi*, dirty alleyways, rags and people devoted to 'sweet idle-ness'. Such films slander an industrious population which is working to raise the social and material quality of life that the regime has imparted. Furthermore, it should be stressed that such films are also lacking in any artistic merit. (Quoted in Bernardini and Martinelli 1986: 71)

The last films to be produced in Naples were Any Films' *Quann'ammore vo' filà!* and *Zappatore* in 1930, while the last Neapolitan film to be released was Miramar's *Fiocca la neve*, which had been shot in 1927 but, significantly, had been blocked by censorship until 1931. When the Fascist regime subsequently began investing in the cinema, the drive was towards centralisation and the creation of a national industry in Rome based around the studios of Cinecittà, which were inaugurated in 1933. The few films that took Naples as their setting and theme (Armando Fizzarotti's *Napoli verde-blu* in 1936 and Amleto Palermi's *Napoli d'altri tempi*, 1937, and *Napoli che non muore*, 1939) were shot in studios in Rome, produced by Rome-based companies and avoided the use of local actors and dialect.

Roberto Amoroso, a photojournalist who had served as a documentary film-maker during the war, was responsible for resurrecting Neapolitan production and re-launching the NF with *Malaspina* (1947), for which he hired genre veteran Armando Fizzarotti to direct.[4] He sold the film cheaply to exhibitors from Pozzuoli and it went on to become a huge success. As in the silent era, it was also sold to an American distributor who screened it to Italian-American audiences in New York. According to Amoroso it cost between 6 and 7 million Lira and grossed about 180, of which he saw very little (Migliaccio 1985: 55). He then founded Sud Film, which would produce ten films, predominantly Neapolitan melodramas, at the rate of one per year. When the NF dried up, Amoroso created Ramofilm and diversified into new genres. On the back of

Amoroso's success, Natale Montillo, a successful exhibitor from Castellamare di Stabia, turned to production with *Calamita d'oro* (1949).[5] He formed S.A.P. [Sant'Antonio Proteggimi!] Film, made four Neapolitan films and also tried his hand at directing and acting. Enzo Di Gianni, who had previously worked as a projectionist, theatrical impresario and writer of lyrics for Neapolitan songs, also turned to production with *Le due Madonne* (1949), which he co-directed with Giorgio Simonelli. In 1951 he founded Eva Film, for which he produced six films set in Naples, all starring his wife, the singer Eva Nova. In 1952 Antonio Ferrigno and his wife Rosalia Calabrese founded Aeffe Produzione Cinematografica, which was responsible for nine films, mostly within the NF, before Ferrigno's untimely death. Together with the Sicilian Fortunato Misiano's Rome-based Romana Film, these five producers were responsible for the post-war NF. Theirs were small, regional companies specialising in a particular type of film as long as the market supported it. The films they made were producer-centred; the director and crew were usually selected by the producer and the films they made all fitted into the mould typical of the company. Indeed, rather like the studio product of classical Hollywood, the credits of *Malaspina* describe it as, 'A film by Roberto Amoroso. Directed by Armando Fizzarotti.' Throughout this period Naples remained a significant centre for film production and these figures were flanked by a large number of small, short-lived companies under producers like Nazzareno Gallo, Giuseppe Lombardi and Carlo Caiano, which produced films not necessarily set in Naples.

By the end of the 1950s the NF had dried up and several of these producers returned to other activities, while others created new companies and diversified into new genres. Meanwhile, a new generation of Neapolitan companies, like Mario Caiano's Stella Film, Nike Cinematografica and Cinematografica Emmeci, participated in the proliferation of low-budget genre filmmaking that characterised Italian cinema in the 1960s. Throughout the 1970s there were no significant Neapolitan producers, only a handful of companies which produced one or two films each, mostly exploiting the vogue for stories of *camorra*, a fertile offshoot of the *poliziesco* initiated by the success of Umberto Lenzi's *Napoli violenta/Violent Naples* in 1976. Although short-lived, companies like Ci.Pa. (Cinematografia Partenopea; *Sgarro alla camorra*, 1973, Ettore Maria Fizzarotti), Europhilia (*Figlio mio, sono innocente*, 1978, Carlo Caiano), October 77 Films (*Napoli: i 5 della squadra speciale*, 1978, Mario Bianchi), Falco Films (*I guappi non si toccano*, 1979, Mario Bianchi) and M.D.V.Film (*Napoli, storia di amore e di vendetta*, 1979, Mario Bianchi) represented a significant return to the production of films set in Naples by Neapolitan companies, something entirely lacking in the 1960s. In the 1980s, Ninì Grassia founded two companies, Giada Cinematografica and Ninfea Cinematografica, which launched the film career of neomelodic singer Nino D'Angelo, who also went on to star in all six films produced by Francesco Calabrese's Gloria Cinematografica. The decade also saw the emergence of a number of figures who would later become associated with the NNC of the 1990s; however, the partnerships of both Antonietta De Lillo-Giorgio Magliulo and Salvatore Piscicelli-Carla Apuzzo based their production companies (An.Gio Film and Falco Film respectively) in Rome, even though they chose to shoot some of their films in Naples. In 1982 Falso Movimento, an independent theatrical collective formed in 1979, shot their production of *Tango glaciale* on video and presented it at the Venice Festival. Five years later they joined with Teatro dei Mutamenti and Teatro Studio di Caserta to become Teatri Uniti, which would eventually turn to feature film production in 1992.

Most of the production companies in recent years reflect two tendencies partially exhibited in the preceding two decades: firstly, they are mostly companies formed by directors in order to make their own films, and secondly, they are mostly ephemeral companies responsible for only one or two films. The most significant case is Teatri Uniti, an independent collective that has undoubtedly been the principal point of reference for Neapolitan production over the past two decades, not only because it has produced the most films but also because it has served as a training ground for future producers, directors and technicians. Here are just some of the people who received their formative experiences within Teatri Uniti and went on to work on numerous other films, both Neapolitan and not: Mario Martone, Stefano Incerti, Sandro Dionisio, Nina Di Majo, Valia Santella and Vincenzo Marra (direction); Angelo Curti, Nicola Giuliano, Giancarlo Muselli and Luigi Boscaino (production); Pasquale Mari, Cesare Accetta and Renaud Personnaz (cinematography); Jacopo Quadri (editing); Mario Iaquone, Daghi Rondanini and Silvia Moraes (sound); Metella Raboni (costume design). Furthermore, numerous actors of Teatri Uniti have appeared in other Neapolitan films. In fact, the cast of Teatri Uniti's first production, *Morte di un matematico napoletano*, contains virtually every actor who has made a significant contribution to the NNC: Carlo Cecchi, Renato Carpentieri, Anna Bonaiuto, Licia Maglietta, Toni Servillo, Roberto De Francesco, Andrea Renzi, Enzo Moscato, Antonino Iuorio and Tonino Taiuti. In fact, the only names missing are Iaia Forte, Peppe Lanzetta and Italo Celoro, all of whom feature in Martone's other Teatri Uniti productions. These lists are perhaps unsurprising given the group's origins as a theatrical collective and the fact that they have continued to work together on both stage and screen since their formation in 1987 (or since 1979 in the case of those belonging first to Falso Movimento). The existence of such a network of artistic and technical personnel is important, as producer Nicola Giuliano has emphasised:

> Working with the same group of people, who get on well together and who know each other's strengths and weaknesses . . . creates a protective

and harmonious working environment. . . . We created a network [of personnel] that understands the territory and this helps reduce production costs. (Author's interview, Naples, 3 July 2003)

The collective nature of Teatri Uniti's work provides the strongest argument that the NNC should be considered a distinct and coherent movement, as opposed to a group of individual filmmakers who just happen to be working in the same city. In the interests of establishing the nature and extent of this network, Appendix 8 provides a list of the key personnel of the NNC and details the films on which they worked.

In 1992 Antonietta De Lillo and Giorgio Magliulo abandoned the Rome-based An.Gio Film to take advantage of Government subsidies encouraging the development of enterprises in the South and formed Megaris. As a producer, Megaris's work has been limited to *I vesuviani*, the low-budget digital video feature *Non è giusto*, and a number of shorts, many directed by De Lillo. However, its work as a post-production facility has been significant, given that the lack of film studios, laboratories and post-production facilities has always been one of the primary limitations of film production in Naples.[6] Megaris was among the first Italian companies to be equipped with an Avid suite and it has supplied this resource, together with resident editor Giogiò Franchini, to numerous Neapolitan productions over the past decade (see Appendix 8). Unfortunately, the company closed down in 2003.[7] Nicola Giuliano's Indigo Film was created in 1994, immediately after he graduated from the CSC, although it did not actually begin production until 1998. Having worked in various production capacities for Martone, Capuano and De Lillo, Giuliano met Paolo Sorrentino on the set of *Il verificatore* and the two decided to make their debut together, producing and directing the 1998 short *L'amore non ha confini* and later the feature *L'uomo in più*. Since then Indigo Film has produced all of Sorrentino's subsequent features, as well as Capuano's *La guerra di Mario*. At first, Indigo Film operated out of Teatri Uniti; it now has its own offices in Rome and has begun producing films not set in Naples, including *La ragazza del lago/The Girl by the Lake* (2007, Andrea Molaioli) and *La doppia ora/The Double Hour* (2009, Giuseppe Capotondi). Also worth mentioning is Artimagiche, which since 1999 has made a number of lesser-known, low-budget Neapolitan films and shorts, sometimes in collaboration with its sister company Thule Film, and Figli del Bronx, an independent production company formed by Gaetano Di Vaio, which produced Carlo Luglio's second feature, *Sotto la stessa luna*, Abel Ferrara's docu-fiction *Napoli, Napoli, Napoli* (2009), and several documentaries and shorts. Figli del Bronx, which is named after Peppe Lanzetta's collection of short stories dealing with life in the Neapolitan periphery, began life as an independent collective promoting cultural activities as an engine for change in the Neapolitan periphery, and its film productions have maintained this focus on the difficult peripheral territories that have been such a recurrent feature of the films of the NNC.

Appendix 1 demonstrates that there has been more of a production 'industry' in Naples over the past two decades than at any point since the post-war years. Moreover, Teatri Uniti, Megaris, Artimagiche/Thule Film and Figli del Bronx are the first Neapolitan companies to specialise in films set in Naples and directed by Neapolitan filmmakers since the heyday of the NF. However, most of the recent companies have produced far fewer films (see Appendix 8) than Sud Film (10), Aeffe Produzione Cinematografica (9) or Eva Film (6) did in a shorter period of time. Nevertheless, the 1990s have seen a marked increase in the number of films set in the city, and numerous filmmakers have consistently chosen to work there. There are a number of reasons for this, some of which are cultural, and these will be explored in subsequent chapters; but there are also a number of industrial and institutional factors that have favoured such a resurgence in regional filmmaking.

Institutional Factors Affecting Regional Production: the Film Industry, Legislation and Mode of Production

The passing of Law 203 in May 1995 entailed a 'rearrangement of the functions pertaining to tourism, entertainment and sport', splitting the Ministry of Tourism and the Performing Arts, whose responsibilities included administration of the film industry, into six departments and transferring some of their activities from Rome to the regions. In practice this instigated a 'separation between political direction and administrative management' and a 'decentralisation of functions and structures', so that while general policy for the sector would continue to be decided at national level, many of its administrative functions would be delegated to the regions (Cardoni 1998). For example, the division of the Fondo Unico per lo Spettacolo meant that distribution of funds for the sector as a whole, including the various financial incentives to film production, would remain at national level, while support for local operations like film festivals, incentives to cultural activities and support for the exhibition sector, would be managed at regional level.[8] While this system does not directly encourage the development of regional film production, it does help to foster cinematic culture at a regional level, which may in turn feed back into the growth of regional filmmaking.

Another important influence on regional cinema has been the creation of film commissions – non-profit organisations devoted to attracting and supporting film production in individual regions with an eye to the cultural and economic benefits that they bring to the area.[9] In numerous countries such organisations have been in operation for many years; however, the launch of the Emilia-Romagna Film Commission in 1997 marked the first in Italy. Now there are twenty-seven film commissions, covering practically every region in Italy. Film commissions encourage producers to shoot in the region, help identify potential locations, co-ordinate local resources and put producers in contact with local technicians and equipment suppliers. They also offer support to film festivals and other activities connected to the sector. These services have undoubtedly encouraged the decentralisation of Italian cinema in recent years. In 1998 Rino Piccolo set up the Campania Film Commission, a private company not funded by either the region or the local city council, in Giugliano in Campania. Although it provided assistance for a number of Neapolitan productions, its work was above all with foreign productions shooting in the area, including *Star Wars Episode 1 – The Phantom Menace* (1999, George Lucas) and *The Talented Mr. Ripley* (1999, Anthony Minghella). Indeed, relations between the Campania Film Commission and Neapolitan producers do not appear to have been as healthy or productive as they might have been and Indigo Film's Nicola Giuliano complained about the lack of institutional support for production in the city:

> In Naples there isn't even a film office you can approach to ask how to shoot in a particular location or who to talk to. There are people in the city who have always dealt with the cinema and they can expedite matters for you, but there is no institutional point of reference. There is a film office in Rome, Turin and all the major Italian cities except Naples; yet it is one of the cinema's most important locations. (Author's interview, Naples, 3 July 2003)

In the late 1990s there were repeated calls for film commissions to play a more active role in stimulating production by offering direct financial support to producers who shoot in the region, as was already the case in France (see, for example, Martini and Morelli 1997: 260). As a result, since the early part of the new millennium many film commissions have offered regional or municipal finance to producers via specially designated 'film funds'. The Campania Film Commission soon closed and was replaced in 2004 by the Film Commission della Regione Campania, which is based next to Piazza del Gesù in the historic centre and, as its name suggests, is funded by the region. It has therefore been able to offer more direct financial and logistical support to film production in Campania than its predecessor.

While the restructuring of the Ministry of Tourism and the Performing Arts and the creation of film commissions undoubtedly had an impact on the resurgence of regional cinema in the 1990s, in order to understand fully the characteristics of the NNC we need to take a broader view of both the film industry and government legislation, and the changes these have undergone since Neapolitan cinema's last heyday in the post-war period. In the mid-1950s there were over 10 500 cinema screens in Italy and annual cinema attendances exceeded 819 million, accounting for 68% of Italian expenditure on leisure activities (Corsi 2001: 124, 125 and 127). Given that the exhibition sector was divided into first-, second- and third-run cinemas, films circulated in the theatrical market place for over 5 years. Producers were able to cover their costs through minimum guarantees from distributors and box-office revenue and they therefore spread financial risk over a number of films, using the income generated from previous films to help pay off loans and finance new productions. However, by the mid-1990s the number of cinemas had fallen to 4000 and cinema attendances were only 96.5 million, which accounted for a mere 12% of expenditure on leisure activities (Corsi 2001: 124, 125 and 127). The second- and third-run cinemas had gone, shortening a film's theatrical life to a maximum of 4–12 months (Cauli 1993). In 1990 a film could expect to recoup a mere 20% of its revenue from theatrical receipts, and it therefore became much more difficult for a company to offset the production of new films with revenue from past productions that it had in distribution. Instead, the sale of television rights constituted over 50% of a film's revenue, while other sources such as home video accounted for a further 25% (Corsi 2001: 152). For many films the theatrical release now constitutes little more than a launching pad to raise awareness and, hopefully, generate some positive criticism and the occasional festival prize. Contemporary producers thus attempt to balance a film's budget against potential revenue from a variety of outlets in order to minimise the financial risk before a film is even produced (see Martini and Morelli 1997: 262). The principle sources of finance include government loans and incentives, contributions from co-producers (including television), pre-sale of television rights, minimum guarantees from theatrical distributors, and sale of foreign distribution rights. Revenue from theatrical receipts arrives much later, and only if a film is commercially successful. This situation has created a two-tier system of film production. On the one hand there are large companies like Filmauro, the Cecchi Gori Group and Medusa, which is the film production arm of Silvio Berlusconi's Mediaset Group and thus, like the Hollywood majors, is part of a large corporation operating across the entertainment sector as a whole. On the other, the medium-sized companies based around entrepreneurial producers that proliferated in the 1950s have been replaced by smaller, more ephemeral companies often based around the director himself. These smaller companies are more concerned with obtaining State funding than with producing films with strong commercial potential. Thus 190 billion of the 287 billion Lira invested in the 116 films produced in 1991 came from State funding ('Considerazioni del Ministro Tognoli' 1991). Moreover, directors have assumed increased importance, as it is frequently they who must come up with a valid script and negotiate the bureaucracy in order to access State finance (Corsi 2001: 145). Fania

Petrocchi, citing Salvemini and Delmestri, provides a good description of this situation:

> According to one estimate, in 1995 . . . there were 95 production companies operating in Italy . . . each making on average less than one film per year, and thus presumably registering an annual turnover of under 3.5 billion Lira a year . . . Companies are often set up to produce a single film so as to reduce the risk that a commercial failure will jeopardise the producer's other assets. The sector is dominated by numerous small, independent companies, which act like protective cocoons for new directors. These companies are heavily reliant on State funding, television finance and occasionally foreign co-production deals, and they have little autonomy in choosing scripts or directors. (Repetto and Tagliabue 2000: 53–4)

Rather than a business enterprise, the production company is often an ephemeral structure designed to co-ordinate the financing of an individual film; it is now a function of the film, rather than vice versa. This shift from a producer-centred, market-driven cinema to a director-centred, subsidised one helps explain both the evolution of Neapolitan production companies described above and the shift in the kinds of film they have produced, which will be the subject of subsequent chapters.

Aware of the difficulties facing Italian cinema, the Italian Government has repeatedly attempted to support the industry. The first and last of the three significant reforms in post-war Italian cinema legislation came shortly after the start of the two moments in Neapolitan cinema with which we are concerned. Both the post-war NF and the NNC emerged at moments of industrial crisis and, as we have seen, can be understood partly as a response to the temporary vulnerability of the centralised, national film industry. However, the success of both movements was then influenced by the new legislative reforms that aimed to resolve these crises. Let us consider, then, the differences between these two pieces of legislation and the effect they had on the direction Neapolitan cinema was to take.

Following the end of the Second World War and the reintroduction of American films into the Italian market, the Italian Government passed the 'Andreotti Law' (Law 958, 29 December 1949), which introduced a series of measures designed to help revive the Italian film industry and protect it from Hollywood dominance. Firstly, a tax rebate equivalent to 13% of box-office receipts was awarded to Italian producers to help write off loans incurred during production or to reinvest in future projects. Secondly, a dubbing tax was levied against imported films and the resulting revenue was effectively reinvested in Italian production as a form of disguised subsidy. Thirdly, screen quotas were introduced, obliging exhibitors to show Italian films for at least 20 days per quarter. Finally, a tax rebate equivalent to 10% of gross ticket sales was awarded to exhibitors showing Italian films. The first two measures aimed to stimulate film production and develop a solid, sustainable production base, while the second two were intended to help Italian films find space in a market place awash with American product. The success of these measures can be seen from the fact that in the 5 years after the law was passed, production figures rose from 76 to 201 films per year while the market share enjoyed by Italian films more than doubled, rising from 18% to 39% while American cinema's share fell from 75% to 53% (Assessorato alla cultura del comune di Roma 1979: 389 and Sorlin 1996: 84–5).

In 1965 the Government replaced this law with the 'Corona Law' (Law 1213, 4 November 1965). While maintaining similar protectionist measures for national production as a whole, article 1 of this law also explicitly defined the cinema as 'a cultural and artistic product'. Thus financial prizes were now awarded to films of quality and to screenplays of notable artistic merit. Moreover, article 28 allowed the State to finance up to 30% of the cost of films with cultural or artistic aspirations in which the cast and crew participated in the cost of production. Although this was intended as a loan, it was an unsecured one and was rarely recovered since few article 28 films ever turned a profit. Although initially envisaged as a special resource for filmmakers at the start of their career who were engaged in particularly innovative work, over the next two decades article 28 became, along with television, the main source of finance for Italian cinema.

The Corona Law remained in place with only minor amendments until it was replaced by the 'New Cinema Law' (Law 153, 1 March 1994), which maintained the aims of the previous law but also added the goal of freeing producers from the dependence on television finance that had characterised Italian production since the mid-1970s. In reality the new law did little more than 'make a few corrections to the existing system' (Zagarrio 2000: 305). The most significant change was contained in article 8, which modified the old article 28 by introducing two categories of 'films in the national cultural interest' and thus effectively widening such support to a much broader segment of Italian production. Indeed in 1998 the State invested 28% of all finance for film production, and Umberto Rossi suggests that this figure may actually be as high as 50%, given that the figures for private investment are based on budget estimates (Zagarrio 2000: 294–5). Furthermore, by offering such films guaranteed loans of up to either 70% or 90% of the film's budget at rates of interest equivalent to 30% of the commercial rate, the State essentially assumed part of the risk and became a de facto co-producer. Thirty-two of the fifty films of the NNC were made with State finance and virtually all of the directors in question have produced 'films in the national cultural interest' (see Appendix 8 for a full list). The Neapolitan filmmaker Salvatore Piscicelli has explained his reasoning behind using this mode of production both for his first film, *Immacolata e Concetta: l'altra gelosia* (1980), and for more recent projects:

> I currently see two possible production strategies. On the one hand, you can aim for the international market, which the contraction of national markets has made an important objective. However, this necessitates co-productions, foreign actors and filming in English and runs the risk of creating a lack of cultural specificity. On the other hand, you can scale things to the domestic market, in which case [State funding through] article 28 becomes an essential resource. (Detassis 1987: 53)

Both the 1965 and 1994 laws have been repeatedly criticised for the way public funds have been invested in films that turned out to be commercial failures. However, as Franco Montini points out, such criticism ignores both the high-risk nature of the film industry and the fact that article 28's remit was cultural and artistic, not economic, and thus a film's commercial potential was never a primary consideration (Zagarrio 2000: 307). However, there have also been criticisms about the management and implementation of these funds. Gianni Minervini, the Neapolitan producer whose Rome-based company A.M.A. Film produced a number of Neapolitan films like *Mi manda Picone* (1983, Nanni Loy), *Se lo scopre Gargiullo* (1988, Elvio Porta) and *Pianese Nunzio: 14 anni a Maggio*, described the kinds of problem faced by producers seeking to take advantage of this law. He notes that it typically takes one year for the Cinema Commission to recognise a film as being in the national cultural interest and then a further year before financing is actually approved. *Pianese Nunzio* was awarded a screenplay prize and subsequently applied for financing under the new article 8. However, the commission prevaricated at length and the production was obliged to proceed without State support because of actor Fabrizio Bentivoglio's prior commitments. Funding was approved only after filming was complete and Minervini suggested including the following statement in the opening titles: 'Despite being recognised as in the national cultural interest, this film was not able to take advantage of the State finance envisaged by law' (Cauli 1996). He ultimately refrained from doing so, presumably for fear of jeopardising his chances of obtaining future funding. Criticisms about the distribution of article 8 funds eventually led to accusations of fraudulent mismanagement, which were subsequently dismissed in September 1997 (see Lucente 1997). Similar difficulties later befell *Ossidiana*, which was awarded State funding in 2003 but fell foul of legislative changes the following year. Production did not go ahead until 4 years later, following a campaign to reopen the debate on public finances and an appeal by the production company Artimagiche against the Direzione Generale per il Cinema's decision.

A more serious problem with this system is that, because the loans are unsecured, there is less of an incentive for producers to concern themselves with the commercial success of the film or to develop a coherent long-term strategy, and this hinders the development of a sustainable film industry. This problem is compounded by the fact that State support is now directed almost exclusively towards cultural prestige products, rather than the film industry as a whole, as under the Andreotti Law in the 1950s. Article 28 was originally introduced at a time when the Italian film industry was extremely healthy – in 1964 production levels were at an all-time high of 315 films per year and Italian cinema occupied 50% of the market share (Assessorato alla cultura del comune di Roma 1979: 389 and Corsi 2001: 82) – and it was therefore intended to complement the commercial industry by helping to develop the kinds of film and talent that would not be easily supported by market forces but were necessary to maintain innovation and artistic prestige. However, 30 years later the commercial film industry is as much in need of support as such cultural and artistic projects – in 1995 production slumped to just 95 films, the lowest level since the Andreotti Law was passed, while in the 1993–4 season Italian cinema occupied a mere 14% of the market, the lowest figure ever – and the New Cinema Law did not address this need.[10] Moreover, allocation of unsecured reduced-rate loans, which constitute the only real support to which national productions not deemed in the cultural interest are entitled, have been largely restricted to large or medium-sized firms and have become increasingly difficult to access due to a complicated series of legal restrictions and guarantees (see Martini and Morelli 1997: 259). Thus smaller independent producers are more or less obliged to produce the kind of film likely to be judged in the national cultural interest if they wish to take advantage of the virtually indispensable support of State financing.

The legislative question is an enormously complex one and it is impossible to do it justice here. This somewhat schematic overview seeks solely to emphasise a broad shift in legislative agenda from the late 1940s to the early 1990s, for this has implications for the kinds of film Naples has produced. In the early 1950s, protectionist measures supported national production regardless of subject or quality and encouraged exhibitors to show Italian films at the expense of American ones. Within such a system the kind of low-budget genre filmmaking exemplified by the NF could flourish, particularly given the explosion of cinema audiences during this period. In the 1990s, on the other hand, attention has been directed towards a cinema of artistic and cultural value, largely irrespective of market forces. Potential projects are assessed primarily on the basis of the director-scriptwriter and the funding is similarly directed, reducing the producer to a largely functional role (Corsi 2001: 145). Thus the kind of auteur-centred, culturally prestigious filmmaking exemplified by the NNC has been encouraged, while traditional forms of producer-centred genre filmmaking like the NF have become increasingly marginalised. More recently, debates have stressed the need to create an environment in which producers are able to take a more active role in the financing and development of their own films, and to shift State finance away from production towards promotion, distribution and exhibition (see Lucisano 2001). These considerations invite us to turn our attention to the role played by distribution and exhibition in relation to Neapolitan films.

Regional Disparities and Film Exhibition

The success of the NF in the post-war years derived partly from the characteristics of film exhibition during the period, at least two of which require some comment here. In the post-war years the exhibition sector expanded rapidly to become the principal leisure activity of Italians, accounting for approximately 70% of leisure expenditure (Corsi 2001: 127). Cinema attendance rose from 470 million in 1942 to 662 million in 1950, and reached a peak of 819 million in 1955 (Sorlin 1996: 72). Cinema-going became a habit, what Gian Piero Brunetta has called a 'ritual' for the majority of Italians (Brunetta 1993: 196–219), and this created a massive demand for product, making space for both high- and low-budget films and favouring the development of popular genres through which films based on recognisable conventions could be produced quickly and cheaply. Italian cinema's characteristic division between first-, second- and third-run cinemas, which charged different prices and favoured different types of film, encouraged the development of a two-tier system. On the one hand there were the big-budget, ambitious star vehicles aimed at the first-run cinemas, while on the other were the low-budget films lacking publicity campaigns and big-name actors aimed at the second- and third-run cinemas.[11] This division of cinemas was based around a series of geographical distinctions – rural/urban, central/peripheral, North/South – and most popular genre films recouped their investment slowly from those cinemas concentrated primarily in rural areas, in the periphery of large cities, or in the South, a procedure referred to as 'exploitation in depth' (Caldiron and Della Casa 1999: 83). During this period it was not unusual to find a third-run cinema playing a film that was well over 5 years old. However, while the audience for most of the genre films aimed at the second- and third-run cinemas came from rural and peripheral areas throughout Italy, the same was not true of the NF:

> Of all the genres of popular film, it is only those films that explicitly emphasise their regional traits (in other words Neapolitan films), which were conceived exclusively for the Southern market . . . Northern audiences always respond negatively to these films because of a disinterest in the genre, a somewhat parochial prejudice, and the obvious difficulty in following dialogues frequently in dialect. (Ibid.: 128)

Thus the NF exploited the North–South divide to a much greater extent than the other cycles that relied on exploitation in depth, and some of the NF never even made it as far north as Rome. However, the extent to which the NNC also exploits such a regional disparity is open to question, since the exhibition sector has changed radically over the past 50 years. Let us now examine these changes and the way the NNC has been distributed and exhibited at both national and regional levels.

The Italian press continually laments the crisis facing Italian cinema, usually citing the failure of Italian films at the national box office and the dominance of Hollywood product as evidence, and not without reason. Between 1990 and 2000 annual cinema attendances in Italy averaged 98 million: fewer than France, Germany, Spain and the UK, not to mention much larger markets like the USA and Japan.[12] Moreover, in 1994 Italian cinema occupied on average 24% of the market share, compared to the 66% enjoyed by American films, a figure roughly consistent with European films across the continent a whole.[13] However, these figures do not compare favourably with 1950, when cinema attendances were over eight times as high and Italian cinema enjoyed nearly twice the market share (Sorlin 1996: 72 and 85). Italy's current market share can be understood partly in terms of production volumes; in the 1997–8 season, 97 Italian films received a censorship certificate, as opposed to 312 foreign films, of which at least two-thirds were of American origin, so it is unsurprising that they occupy a smaller market share (Repetto and Tagliabue 2000: 56). However, the problem is also one of distribution and exhibition. In 1996, 40% of Italian films failed to gain theatrical distribution, and of those that did, 45% were shown in fewer than 50 cities (Cianfarani 1997). Of the 156 Italian films shown in 1999, only 15 earned over 2 billion Lira, and only 39 of the 88 films actually released that year were shown in more than 10 cities (Lucisano 1998). In short, many Italian films struggle to be given a proper theatrical release and to find space in a market saturated with Hollywood product. Despite these facts, over 63% of Italian cinema-goers questioned in a survey by the CSC claimed to 'quite like' Italian films (Repetto and Tagliabue 2000: 39). An explanation for this failure at the domestic box office should therefore be sought primarily through an examination of industrial factors like the monopolistic practices of the Hollywood industry, and only secondarily through a consideration of the quality of the films themselves and their potential audience appeal.

Since Italian cinema's market share between 1990 and 2000 actually fluctuates annually from anywhere between 10% and 29%,[14] newspapers periodically temper such pessimism with accounts of a revival. However, such claims are usually short-lived since these fluctuations are largely the result of the runaway success of a few high-profile films and are thus temporary. Indeed, if one examines the box-office rankings it soon becomes clear that the years in which Italian cinema enjoys an increased market share are invariably the years in which a single Italian film tops the box-office charts.[15] The relationship between 'blockbuster' hits and Italian cinema's overall market share is particularly evident in the 1996–7 season, in which Italian cinema occupied 22% of the market share but a staggering 8% was due to the top-ranking film, *Il ciclone* (1996, Leonardo Pieraccioni).[16] In 1997 Italian films achieved a record 29% of the market; however, 78% of this share was due to just five films, while 118 of the Italian films released earned less than 7.3 million Lira each ('Conferenza stampa' 1998). The Italian box office is thus dominated by a handful of high-profile films, rather than the successful market penetration of a wide range of films. These blockbuster successes are almost exclusively comedies, from the *cinepanettoni* (Christmas comedies) to the films of actor-directors like Roberto Benigni, Leonardo Pieraccioni and Carlo Verdone, or television and stage comics like Aldo, Giovanni and Giacomo. The rest of the box-office hits are American films and international co-productions, typically shot in English. The only Neapolitan presence at the top end of the box-office spectrum is the late Massimo Troisi, who belongs to the actor-director comedians listed above.

It is worth briefly considering the role played by distribution and exhibition in this situation. In 1996–7 the two largest distributors were Cecchi Gori with 27% of the market and UIP with 13%; between them five Italian and five American firms controlled 97% of the market (Pasquale 1997). Margherita Pagani points out that 66% of distributors are concentrated in Rome and only 34% are located in other regions (Martini and Morelli 1997: 257). However, if we look more closely at this data, we can see that 92% of firms are based in Rome or Milan, and less than 2% (one single firm) is located in the South of Italy (in Puglia). This reveals a strong concentration of the distribution sector in the hands of a few large firms and a massive centralisation of this sector around the political and economic capitals of Rome and Milan, which are also the largest exhibition markets (see below). The remaining 8% consist primarily of the 'regional independents', which are not tied to particular production companies and tend to handle smaller film, which generally fail to achieve a wide national release. In 1998 the regional independents handled 14 of the 333 films released that year, and obtained less than 0.1% of the spectators.[17] Such a concentration of power in the hands of a few large distributors obviously has an impact on the range of films that receive distribution. Given this situation, the creation of a Neapolitan distribution company, Thule Film, in 2000 constitutes a striking development. However, we should be careful not to attribute too much importance to this event. Indeed, Artimagiche/Thule Film's Vincenzo Di Marino has suggested that the decision to base the company in Naples was motivated purely by personal reasons and the separation from Rome constitutes a significant commercial disadvantage (Author's interview, Naples, 3

December 2009). Distributors' targeting of a specific Southern market in the 1950s no longer seems to be a viable strategy within the context of the modern film industry. Indeed, Artimagiche/Thule Film's production, *Ossidiana*, screened in numerous Italian cities following its release in November 2008, but surprisingly not in Naples until December of the following year.

Between the mid-1970s and the late 1990s the number of cinema screens in Italy declined from over 8000 to 2400 (Repetto and Tagliabue 2000: 52). In 1997 fewer than 15% of municipalities had more than one cinema, and this explains why 45% of Italian films released that year reached fewer than 50 cities (Cianfarani 1997). Given that the majority of the cinemas that closed belonged to the second- and third-run chains, this decline must also be understood as a concentration of the exhibition sector in first-run cinemas, typically located within urban centres. This concentration parallels the global trend following the rise of the blockbuster phenomenon, which aimed to squeeze higher revenue from a smaller number of films in a shorter period of time; such films would open wide, backed by a massive advertising campaign, and could generate huge profits in the opening couple of weeks of release before being pulled from distribution relatively quickly. This is the complete opposite of the way the Italian film industry used to function, with the 'exploitation in depth' on which the NF relied. This situated is exacerbated by the multiplex phenomenon, which actually reached Italy relatively late. Nevertheless, by 1997 Italy boasted 168 multiplexes, which accounted for 8% of cinemas (Repetto and Tagliabue 2000: 56). In 1988 Naples had 18 first-run screens and 2.7% of the market, compared to Rome's 61 screens and 12.9%. Ten years later, Naples had 35 screens and 3.1% of the market, compared to Rome's 138 screens and 13.1%.[18] Both cities effectively doubled their number of first-run screens, but it should be stressed that this is an expansion of the number of screens, and not cinemas, in the first-run sector alone and thus can be explained in terms of the concentration of cinemas and the multiplex phenomenon described above rather than as an expansion of the exhibition sector as a whole. Il Modernissimo was the first multiplex to open in Naples.[19] Originally a theatre, just off via Roma and close to Piazza Dante, in 1956 it became one of Naples' most prestigious cinemas. It passed from ECI to Gaumont and finally in the late 1970s to Canon, which converted it to second-run. It subsequently closed for 10 years before reopening in August 1994 as Naples' first multiplex. It comprises one large auditorium (1500 seats), two smaller ones (110 and 105 seats) and one extremely small one (35 seats) dedicated to art-house and independent productions. Whether or not such a cinema can truly be called a multiplex is debatable. However, a more conventional multiplex opened in Afragola in the Province of Naples in June 2002: the Happy Maxicinema with 13 screens, the largest of which has a 20-metre screen equipped for 70mm projection and seats 534 spectators. It was subsequently joined by the 11-screen,

2700-seat Med Maxicinema in Naples, and 13- and 11-screen cinemas in Caserta and Casoria. As of 2009, Naples boasts 19 single-screen and 9 multi-screen cinemas.

Having established the national context for the exhibition of Italian cinema, we can now consider regional variations within that market. The distribution of screens across the country is dramatically uneven; over three-quarters of cinemas are located in North or Central Italy, leaving less than a quarter to serve the South, which contains 34% of the population (Repetto and Tagliabue 2000: 55–6). Moreover, the South is responsible for less than 15% of national box-office receipts, less than the single region of Lombardy in the North.[20] There is also a discrepancy in terms of the frequency with which people attend the cinema; only 10% of regular cinema-goers are located in the South, compared to 39% in the centre and 35% in the North. Conversely, 48% of occasional cinema-goers are based in the South (Repetto and Tagliabue 2000: 18). As far as individual cities are concerned, Rome tops the chart with 13% of the market and 138 screens, followed by Milan with 8% and 60 screens. Naples is the highest-ranking city in the South, with 3% and 35 screens.[21] In short, the South contains fewer cinemas and less assiduous cinema-goers, and contributes a smaller percentage of the national box office. Large cities and the *capozona* (regional capitals) in particular are disproportionately important. Naples can be considered the cinematic capital of the South.

Do such regional disparities affect the performance of individual films? We have already seen how, within the flourishing market of the 1950s, the films of the NF were aimed exclusively or primarily at the third-run cinemas of the South, but what about the NNC, which operates within a drastically reduced market based primarily around first-run cinemas? In a short but provocative article, Barbara Corsi and Claudio Zanchi analyse regional disparities by examining the relative performance of a number of films that enjoy a special relationship with a particular city (Corsi and Zanchi 2000). For example, given that Milan occupies 8% of the national market, one would expect that a film would achieve approximately 8% of its audience in that city; but Corsi and Zanchi demonstrate that for some films this is not the case. In addition to expressing the spectators as a percentage of the overall national audience, they also choose to express them as a percentage of the total audience obtained in the 12 *capozona*. This is because some films enjoy a trickle-down success, achieving a very wide national distribution. For such films the regional per-centage compared to the national audience would be relatively smaller than for a similar film whose distribution was limited to the major cities; however, the percentage in relation to the *capozona* would remain high. I have adopted this method for a more systematic analysis of Neapolitan films for the period in question. In addition to expressing Neapolitan cinema's performance in Naples, I have also shown its performance in Milan; this serves as a control, given that Milan is a Northern city with the second largest market share after Rome, and would not be expected to exhibit a particular preference for Neapolitan films.

The results of this analysis are shown in Appendix 2 for the NNC, and in Appendix 3 for a selection of other Neapolitan genre films of the period sub-divided into recent examples of the NF, the work of Neapolitan comics like Vincenzo Salemme and Massimo Troisi, and the Neapolitan-set films of more established non-Neapolitan directors like Lina Wertmüller and Nanni Loy. For the sake of clarity, these results are also represented graphically in Appendices 4 and 5. Given that Naples occupies approximately 3% of the national market and Milan 8%, we would expect that, if all other factors were equal and there was no particular preference on the part of spectators for these films, then a Neapolitan film would achieve approximately 3% of its total audience in Naples and 8% in Milan. This is not the case. The average audience in Naples for a film of the NNC is 14.7%, while for popular Neapolitan films it is 16.1%. The comparable figures for Milan are 11.5% and 5.2%. Thus Neapolitan films fare about five times better than expected in Naples, with a slight preference for popular films such as those of the comics over the NNC, but a massive preference for the NF (37.4%). In the larger Milanese market the NNC fares only slightly better than expected and popular Neapolitan films much worse. In relation to the *capozona* figures, we would expect films to achieve about 7% of their audience in Naples, yet the NNC actually achieves almost three times that amount (20.3%), while popular Neapolitan films achieve almost five times that amount (32.7%) and the NF an extraordinary 13 times (94%). We would expect the films to achieve about 19% of the *capozona* audience in Milan, yet the NNC achieves slightly less (15.9%) while popular Neapolitan films achieve just 10.5% and the NF a mere 0.2%. We can immediately draw two conclusions from these figures: firstly, that recent Neapolitan films fare much better in Naples than they do in Milan, and secondly that this difference is particularly marked for the films of the NF. Before considering the implications of this in relation to overall box-office success let us first speculate as to the factors that might cause this variation and then test our hypotheses against individual films.

The first factor is limited or uneven distribution. The most extreme example of this is a film like *Baby Gang*, which only played in Naples and thus achieved 100% of its audience there. In this case the uneven box-office performance does not reflect audience preference but rather the marginality of the film and its limited distribution. Nevertheless, it is obviously likely that the distributor deliberately chose to release the film just in that city because he felt it would only perform well there. While it would be difficult to discover how many copies of a particular film were distributed in different parts of the country, we can get a further sense of its distribution pattern by looking at the number of cities in which it screened and where it premiered. Some films open wide, others in the capital and others in Naples. This last group suggests that distributors recognise the relationship between certain films and the city, and presumably anticipate a better box-office success there. Most of the early films by new Neapolitan directors tend to open in Naples but their later films, once the directors have established a reputation, tend to open wide (see Appendix 2). A particularly notable case is Vincenzo Salemme, an actor-director of popular Neapolitan comedies, who was already well established in Neapolitan theatre before his film debut, *L'amico del cuore*, was released by Cecchi Gori in Naples during the 1998 Christmas season as a kind of Southern counterpart to their stable of Tuscan comics. Only when it had enjoyed an enormous success in Naples, more than two weeks later and after the festive period had ended, did it open in other cities, where it enjoyed a reasonable, but less pronounced success.

The second cause of regional variations is differences in taste, and a number of factors come into play here. Actors are an extremely important factor in influencing a spectator's decision to see a given film; the survey carried out by the CSC revealed that 21% of interviewees were influenced in their choice of film by the actor(s) very often, 29% fairly often and only 13% rarely or never (Repetto and Tagliabue 2000: 39). Appendix 3 reveals that Neapolitan comics like Massimo Troisi and Vincenzo Salemme have considerable appeal for Neapolitan audiences. However, while Troisi's appeal also extends to the national market, the same is not true of Salemme; 53.7% of the *capozona* audience for his first film came from Naples, while the figure for *Cose da pazzi* is 56.7%, despite the fact that it enjoyed wide national distribution and the full support of a Cecchi Gori publicity campaign.[22] The CSC survey reveals that genre is even more important than actors in determining the choice of film; 69% of those interviewed based their choice on the film's subject or genre very often, and only 2% rarely or never (Repetto and Tagliabue 2000: 39). The generic predilection for the NF is reflected in the statistics for films like *Fatalità* (55.4% of total audience/83.4% of *capozona* audience), *Annarè* (66.4%/98.5%) and *Cient'anne* (61.7%/100%).[23] Another factor that could influence taste is the use of themes or events linked to the city, as in the case of *Totò Sapore e la magica storia della pizza* (2003, Maurizio Forestieri), an animated feature about the birth of the pizza which earned 10.8% of its total audience and 24.2% of the *capozona* audience in Naples, compared to 4.7% and 10.5% in the much larger Milanese market.[24] Similarly, the *camorra* drama, *Pater familias*, earned 35.2% of its total audience and 43.1% of the *capozona* audience in Naples, as opposed to an extraordinarily low 4.2% and 5.1% in Milan. The final factor in determining taste is location; it is entirely possible that a Neapolitan audience might choose to see a film because it is set in Naples, and this might be borne out by the relative performance of films like

Autunno (20.6%/26.7%), *Rose e pistole* (20.9%/20.9%) and *Il verificatore* (24.7%/31.4%). These are all films by first-time directors, which do not feature a particular Neapolitan star or rely on a genre conventionally associated with the city, and have all enjoyed reasonably wide distribution. However, they have still done disproportionately well in Naples. It is possible that the location plays a part in this, although one would probably have to look quite closely at how the films were promoted. Did the audience know that these films were set in Naples before entering the cinema? It is also interesting to examine the performance of films that make reference to Naples in their title, like *Morte di un matematico napoletano* (12.3%/16.6%), *Polvere di Napoli* (26.4%/27.4%) and *I vesuviani* (27%/43.1%).

The films listed above are merely intended to highlight some of the reasons why Neapolitan films might fare better in Naples. Clearly, the success of any one film is the result of a complex of factors that cannot be easily separated. Nevertheless, these statistics lend considerable weight to claims that have traditionally been made about earlier Neapolitan films without any real empirical evidence and reveal that such claims remain valid for the NNC. However, it is important to note that this is not the case solely for Neapolitan cinema. Corsi and Zanchi's article includes figures for a number of films closely associated with other regions and the figures are just as striking as those for Neapolitan cinema; this begs the question of whether Neapolitan cinema constitutes a special case. I would suggest that it does because, although there are non-Neapolitan films that highlight their regional roots and are disproportionately successful in their place of origin, they are comparatively few in number; it is the sheer number of Neapolitan films displaying such regional variation that makes them a special case.[25] Moreover, it appears almost always to be the case that a Neapolitan film will perform better in Naples than elsewhere, while the same is only occasionally true for films set in other cities. One possible explanation for this is that many Neapolitan films elevate this emphasis on regionalism to the level of a textual strategy, whereas the same does not generally occur in films from other regions. This is a practice that will be explored in depth in subsequent chapters.

The Performance of Neapolitan Films in the Theatrical and Non-Theatrical Market Place

The fact that the NNC has been so disproportionately successful in Naples, which constitutes a mere 3% of the national market, begs the question of how successful they have been in absolute terms. Appendices 2 and 3 demonstrate that the answer is not very. The average national audience for a film of the NNC (32 720) is slightly less than that for recent examples of the low-budget NF (36 740), but well under half of that for other recent Neapolitan-set films

(89 818) and less than a twentieth of that for comics like Salemme and Troisi (738 019). The year 2001–2 apparently reconfirmed the significance of the NNC since numerous films were screened at the Venice Film Festival that year and much was made of this fact (see p. 36). However, *Chimera* was rated 212 in the national box-office charts with just 21 343 spectators, *Luna rossa* 246 with 14 415, *Tornando a casa* 223 with 19 556 and *L'uomo in più* 234 with 17 306. This is, perhaps, not surprising given the types of film that we are dealing with, but these figures none the less emphasise the fact that the NNC belongs to that portion of Italian production which struggles to achieve distribution or a market share. Indeed, there are a number of new Neapolitan films not even included in these appendices since they failed to achieve any theatrical distribution whatsoever, or because their release was so limited that *Il giornale dello spettacolo* lists no data.[26] The most successful Neapolitan-set films during this period, both in Naples and nationally, are not titles that are generally associated with the NNC, but rather those of comics Massimo Troisi and Vincenzo Salemme, of established non-Neapolitan directors like Lina Wertmüller, or genre films like the comedy *Incantesimo napoletano* and the animation *Totò Sapore e la storia magica della pizza*. The only new Neapolitan films to achieve six-figure audiences are *I buchi neri*, Martone's first two films, and Sorrentino's international hit, *Le conseguenze dell'amore*.[27] This discrepancy between the critical perception of a flourishing NNC and the commercial reality is perhaps best brought home by the relative success of *I vesuviani*, which critics have often interpreted as the 'flagship film' of the NNC, and *Annarè*, yet another low-budget example of the NF starring the neomelodic singer Gigi D'Alessio; *Annarè* attracted almost twice as many spectators as *I vesuviani* on a national level, and over four times as many in Naples. Even if the NNC is successfully reinvigorating the conventions of Neapolitan cinema, the mainstream cinema-going public still seems to favour more traditional forms of Neapolitan cinema.

It was suggested above that non-theatrical outlets have become increasingly important to the cinema industry over the past two decades. Undoubtedly, the NF now relies as much on these sectors as it does on theatrical distribution, and this is largely due to the decline in the second- and third-run cinemas that traditionally constituted its primary exhibition site. Quality Sound Video is a Neapolitan company specialising exclusively in distributing this kind of product. They have been responsible for video releases of films starring neomelodic singers like Nino D'Angelo and Gigi D'Alessio, as well as a number of video productions of Mario Merola *sceneggiate*. Many of these cassettes and DVDs do not enjoy a regular nationwide distribution, but remain concentrated in Southern cities like Naples, particularly in specialist shops and cheap market stalls. While such productions are guaranteed a home video audience without a theatrical release because of their reliance on an established generic template and actors famous for their musical career, the same is not true of most of the films of the NNC that have failed to obtain a theatrical release, such as *Malemare*, *Tatuaggi* or *Sotto la stessa luna*. Such films, together with many theatrically distributed films like *Polvere di Napoli*, *Il verificatore* and *Per tutto il tempo che ci resta*, have failed to find their way on to the home video platform. While the NF frequently screens on regional television stations, the films of the NNC tend to be shown either on the national network, especially the arts-focused RaiTre, or occasionally on subscriber channels such as Tele+. Again, a theatrical release is important in gaining a television screening, although it is important to bear in mind that some of the films are co-financed by television stations, which virtually guarantees them a television airing even without a theatrical release. On occasion, these media have even provided an outlet for films denied proper circulation; thus, after an eight-year wait and a lengthy petition, *La volpe a tre zampe* finally achieved its first post-festival screening in March 2009 thanks to RaiUno, while *E io ti seguo*, which only played briefly in two cinemas in Campania, is now being independently distributed on DVD via the internet and as a supplement to the magazine *Chiaia*. Although the revenue from such distribution must be negligible, it does at least mean that the films are receiving some visibility.

Festival screenings have also been of key importance to the NNC, even contributing to the idea of its very existence. *Vito e gli altri* received its premiere at the Venice Film Festival in 1991, where it won the International Critics' Prize, and many subsequent films have also received their premieres there, including *Pianese Nunzio: 14 anni a Maggio* and *Isotta* in 1996, *Giro di lune tra terra e mare*, *I vesuviani* and *Tatuaggi* in 1997, *Appassionate* and *Autunno* in 1999, and *Lontano in fondo agli occhi* in 2000. Amongst the eight Italian films shown at the London Film Festival in 1995 were three Neapolitan ones (*L'amore molesto*, *I buchi neri* and *Il verificatore*) and the festival brochure described 'the new Partheneon [*sic*] culture, which has made a decided breakaway from traditional themes' (London Film Festival Catalogue 1995: 82). In 2001, the Venice Film Festival included screenings of *Tornando a casa*, *Luna rossa* and *L'uomo in più*, together with Tonino De Bernardi's partially Neapolitan-set *Farelavita* (later re-edited and released as *Rosatigre*), the shorts *Della Napoli di Luca Giordano* (Mario Martone), *Scalamara* (Giuseppe Gaudino) and *Un paio di occhiali* (Carlo Damasco), together with the restoration of the Neapolitan-set American production, *Santa Lucia luntana* (1931, Harold Godsoe). The presence of so many Neapolitan films was commented on in the festival brochure and also formed the subject of a full article in *Cinema d'oggi*'s report on the festival (Zocaro 2001). Festivals present a large number of recent films to critics and a ciné-literate audience, and thus contribute to the critical perception of the state of contemporary cinema. The strong presence of these new Neapolitan films in festivals has thus been instrumental in propagating discussions about the emergence of an NNC.[28] The vogue for Neapolitan retrospectives in the early 1990s may also have played a role. In 1991 the Rencontres d'Annecy devoted a section to 'Naples au Cinéma', while the Festival du Film Italien in Villerupt ran a similar retrospective two years later. In 1994, the Festival of Neapolitan Cinema was launched in Naples itself, the first year being devoted to the 1930s, while subsequent years looked at following decades. A more prestigious retrospective on 'Naples and the Cinema' was held at the Museum of Modern Art in New York and the Centre Georges Pompidou in Paris in 1993, for which large-format volumes on the history of Neapolitan cinema were commissioned (Aprà 1994, Aprà and Gili 1994). An exhibition devoted to Neapolitan cinema held in Naples in 1995 also led to the publication of another book on Neapolitan cinema, which included a chapter on the NNC (see De Crescenzo 1995: especially 65–78). The year 1999 saw the launch of the Napoli Film Festival, which features both international films as well as Italian and Neapolitan productions, and from 2004 a selection of films from the festival played in New York as 41° Parallelo. In 1999 the Comune di Napoli and the Mediateca di Santa Sofia teamed up to launch 'O curt, a mini-festival showing shorts and videos produced in Naples during the past year. The festival has shown everything from films by established filmmakers like Antonio Capuano (*Pallottole su Materdei*, 1995) or young filmmakers soon make to their feature debut like Eduardo Tartaglia (*Impara l'arte*, 1998) and Carlo Luglio and Diego Olivares (*Les Jeux sont faits*, 2000) to collective works made by non-professionals such as *Il lavoro dei minori uccide l'infanzia* (1999, Consorzio scuole città di Marano), *'O 'nnfammone* (2000, Laboratorio multimediale della casa circondariale di Lauro) and *Poesia criminale* (2000, Associazione culturale Mario Pesce a Fore). The interest of film festivals both in screening new Neapolitan films and in retrospectives of the history of Neapolitan cinema is clearly part of the movement towards the cultural regeneration of Naples in the 1990s and undoubtedly contributed to the perception that an NNC was emerging. Furthermore, in an industry in which financing production is so difficult and achieving visibility in the market place even more so, the festival success of the NNC helps explain the continued expansion of the phenomenon, even if the films have not been particularly successful in absolute, commercial terms. Nicola Giuliano of Indigo Film is clear on this point:

> You can count on the fingers of one hand the number of films that turn a profit, especially if you eliminate the 'national genre' of comedy . . . What, then, determines whether a young filmmaker continues to make films or is forced to give up? The determining factor is whether he is successful on the international festival circuit and whether he enjoys favourable notices in the national press. In this way, you can see whether a director

has something to say and therefore whether he is worth investing in, even if he has not been commercially successful. . . . A study reveals that, since 1983, 950 Italian directors have made their debut, but 830 of these have yet to make a second film. So it's clear that if *Libera*, *Morte di un matematico napoletano* and *Vito e gli altri* had been critical fiascos . . . they would not have released this potential. . . . It's a self-propagating mechanism. (Author's interview, Naples, 3 July 2003)

CONCLUSION

In terms of its mode of production the NNC is a marginal cinema both geographically and economically, favouring medium-/low-budget, State-financed production by small independent companies. As Capuano has observed, such a production strategy is an inevitable correlative to the films' marginalisation within the exhibition sector and lack of commercial success (Tassi 2006: 24). Similarly, in writing about *I cinghiali di Portici*'s mode of production, stylistic choices and lack of distribution, Emiliano Morreale has suggested that 'humility and tenacity' constitute an 'example of an ethics based on modest *mise-en-scène*' and that the film exemplifies 'a medium-sized cinema worthy of such a name' (Morreale 2006: 24). In this respect, at least, the NNC is consistent with traditional Neapolitan cinema. It is interesting that Corsi and Zanchi end their article by suggesting that exploiting regional variations in preference is one way in which contemporary Italian cinema might deal with its marginalisation within the market place, as if this were a new idea when it is anything but that; indeed, it is precisely the strategy that the NF pursued in the post-war years. However, as we have seen, given the limited box-office success of 'films in the national cultural interest' and the limited size of the market constituted by even such a large city as Naples, this strategy is not without problems. Nicola Giuliano has, in fact, suggested that his films are not aimed primarily at a Neapolitan audience:

We all know that a film made in Naples can exert a certain attraction here. However, I don't believe that a film can only target the Neapolitan market, because it is too small an area . . . That 27% [the percentage of the total number of spectators for *I vesuviani* located in Naples] is equal to box-office receipts of about 250 million Lira, which is next to nothing. (Author's interview, Naples, 3 July 2003)

The NNC is primarily the product of a network of filmmakers, actors and technicians working at regional level and gravitating around local, independent production companies supported by State funding. The films they produce clearly appeal more to local audiences than they do to national ones. It would seem to be legitimate, then, to talk about a distinct 'Neapolitan cinema'. However, the NNC can no longer be considered an exclusively regional phenomenon in the way that the NF was. Changes in the mode of production and the opening up of Neapolitan cinema to a broader national and, to a lesser extent, international context have had a dramatic impact on the characteristics of the films themselves. Before we can assess the nature and extent of this change it is necessary first to identify the characteristics of earlier Neapolitan cinema – and this will form the subject of the next chapter.

NOTES

1. It would probably be unwise to attribute too much weight to the sudden drop to three companies in the late 1980s, given the relatively small size of the sample and the fact that the number of companies suddenly rose again in the early 1990s, although it is obviously symptomatic of the overall difficulties facing production at the time.
2. For a more detailed history of Neapolitan production in the silent era see Foglia et al. 1995, Grano and Paliotti 1969, Grano 1996, and Masi and Franco 1988.
3. On Dora Film, see Troianelli 1989 and Bruno 1993.
4. For a more detailed history of post-war film production in Naples see Curcio and Bonamassa 2004, De Crescenzo 1995: 117–25, Grano 1996: 63–72, Grano and Paliotti 1969: 175–86 and Iaccio 2000: 98–107.
5. Apparently, as an exhibitor he capitalised on his other career as a baker to beat his competitors by handing out free pastry at his screenings (Aprà 1994: 202)!
6. Plans are now under way for the construction of film and television studios on the site of the former industrial complex at Bagnoli. Whether or not these reach fruition remains to be seen.
7. By this time Magliulo had split from De Lillo and formed his own Rome-based company, Dodici Dicembre, which has since produced the films of his new partner, Nina Di Majo. Since then Franchini has opened his own studio and continues to edit much of the NNC.
8. This is similar to the situation in England, where the Film Council is responsible for film-funding, and the Arts Council for England, via the various Regional Arts Boards, finances activities at a local level.
9. Maria Marcucci, Vice-President of the local council in Tuscany, has observed that a medium-budget film production can bring economic benefits of 5–6 billion Lira to the area in which it is shot, as well as contributing to the development of local skills ('Film Commission anche in Toscana' 2000: 7).
10. These statistics are derived from production figures published by the Associazione Nazionale Industrie Cinematografiche Audiovisive e Multimediali (ANICA) on their website and the reports published by the Associazione Generale Italiana dello Spettacolo (AGIS) published at the end of every cinema season in *Il giornale dello spettacolo*.
11. For a more detailed account, see Wagstaff 1992.
12. Elaborated from data from the European Audiovisual Observatory quoted in *Cinema d'oggi* 33:8–9, 10 May 1999, p. 24 and 35:8–9, 5 May 2001, p. 32.
13. Based on data from the European Audiovisual Observatory quoted in *Cinema d'oggi*, 33:8–9, 10 May 1999, p. 24.
14. Based on data compiled from the AGIS reports published by *Il giornale dello spettacolo* at the end of every season.

15. Based on an analysis of the box-office tables published in *Il giornale dello spettacolo* at the end of every season.
16. Figures quoted in *Il giornale dello spettacolo: Borsa Film*, 53:22, 18 July 1997, pp. 14 and 16.
17. Data elaborated from figures in *Il giornale dello spettacolo: Borsa Film*, 54:22, 17 July 1998, pp. 2–13.
18. Figures quoted in *Il giornale dello spettacolo: Borsa Film*, 44:23, 20 June 1988, pp. 33–4 and 54:22, 17 July 1998, p. 15.
19. Il Modernissimo has staged the premieres of many films of the NNC including *Pianese Nunzio* and *Pater familias*. According to Stefano Incerti, they showed *Il verificatore* on the smallest screen constantly for 3 months (Author's interview, Rome, 17 June 2003).
20. Based on figures from the Società Italiana degli Autori ed Editori (SIAE) quoted in *Il giornale dello spettacolo*, 50:26, 29 July 1994, p. 19.
21. *Il giornale dello spettacolo*, 54:22, 17 July 1998, p. 15.
22. Due to the extremely wide distribution of these films it is more revealing to consider the *capozona* figures rather than the overall national totals. The reduced percentages in relation to the total audiences, 30.9% and 14.6% respectively, possibly reflect the importance of the other cities in the South to his success.
23. It should be pointed out that star appeal also plays an important role in these films' success, given that they all feature neomelodic singers like Nino D'Angelo or Gigi D'Alessio. Furthermore they received a relatively narrow distribution: 3–15 cities, presumably predominantly in the South.
24. Again, this is a film that received very wide distribution (214 cities) and thus the regional preference is more marked in the *capozona* figures.
25. Here I am assuming that the conclusions drawn for the post-1990 era are also valid for the earlier periods in which Neapolitan cinema achieved success, which seems highly likely; if anything, the variation is likely to be more pronounced.
26. *Tatuaggi, Malemare, La volpe a tre zampe, I cinghiali di Portici* and *Sotto la stessa luna*.
27. The figures for *Le conseguenze dell'amore* refer to its initial release run. After its victory at the David di Donatello awards the film was re-released and achieved even higher audience figures.
28. See, for example, Alberto Castellano's essay in the 1997 Venice Film Festival catalogue, which is the first really significant discussion of the NNC (Castellano 1997a).

2. CHARACTERISTICS AND FUNCTIONS OF THE NEAPOLITAN FORMULA

Traditionally, Neapolitan cinema has been identified primarily with two genres: comedy and melodrama. Neapolitan comedy derives from a rich stage tradition and is exemplified by the work of playwright-actors like Eduardo and Peppino De Filippo and of comics originating in theatrical revues and cabaret like Totò and Massimo Troisi. These figures occupy a position of great significance within Neapolitan culture and have become virtual synecdoches for the city, their photos appended to *pizzerie* around the world. However, most of their films cannot really be considered examples of regional cinema; while they play Neapolitan characters and construct jokes based on 'Neapolitanness', most of their films are produced by the Rome-based national film industry and either use Naples as a mere location or are set elsewhere. Moreover, they are not really distinct from national productions in either narrative or stylistic terms. While it would certainly be possible to analyse the personae of these comic actors in terms of their *napoletanità* ('Neapolitanness') and examine how they contributed to cultural perceptions of Naples, such an operation would lie outside this book's remit. Neapolitan melodrama, on the other hand, is a different matter since the majority of these films were produced at regional level and made predominantly by Neapolitan filmmakers. They also display characteristics that clearly distinguish them from the national tradition of film melodrama in that they typically structure their melodramatic narratives around the concept of *napoletanità*. Let us call these films the 'Neapolitan Formula' (hereafter NF).[1]

The NF began in the silent era when film production flourished in Naples, but it was abruptly curtailed by the arrival of synchronised sound and Fascist censorship. It resurfaced in the post-war years, before dying out once more at the end of the 1950s, to be replaced by a series of action-adventure formulae like the peplum and the spaghetti western. It received a new lease of life in the mid-1970s, thanks to the success of actor-singer Mario Merola and this success continued into the early 1980s with the films starring neomelodic singer Nino D'Angelo, before more or less dying out once more at the end of the decade.[2] This chapter will focus primarily, but not exclusively, on the post-war cycle (1946–59), arguably the period in which the NF achieved its fullest expression. It will begin by describing the principal sources of influence on the NF: Neapolitan song, the *sceneggiata* and melodrama. It will then describe how the NF performed an almost ritualistic function for spectators in the popular quarters of Naples and other Southern Italian cities, generating audience participation by reflecting their 'world-view' and providing a cathartic release for pressures specific to Naples and the South through a deliberate use of *napoletanità*. The chapter will then briefly describe the NF's principal narrative typologies and its thematic and stylistic characteristics before concluding with a critical (re-)interpretation of the genre and its functions.

ORIGINS: NEAPOLITAN SONG, THE SCENEGGIATA, AND FILM MELODRAMA

To gauge the importance of Neapolitan song (*la canzone napoletana*), the most famous of Naples' cultural exports, one need only think of *'O sole mio*, a song so widely known throughout the world that it is has virtually become a second Italian national anthem.[3] Internationally renowned tenors like Enrico Caruso and Mario Lanza brought Neapolitan song to an international audience and created an instant recognition of, and appetite for, Neapolitan culture, which continues to this day. Although its origins can be traced back much further, the modern conception of Neapolitan song really evolved in the nineteenth century. Musicologist and historian Pasquale Scialò defines it in terms of its emphasis on 'poetry and melody', and this dual focus is reflected in the fact that Neapolitan songs usually bear two signatures of equal importance: one responsible for the lyrics, the other for the music (Scialò 1995: 13). Unlike opera, where the librettist is secondary to the composer, the contribution of famous poets, playwrights and authors like Salvatore Di Giacomo, Libero Bovio, E.A. Mario and Gabriele D'Annunzio is of equal importance to that of musicians like Francesco Paolo Tosti, Eduardo Di Capua and Vincenzo Valente. Thus Neapolitan songs typically contain a strong narrative element and are designed to give musical expression to the emotion contained in that narrative situation; for example, *Marechiaro* expresses a sense of wonder at the natural beauty of Naples, *Fenesta ca lucive* reflects the pain of the loss of a loved one, *I te vurria vasà* and *Aggio perduto 'o suonno* express romantic yearning, and *Malafemmena* expresses the torment over being betrayed by one's lover.

This narrative dimension means that Neapolitan song lends itself particularly well to the stage and screen, most obviously in the *sceneggiata*. Strictly speaking, a *sceneggiata* is a staged work whose title and narrative derive from a popular Neapolitan song; the song is literally 'sceneggiata' (scripted) and the resulting narrative is then punctuated by a series of musical numbers culminating in the title song. *Sceneggiate* are typically melodramatic in conception and extremely formulaic, invariably revolving around a triangular narrative matrix often referred to as 'isso, essa and 'o malamente' ('him, her and the bad-guy' in Neapolitan dialect). This fixed narrative structure is dependent on stock character types: *'o guappo, 'a malafemmena, 'a mamma, 'o nennillo* and *i comici*. A figure profoundly rooted in Neapolitan culture, the *guappo* is a man who commands respect; he is immaculately dressed, abides by a particular moral code, and is ready to defend his family and friends, his honour and his code through violence when necessary. Equally important is the *malafemmena*: a woman of loose virtue capable of bringing a man to ruin through her treacherous nature and the passions she provokes. These figures are flanked by *'a mamma* (the protagonist's mother) and *'o nennillo* (the child), who contribute to the pathos, and *i comici* (the comic duo), who provide much needed light relief and offer a commentary on the action, much like the chorus in Greek tragedy. The narrative also revolves around fixed dramatic situations: the *malafemmena*'s betrayal of the *guappo* and his subsequent retribution by *sfregio* (scarring of her face) or *zumpata* (duel) with *'o malamente*; the *guappo*'s emigration from Naples, either to escape the shame and suffering of his betrayal or to evade capture after taking revenge; and the illness or death of *'a mamma* or *'o nennillo*, which typically coincides with the narrative resolution and contributes to the climactic pathos. These characteristics are apparent in *Pupatella*, arguably the first *sceneggiata*, which was based on the song by Bovio and Buongiovanni and first staged by the Maggio-Coruzzolo-Ciaramella company in 1916. They also reoccur in the most famous *sceneggiate*, such as Enzo Lucio Murolo's *Guapparia* (1925) and Gaspare di Majo's *Lacreme napulitane* (1926).

The *sceneggiata* was performed in the popular quarters of Naples and other Southern Italian cities in small theatres like the Trianon, the San Ferdinando and the Duemila, and was also exported to New York, where it played to the Southern Italian emigrant population;[4] however, it never reached more respectable theatres, or those of Northern Italy and the rest of Europe. This socio-geographic context is important for understanding both the *sceneggiata*'s characteristics and the way it has been interpreted by the critical establishment. A short-lived revival of the waning *sceneggiata* led to a series of performances and round-table discussions at the Festa dell'Unità in Naples in 1976, where the *sceneggiata* and the NF were systematically studied for the first time.[5] The interest was primarily sociological, examining the phenomenon as an authentic expression of local and popular culture in an age of increasing cultural homogeneity and mass-media dominance. However, this newfound interest did not result in an uncritical celebration of the form, and ideological critiques pointed to its patriarchal conception, conservatism, passive acceptance of the social status quo and celebration of a potentially criminal value system. If such criticisms contain a hint of class (and geographic) prejudice, it is also significant to note that this newfound interest in the *sceneggiata* on the part of outsiders also resulted in the first significant challenges to its form and values.[6] However, these changes also coincided with the *sceneggiata*'s ultimate decline.

The influence of Neapolitan song and the *sceneggiata* on Neapolitan cinema is immeasurable but can perhaps be glimpsed in the plethora of films that take their titles from popular songs: *Marechiaro* (1949, Giorgio Ferroni), *Luna rossa* (1951, Armando Fizzarotti), *Core 'ngrato* (1951, Guido Brignone), *Santa Lucia luntana . . .* (1951, Aldo Vergano) and *Malafemmena* (1957, Armando Fizzarotti), to name but a few. Many films are based around the star appeal of popular singers like Giacomo Rondinella, Mario Merola and Nino D'Angelo, or feature Neapolitan songs either on their soundtrack or in on-screen performances. There are even a few films that revolve almost entirely around such performances, most famously *Carosello napoletano* (1953, Ettore Giannini), which is often described as the only true Italian musical (Arcagni 2006: 14). More importantly, numerous films turn to the narratives of Neapolitan songs for inspiration, either reworking existing *sceneggiate* or adapting songs into screenplays in an analogous fashion. Although the NF is sometimes referred to as the *film-sceneggiata*, the relationship between these two forms is actually rather complex and it is worth keeping them distinct. While many films borrow from the *sceneggiata*, few display all of its characteristics or adhere quite so rigidly to fixed character types or plots. Roberto Amoroso, the producer directly responsible for the post-war revival of the NF, has observed a difference between his films, which borrow narratives and even some dialogue from Neapolitan songs but usually only feature songs on the soundtrack, and those films which feature actual on-screen performances by actor-singers (Migliaccio 1985: 59). It is also worth recalling that Neapolitan cinema's borrowings from Neapolitan song actually predate the *sceneggiata*,[7] and that the *sceneggiata* itself borrowed from the NF. Rather than a direct equivalence it is more appropriate to talk about a process of reciprocal influence, evident above all in those figures that moved back and forth between the two forms, like producer Enzo Di Gianni, impresario-director Ciro Ippolito, and actor-singer Mario Merola.

In addition to such specifically Neapolitan extra-cinematic cultural forms, the NF's roots can also be traced back to film melodrama, the dominant genre of post-war Italian cinema. If the NF is distinguished by its culturally specific reliance on *napoletanità*, then other sub-genres of Italian film melodrama can also be distinguished by examining their sources of inspiration. There are adaptations of popular literature, and in particular nineteenth-century *feuilletons* like Francesco Mastriani's *La sepolta viva* (1948, Guido Brignone) and *La cieca di Sorrento* (1952, Giacomo Gentilomo), films adapted from or inspired by opera, such as *Rigoletto* (1946, Carmine Gallone) and *Aida* (1953, Clemente Fracassi), and social-realist melodramas such as the films of Raffaello Matarazzo and those of Neorealism. However, providing a clear definition or typology of Italian film melodrama is not straightforward. Indeed, the definition of melodrama itself has always caused critics problems. Etymologically, the term describes the fusion of music and drama, as in the Italian use of the term to refer to opera, or the French *mélodrame*, apparently first used by Rousseau to describe his play with orchestral accompaniment, *Pygmalion*. At its most general, melodrama has been seen as a literary or theatrical form in which heightened emotional effects are created through the use of music or other stylistic devices. Under such a conception, melodrama must be considered a style or mode rather than a genre (Gledhill 2007: 316). However, many critics have seen melodrama as more historically and socially circumscribed. Peter Brooks describes it as a product of the French Revolution, when the bourgeoisie took power from the aristocracy, and thus describes it as,

> a response to the loss of the tragic vision. It comes into being in a world where the traditional imperatives of truth and ethics have been violently thrown into question, yet where the promulgation of truth and ethics, their instauration as a way of life, is of immediate, daily, political concern. (Landy 1991: 60)

Similarly, Christine Gledhill observes that, 'family melodrama is nevertheless frequently defined as the dramatic mode for a historical project, namely the centrality of the bourgeois family to the ascendancy and continued dominance of that class' (Gledhill 2007: 316). Under such a definition melodrama should be considered an acutely political form bound to a specific set of contemporary concerns. For John Cawelti, melodrama is distinguished from other popular formulae by the 'moral fantasy' it provides – that of 'a world that operates according to our hearts' desires' (Cawelti 1976: 45). Thus he defines melodrama as 'narratives of a complex of actions in a world that is purportedly full of the violence and tragedy we associate with the "real world" but in this case seems to be governed by some benevolent moral principle' (ibid.: 44–5). Cawelti's conception of melodrama unifies a number of elements that are popularly seen as characteristic of melodrama (unbelievable plots, sensationalism, heightened emotions) with a fairly convincing explanation of its general narrative characteristics. Cawelti also talks about 'social melodrama', which 'gradually shifts its formulae as each generation seeks its own means of resolving the tension between changing perceptions of the social scene and the moral ideals that define what is right and significant in life' (Landy 1991: 47). This definition acknowledges melodrama as a broad category with a long history, but also recognises the historically contingent way in which it has been articulated at certain times. Cawelti's emphasis on the 'ways in which specific cultural themes and stereotypes become embodied in more universal story archetypes' (Cawelti 1976: 6) also helps explain the appeal of the four tendencies of Italian film melodrama described above. The *feuilleton* adaptations set the conventional melodramatic narrative of a world under threat against the backdrop of historical change, most frequently the events leading up to the collapse of the Bourbon Empire and the Unification of Italy, and thus narrate the process by which modern Italy came into existence. The opera films also frequently articulate a discourse about (national) identity, in particular through the use of Giuseppe Verdi, who has great significance in terms of Risorgimento politics, or the linking of opera to recent historical and political events, as in *Davanti a lui tremava tutta Roma* (1946, Carmine Gallone).[8] The 'social realist' tendency sets its generic narrative against contemporary concerns about the effects of the Second World War and issues like emigration, poverty and homelessness. The NF owes its success in part to its ability to draw on elements characterising all three of these other tendencies, through Naples' role as the capital of the pre-Unification Bourbon Empire, through questions of national and regional identity raised by the discourse around *napoletanità*, and through the particularly acute social problems Naples faced after the war. The NF can thus be considered one of the most successful and readily identifiable embodiments of melodrama in post-war Italian cinema. It is possible, then, to see the NF as both an expression of Italian film melodrama and a version of it specifically tailored to the culture of twentieth-century Naples and Southern Italy.

POPULAR FILM AS RITUAL: ARTICULATING THE NEAPOLITAN WORLD-VIEW

Chapter 1 described how, in Italy in the post-war years, the cinema constituted a privileged social space, and film-going became a ritual for much of the population. This idea of cinema as a ritual can also be extended to the kind of experience that popular films of the period offered and the function they served. Although the relationship between ritual and popular entertainment forms such as the theatre or cinema is complex and controversial, there are many points of similarity: the communal experience, the use of a circumscribed and defined space, the (relatively) fixed and invariant nature of the event, and the emphasis on performance (see Rappaport 1999: 37–46). Although filmgoers do not directly participate in the spectacle like the congregation during a Catholic mass, their emotional involvement and the physical response it can produce (laughter and tears), the use of the cinema auditorium as a site of social interaction, and the role played by the spectator in constructing meaning as described by spectatorship theories all indicate that the spectator is not restricted to an entirely passive role. Moreover, ritual's goal of transforming and purifying the individual and community by purging it of negative elements, codifying belief and reconfirming the social or moral order is not that dissimilar from the way in which popular films function. Indeed, Cawelti has argued that ritual (the cathartic working-through of psychological and social tensions) constitutes one of the main functions served by popular fiction, together with game (the play with generic convention) and dream (the pleasure of fantasy and escape from reality) (Cawelti 1975: 33).

In order to generate such 'participation' and fulfil a ritualistic function, popular films mirrored the beliefs and value system of their intended audience. There is some evidence of a deliberate and conscious desire to achieve such an effect in the (rare) interviews left by filmmakers of the NF. For example, Enzo Merolle, the owner of Glomer Film, which produced *Cuore di mamma* (1954, Luigi Capuano), described his criteria thus:

> Success is determined by the story, by the sentiments. Artistic criteria are not readily accessible to the broad public and daring theories can only be grasped by audiences in the first-run cinemas. In order to be understood by everyone you need simple emotions: love, faith, religion, honour, and national pride. (Caldiron and Della Casa 1999: 83)

Similarly, Luigi Capuano, director of *Cuore di mamma* as well as *Scapricciatiello* (1955) and *Maruzzella* (1956), stated his philosophy thus:

> [Popular films] must be immediately intelligible and easily digestible. They must be compatible with the spectator's sense of morality. After all, popular films are aimed at families: it is the Saturday and Sunday audiences that guarantee their success. (Ibid.: 125)

The Sicilian, Fortunato Misiano, whose Romana Film was the only firm not based in Naples to specialise in the NF, also recognises that the simplicity and clarity of the emotional characteristics of his films are one of their key facets: 'The spectator is moved only by dramatic situations that appeal to the most basic of feelings' (quoted in Faldini and Fofi 1979: 169–70). This process results in the audience's perception of the films as 'realistic' or 'plausible' despite their conventional and formulaic nature (see Masi 1979a: 274). For example, Roberto Amoroso gives an interesting account of the response of contemporary audiences when he describes one viewer's reaction to *Malaspina*: 'watching this film, it felt as if I were in my own home' (Caldiron and Della Casa

1999: 90). A similar process underpins the *sceneggiata* in which the separation between stage and stalls is blurred and the audience interacts verbally or even physically with the performers. Indeed, it was not uncommon for someone to get so caught up in the drama that they would invade the stage and lunge at *'o malamente* (see Scialò 2002: 5).

This replication of the audience's 'world-view' could best be achieved through the application of a melodramatic framework and this helps explain melodrama's pre-eminent position within the popular formulae of the period.[9] The reliance of the NF on a melodramatic framework can be explained in a number of other ways, too. On one level, the range of clichés and stereotypes typically associated with Naples imbue the city with melodramatic qualities: the emotional character of Neapolitans, their use of an expansive, gestural means of communication and the conflictual nature of the city, colourful and full of life yet beset by problems. This superficial similarity should not be ignored, since it is undoubtedly responsible for many of the melodramatic characteristics of the films; it is also one reason why the cinema has adopted Naples as, to borrow Ezio Alberione's phrase, 'the privileged stage for conflicts and emotions' (Caldiron and Della Casa 1999: 63). However, on a deeper level, the structures of melodrama are closely aligned with the world-view of Southern Italian, and in particular Neapolitan, society. As such, the NF can be considered an instance of Cawelti's social melodrama, closely linked to the historical and cultural context in which it evolved. Furthermore, it can be argued that the NF evolves within the context of what Brooks terms the 'loss of the tragic vision' in which 'truth and ethics . . . is of immediate, daily, political concern' (Landy 1991: 60). This becomes clear when one looks more closely at the social structure of Naples during the period when the NF flourished.

In his analysis of Neapolitan society, Percy Allum utilises Ferdinand Tönnies's categories of *Gemeinschaft* (communal) and *Gesellschaft* (associational) societies, which he defines thus:

> *Gemeinschaft* is a social formation based on feeling, in which every individual considers every other individual as an end in himself, knows him personally and shares a great deal in his private life. The individuals who compose it intrinsically value their mutual relationship and the fact that they are a vital part of such a social entity . . . In contrast to it stands *gesellschaft*, the social formation founded on interest, in which the individual considers the others as the means, knows them impersonally, and shares his external life only with them. Individuals value their relationship only extrinsically. (Allum 1973: 5)

Allum argues that Neapolitan society has traditionally been based around *Gemeinschaft* relations and, to a large extent, continues to be so (he is writing in the early 1970s), particularly in the 'Neapolitan casbah', in which apartment blocks function as micro-societies operating autonomously and independently from the wider society. In terms of our enquiry it is significant that the *Gemeinschaft* society is based primarily around the family unit while the wider social organisation is based around friends and neighbours:

> The primary social unit is the family; although it is patriarchal in conception, the central role devolves on the mother. For, if the wife is subject to her husband, it is she who looks after the home . . . The wife, as mother, is the repository of tradition, but at the same time is bound by it. Children brought up in this atmosphere have no social space to acquire personal autonomy and accept family decisions on their future quite easily. (Ibid.: 57)

In such a society, problems are formed and resolved at the level of personal relations, not through public institutions or larger social or political bodies. Clearly, such a social organisation finds expression in melodrama's displacement of social and political tensions on to the family and its reliance on personal and emotional relationships in order to explore and resolve these conflicts.

Allum goes on to argue that, as a consequence of the Unification of Italy in the 1860s, the structures and institutions of a modern *Gesellschaft* society were artificially imposed on Naples, without significantly changing the social fabric of the *Gemeinschaft*. This resulted in a number of tensions and, more importantly, was responsible for what he terms the 'political world-view' of Neapolitans. He shows that out of 120 inhabitants of the Neapolitan casbah interviewed by L. G. Grasso, only 24 saw any relation between themselves and the State, while 90 claimed they had no faith in the State whatsoever (ibid.: 94). He considers these responses as indicative not only of Neapolitans' estrangement from and distrust of the institutions and politics of the modern *Gesellschaft* society, but also of their continued attachment to a patronage polity deriving from the type of social organisation that existed when Naples was the capital of a monarchy and which continues to find expression in the clientelism characteristic of Neapolitan politics. He quotes Naples' vote 80% in favour of a monarchy in the constitutional referendum of 1946 as evidence of this view (ibid.: 96). Allum goes on to argue that the Neapolitan's reaction to this situation takes three different forms: parasitism (a passive acceptance of the patronage system), grievance and riot (the violent response to the patron's failure to perform what is regarded as his duty towards his subject), and quitting (the rejection of any possibility of changing the society and the consequent desire to abandon it, typically through emigration). Organised or coherent political action is rarely an option in such a situation. The reliance on a patronage polity on a secular level finds its correlative on a religious level in the superstition and fatalism of Neapolitan Catholicism:

> The social experience of the patronage polity has long since been ration-alised into a tradition of fatalism . . . The ordinary individual feels that he has no more control over the caprices of human authority than he does over the uncertainties of the physical universe. All he can do in both circumstances is to take what precautions he can: with the deity, through a protector-saint (San Gennaro), against natural disaster and with the *raccomandazione* of the most powerful person he knows to protect him against human cupidity. (Ibid.: 98)

This political and religious world-view finds its perfect correlative in the NF's melodramatic conventions, according to which conflicts typically stem from the actions of a higher authority or events over which the characters have no control. Moreover, the reactions described by Allum are clearly paralleled in the strategies of narrative resolution: parasitism in the masochistic identifica-tion with the characters' suffering, which generates emotional catharsis, and the happy endings, which never alter the existing social order; grievance and riot in the explosions of violence and crimes of passion; and quitting in the emigrations or withdrawals into convents with which the films so frequently end.

In addition to the sense of estrangement from the new *Gesellschaft* order, the consequences of Unification are also the initial source of a sense of shame, regret and nostalgia that is a key facet of the Neapolitan mentality. The transi-tion from capital of the Kingdom of the Two Sicilies to a regional city intro-duced not only a series of economic problems but also psychological concerns about the decline of Naples. Such concerns are articulated by the NF's reliance on narratives in which the traditional social order is beset by the corrupting influences of modernity or non-Neapolitan society, and in which characters become morally corrupted or experience a fall from grace.

This relationship between the NF's melodramatic conventions and the Neapolitan 'world-view' helps explain why viewers perceive these films as realistic, identify with them, and achieve emotional engagement. However, the relationship is actually more complex; these narratives do not simply reflect the common perception of reality, but also constitute a template for representing and interpreting that reality. This is clear in Grasso's interview with Vincenzo B, a 34-year-old, unemployed, unskilled worker with a wife and six children in via Marittima. Vincenzo's story of how his wife was mistakenly arrested by the police and then molested closely mirrors the narrative conventions of the NF in its emphasis on victimisation by the authorities, the attempted violation of an innocent woman, and the desire to avenge one's honour (ibid.: 94–5).

Gabriella Gribaudi also offers an interesting account of this 'circularity of theatre and daily life in Naples' through an exploration of the relationship between popular stereotypes of Naples, their depiction in theatre and literature, and first-hand accounts of real events (Gribaudi 1999: 65). Rather than revealing a more complex reality that contradicts or modifies stereotypes, these testimonies mirror the kinds of narrative and interpretative structure of their fictional counterparts and thus reveal the extent to which the generic and narrative conventions of literature, film and the theatre constitute a means of articulating and interpreting reality. Significantly, Vincenzo B.'s account ends inconclusively (he will not kill the guard who molested his wife, otherwise he would be arrested), and this highlights the way fictional narratives function either as wish-fulfilment, completing the narrative in a more satisfactory fashion, or as a way of making sense of and coming to terms with insoluble problems.

The representation of Naples itself plays a central role in this creation of 'realistic' fictions. It is therefore necessary for us to consider briefly how the city has been represented both in the NF and in the wider cultural sphere. As the largest metropolis in the South and the ex-capital of the Kingdom of the Two Sicilies, Naples exemplifies the South as a whole, but also constitutes a somewhat anomalous case. In the eighteenth century, contradictory images of the South circulated as the Grand Tour writers described it as either a terrestrial paradise, an inferno, or a 'paradise inhabited by devils' (see Lumley and Morris 1997: pp. 84 and 88). Subsequently, the Meridionalisti constructed the South in terms of a 'Southern Problem' (*questione meridionale*), emphasising its negative characteristics, as in Pasquale Villari's description of the appalling living conditions in Naples at the time (Villari 1887). What is important about these interpretations is that they conceive of the South as an other. As John Dickie has observed, this serves an important function in terms of the construction of Italian national identity:

> To define Italy as civilized, one has to have a sense, albeit perhaps implicit, of where that civilization fades at its boundaries into the barbarous. The South was one of Italy's most important banks of images of Otherness. The barbarous, the primitive, the violent, the irrational, the feminine, the African: these and other values, negatively connoted, were repeatedly located in the Mezzogiorno as foils to definitions of Italy. (Lumley and Morris 1997: 119)

Naples not only served as a repository of otherness, like the South as a whole, but also helped to demarcate this borderline, and it soon came to be seen as the point of transition between civilised Europe and the barbarous South. For example, in 1806 Creuze de Lesser wrote, 'Europe ends at Naples and ends badly. Calabria, Sicily and all the rest belong to Africa' (ibid.: 87). Although conceptions of Naples as a paradise and an inferno tend to co-exist, there is a general passage from the former to the latter during the nineteenth and twentieth centuries, as exemplified by the oft-quoted phrase 'vedi Napoli, e poi muori,' which originally meant that once you had seen Naples you could die in peace as there was nothing more beautiful to see, but is now taken to mean that you are unlikely to survive a visit to the city![10]

While the NF never quite goes so far as to depict Naples as a utopian paradise, it nevertheless repeatedly establishes its uniqueness by emphasising a series of positive values ranging from the aesthetic (the beauty of the Bay of Naples) to the cultural (the glories of Neapolitan song), anthropological (the irrepressible vitality and fundamental goodness of its population) and social (the close-knit local community). Such a conception of Naples plays a funda-mental role within the structural economy of the NF's melodramatic narra-tives. In order to see how this takes place in a more concrete fashion, let us now take a closer look at the NF's narrative and stylistic characteristics.

NARRATIVE TYPOLOGIES

Based on the nature of the dramatic conflict underpinning the narrative and the method by which it is resolved, it is possible to identify four broad narra-tive variants within the NF. The first two revolve around a series of obstacles to the consecration of a social order based around the family and romantic exclusivity, while the second two focus on the conflicts generated when the protagonist(s) transgress this social order and its moral values. All four vari-ants articulate narratives in which the Neapolitan *Gemeinschaft* and its values come under threat, and all four conclude with a cathartic resolution.

Internal Challenges to the Establishment of Social Order

The first variant revolves around the opposition of a parental or authority figure or a series of economic obstacles to romantic union. The optimistic reso-lution is brought about by a combination of the protagonist's qualities, usually his vocal talents, which bring him fame and fortune, and a dose of miraculous good luck. Numerous films feature characters who overcome economic dif-ficulties and win over a lover's parents by becoming successful singers; the biopic *Enrico Caruso (Leggenda di una voce)* (1951, Giacomo Gentilomo) is constructed in such terms, as is *Monaca Santa* (1948, Guido Brignone), *Una voce, una chitarra, un pò di luna* (1956, Giacomo Gentilomo) and *Napoli, sole mio!* (1958, Giorgio C. Simonelli). Similarly, in *Vagabondi delle stelle* (1956, Nino Stresa), a young painter only manages to convince his girlfriend's father of the sincerity of his feelings and thus earn his consent by serenading her.

Several other films present economic problems as an obstacle to an aspiring couple but resolve the problem in a different fashion. In *Quel tesoro di papà* (1959, Marino Girolami) a rich family oppose their daughter's relationship with a young chauffeur, only to discover that he is actually rich and was only pretending to be poor in order to ensure that her feelings for him were genuine. Other films present a range of different obstacles to romantic union: *Io, mammetta e tu* (1958, Carlo Ludovico Bragaglia) features both parental opposition and the prospect of impending military service, while *Carcerato* (1951, Armando Zorri) presents a whole range of obstacles (emigration, pregnancy, intercepted letters and a treacherous rival) until the return of the young man and the accidental death of the rival allow the union to occur. *Presentimento* (1957, Armando Fizzarotti) offers an interesting variation in which a man is forced to marry a woman he does not love, only for her to die, allowing him to return to the woman he loves and start a new family with the children of both marriages.

Città canora (1952, Mario Costa) is a good example of this tendency in that it displaces an economic problem (Giacomo is poor) on to an affective one (so he cannot marry Maria) and resolves this problem through the success he achieves as a singer. It is typical of the Neapolitan fatalism described above that, in order to bring the narrative to its happy conclusion, it requires the intervention of a series of fortuitous events (the unexpected arrival of an impresario looking for an unknown Neapolitan singer and the death of his rival for Maria's affections at the hands of his criminal consorts). Crucially, this fantasy of wish-fulfilment is explicitly linked to a celebration of Naples and its culture; Giacomo is chosen by the impresario because he is a poor Neapolitan singer and he obtains success in a show celebrating the musical traditions of the city. Moreover, *napoletanità* is explicitly constructed as a positive character trait; whereas Giacomo is 'the best, and the most Neapolitan, of Neapolitan musicians', his rival, who has lived in the North for many years, is rejected by the community when they recognise his corruption and complain that 'the only thing Neapolitan about you is your name.' The impresario continually expounds the virtues of traditional Neapolitan song and laments its dilution into more modern forms, reinforcing a discourse about the threat posed to Neapolitan traditions by the corrupting influence of modernity and foreign influence.

External Challenges to the Establishment of Social Order

In the second variant, romantic union is obstructed by greater forces over which the protagonists have no control, such as an unscrupulous rival or a piece of fatal bad luck, and this usually results in the protagonist being either suspected of infidelity or convicted of a crime. It is important to note that the protagonists' innocence is only ever questioned by the other characters; the audience must be aware of their innocence in order to share in their suffering. This tendency represents the misfortunes that can befall the innocent member of a *Gemeinschaft* society estranged from the unjust systems of law and authority; the ending is invariably positive and utilises chance or divine providence to prove their innocence miraculously and to consecrate the romantic union. The motif of the innocent accused is a staple of melodrama in general and is probably the most frequently recurrent theme of the NF; it is evident in numerous titles, including *Le due Madonne* (1949, Enzo Di Gianni and Giorgio C. Simonelli), *Lettera napoletana* (1954, Giorgio Pàstina), *Cuore di mamma* (1954, Luigi Capuano), *La Luciana* (1954, Domenico Gambino), *Quel bandito sono io!* (1949, Mario Soldati) and *La trovatella di Pompei* (1956, Giacomo Gentilomo). *Core 'ngrato* (1951, Guido Brignone) takes this device a stage further by having an innocent young woman falsely accused twice before falling in love with her defence lawyer! Several other films feature young women who manage to save their fathers from unjust accusations, including *Madunella* (1947, Ernesto Grassi) and *La figlia del mendicante* (1949, Carlo Campogalliani). This theme is also frequently linked to the actions of an unscrupulous rival; in both *Piscatore 'e Pusilleco* (1954, Giorgio Capitani) and *Suonno d'ammore* (1955, Sergio Corbucci) a man accuses his rival of a crime but his treachery is discovered, freeing the innocent who can then marry his fiancée. In other cases, the rival's acts interfere with the relationship in different ways. In *Cento serenate* (1954, Anton Giulio Majano) a young man becomes jealous of a rival's attentions to his fiancée but ultimately recognises her innocence, while in *Desiderio 'e sole* (1954, Giorgio Pàstina) a young woman is rescued from the persecutions of a prospective lover by the intervention of her fiancé. *Scapricciatiello* (1954, Luigi Capuano) offers another variant in which a young man is accused of being the father of an unborn child, thus endangering his relationship with his true love before the truth comes out.

This variant is most clearly embodied by the 'torna' (return) narrative in which a woman is pursued by an unscrupulous old flame, who induces her husband to suspect her of infidelity, as in *Torna* (1984, Stelvio Massi). In both *Catene* (1949, Raffaello Matarazzo) and, more recently, *Lacrime napulitane* (1981, Ciro Ippolito) the protagonist is driven to emigrate from Naples in order to escape the shame and suffering generated by his wife's presumed infidelity, and this motif obviously had particular resonance for the large Southern Italian population in the United States. Indeed, the films exploit this fact for maximum emotional effect by drawing on classic emigrant songs such as *Lacreme napulitane*. In this way, Naples is once again associated with a series of positive social and moral values and the protagonist's lament for the loss of his family and his homeland also functions as a lament for the erosion of this social and moral order in the face of modernity and historical change. Once again, however, the resolution is a happy one and, following the cathartic performance of the title song, the woman's innocence is established, the rival is dispatched, the protagonist returns, the family unit is reconstituted and the social order is reaffirmed.[11]

The Purging of Serious Transgressions of the Social Order

The third variant revolves around a series of problems created when the protagonist(s) stray from what is perceived as the correct moral or social order and have to deal with the consequences. In the case of a male protagonist, this is usually depicted as a slide into a life of crime (typically stealing or contraband), while for women it usually revolves around the loss of sexual purity. In a *Gemeinschaft* society sexual activity outside wedlock presents a threat to its functioning, particularly when it involves the woman who, as we have seen, constitutes the cornerstone of the system and whose primary role is as mother, rather than wife. This threat is embodied in a number of recurrent figures: the *malafemmena*, or fallen woman, and the *figlio di nessuno*, or illegitimate child. Criminal activity is also a threat to a precarious economic system such as the one operating in Naples; the films define crime in moral rather than legal terms and arrive at a double standard, distinguishing between those activities that are acceptable or even necessary to the society and those that are not. Significant in this regard is the distinction frequently made between the *guappo* and the *camorrista*; the *guappo* represents a supposedly honourable tradition, which is seen as serving an important social function, given the rejection of the institutions and authority of the *Gesellschaft*, while the *camorrista* represents the decline of that tradition into a criminal enterprise based solely around self-interest.[12]

In this third narrative variant, the protagonist either is sacrificed or withdraws from society in order to atone for his/her transgression of the rules of the *Gemeinschaft* society and to permit the social order to continue unchanged; thus the narrative works towards the reaffirmation of the social order by purging it of undesirable elements. The most frequent way in which this variant is embodied is through the figure of the *malafemmena*. In the two adaptations of Salvatore Di Giacomo's 1904 play, *Assunta Spina* (1914, Gustavo Serena and Francesca Bertini, and 1947, Mario Mattoli), the titular character is *sfregiata* (scarred) by her lover for a presumed betrayal. On discovering that she has accepted the patronage of another man during his imprisonment for this act, he kills his rival and Assunta atones for her 'sin' by confessing to the crime of *delitto d'onore* that she drove her jealous lover to commit and thus sacrificing herself to ensure his continued freedom. Similarly, the protagonists of *Femmina senza cuore* (1952, Renato Borraccetti), *Vestire gli ignudi* (1953,

Marcello Pagliero) and *La scogliera del peccato* (1950, Roberto Bianchi Montero) are punished for their infidelities with death, while Anna Zaccheo, in *Un marito per Anna Zaccheo* (1953, Giuseppe De Santis), is abandoned by her fiancé when he discovers she has been seduced by another man. Similarly, the revelation that the protagonist of *Malafemmena* (1957, Armando Fizzarotti) is actually more noble than everyone believed is only arrived at through her ultimate sacrifice. In terms of the male variant, *Una donna ha ucciso* (1951, Vittorio Cottafavi) features a male protagonist who is punished for a casual relationship by losing his life, while in *Passione* (1953, Max Calandri), a man turns to crime and inadvertently steals from his estranged daughter before being killed by his partners.

It was a narrative of this kind that re-launched the NF in the post-war era: *Malaspina* (1947, Armando Fizzarotti), an adaptation of the song by Cioffi and Fusco. While most of the characters remain as fixed types, Maria/Malaspina moves from the role of virginal fiancée to treacherous seductress and, finally, to world-renouncing nun. Such character instability is typical of films of this tendency, which revolve around the protagonist's morality; just as film noir places its femme fatale at the centre of its ostensibly crime-based investigation, so *Malaspina* bases its melodrama around the moral shifts of its female protagonist.[13] Undoubtedly, one of the key functions of this type of film is containment; the character's fall from virginal grace as Maria to the *malafemmena* Malaspina is ultimately resolved by her withdrawal into a convent. Within the confines of a Catholic, *Gemeinschaft* society, sexual activity (and in particular female sexual activity) outside of marriage is seen as a destructive force, and *Malaspina* explores this threat and then defuses it. Significantly, the resolution is constituted as both a renouncing of sexuality and a marriage with God, and this fact is made explicit twice in the film: when Maria promises Andrea, 'I'll belong to you or to God,' and when she later flees from a marriage to his rival to present herself at the convent in her wedding dress. The films that constitute this variant are frequently described as revolving around questions of honour, in which the male protagonist, having been betrayed by a treacherous woman, re-establishes his honour through a *delitto d'onore*. However, although *Malaspina* features both betrayal and a *delitto d'onore*, it is less about re-establishing honour than about working through the threat posed by sexual activity outside of marriage. Indeed, the role played by the *delitto d'onore* is ambiguous; it is Maria's withdrawal into a convent and marriage to God, and not Andrea's killing of Gaetano, which brings about narrative resolution. Indeed, the *delitto d'onore* is presented as the nadir of the protagonist's decline as a result of the woman's treachery, rather than the restoration of his honour, and thus the ending must be considered pessimistic.[14]

The Repairing of Minor Transgressions of the Social Order

The final variant also deals with a moral or social transgression but it has a more positive resolution in which the protagonist repairs his/her wrongdoings and is accepted back into society, suggesting that the transgression is less threatening to the social fabric. The most typical way that this is articulated is in the story of a young man who is seduced and led astray by a sensual yet immoral woman (typically from the world of show-business) before coming to his senses and returning to the innocent girl who loves him. This is the plot of *Napoli terra d'amore* (1954, Camillo Mastrocinque), *Amore e smarrimento* (1954, Filippo Walter Ratti) and *Non sono più guaglione (Oh, mia bella Carolina!)* (1958, Domenico Paolella). Whereas the *malafemmene* described above destroy the men who fall for them before being sacrificed themselves, the films in this last variant concentrate on the drama of their male protagonists and frequently show disinterest in the fate of the women. Several other films feature the redemption of a man who had turned to a life of crime; the protagonist of *Santa Lucia luntana* (1951, Aldo Vergano) ultimately decides to go straight and returns to his fiancée, while the protagonist of *Zappatore* (1950, Rate Furlan), having ruined his peasant family through a life of vice in the city, repents and goes home. While the majority of films featuring a female sexual transgression fall into the third variant described above, there are a few films in which the woman returns, unpunished, to the social fold; in *Lacrime d'amore* (1954, Pino Mercanti) a woman has an affair before returning to her husband and children, while in *Te sto aspettanno* (1956, Armando Fizzarotti), a girl abandons her fiancé for a man who marries another, then returns to the fiancé who is still waiting for her.

A good example of the fourth variant is *Guaglione* (1956, Giorgio C. Simonelli), in which an adolescent is led astray by an immoral older woman. However, he is seduced less by her sexuality than by the exotic luxuriance she represents as a Northern Italian living in a plush and elegant apartment and belonging to the world of show-business. The film depicts the dangers inherent in a pursuit of such illusions before resolving itself when Franco gets together with the girl next door, whom he will presumably marry, and runs to embrace his mother. On one level the film functions as a morality play, warning of the dangers of indulging one's desires, both sexual and economic. Once again this morality is articulated in terms of a contrast between a modern, Northern society typified by the soubrette and a traditional Southern one typified by the girl next door. Thus the film functions both in psychological terms, containing desire, and in social terms, working through the conflict between *Gemeinschaft* and *Gesellschaft* social structures.

These four variants should be considered broad tendencies rather than distinct categories and there are several films that exhibit characteristics of more than one variant. The combination of elements from the first two tendencies simply represents a multiplication of the obstacles faced by the young couple, as in *Giuramento d'amore* (1955, Roberto Bianchi Montero) or *Napoli, eterna canzone* (1950, Silvio Siano). *Siamo ricchi e poveri* (1953, Siro Marcellini), on the other hand, combines elements of the first and last tendency, telling of a young man who is seduced by another woman, but then earns success as a singer, inherits a fortune and returns to his fiancée. Both *Noi peccatori* (1953, Guido Brignone) and *Napoli è sempre Napoli* (1954, Armando Fizzarotti) combine elements of the second and final tendencies, telling of women who become singers in order to help their fiancés; this leads to jealousy, abandonment but ultimately understanding and reconciliation. All of these combinations are perfectly compatible because they all work towards the salvation or redemption of their protagonists and only differ in terms of the obstacles they present. More significant, perhaps, are those films that combine elements of the third and fourth tendencies and which point to a kind of double standard in the way in which different transgressions – male and female, social and sexual – are perceived. For example, in *Monastero di Santa Chiara* (1949, Mario Sequi), while Enrico is able to put his life of crime behind him and go straight, Ester has to pay for falling in love with a German officer with her life.

STYLISTICS

Location shooting is one of the key distinguishing traits of the NF and its absence from Neapolitan-set, Roman-produced films of the 1930s like *Napoli d'altri tempi* (1938, Amleto Palermi) is another reason why this period constitutes a hiatus between the Neapolitan cinema of the silent era and the post-war period. This location shooting is often seen as responsible for creating a distinctive and characteristic 'environmental realism' (Spinazzola 1974: 185). However, the images of the city most frequently deployed are highly stereotypical, and this fact cannot easily be reconciled with the idea that they function as a realist device. Rather, an explanation of their function should be sought in relation to the role that Naples plays within the social and moral economy the films' discourse sets up.

The NF employs three distinct strategies in the representation of the city. The first is to present panoramas of the Bay of Naples, typically shot from Posillipo with the almost obligatory pine tree in the foreground and Vesuvius on the horizon (see Fig. 2.1). The use of such images at the start of the film or as a backdrop to the credit sequence is so common that it constitutes a virtual stylistic motif. Such sequences draw on conventional representational strategies dating back to the seventeenth-century practice of *vedutismo* and, in their aestheticisation of natural beauty, align Naples with the kind of unspoilt, earthly paradise described by the eighteenth-century Grand Tour

Figure 2.1   The quintessential image of the Neapolitan Formula: a panorama taken from the hills of Posillipo. *Disonorata senza colpa* (1954, Giorgio W. Chili) ©General Film Industria Cinematografica.

writers.[15] In this way they immediately and unequivocally establish both the film's Neapolitan setting and the positive interpretation of Naples that the film wishes to present. Another recurrent strategy is to focus on images of crowded *bassi*, teeming alleyways, and courtyards overlooked by the windows of the surrounding apartments. These scenes serve to emphasise communal living and thus draw attention to the *Gemeinschaft* society that plays such an important role within the films' discursive structure (see Fig. 2.2). The third and final strategy is to present travelogue sequences of historical monuments and internationally renowned sites like the cloisters of Santa Chiara, Castel Sant'Elmo, Castel dell'Ovo, Maschio Angioino, Porta Capuana, Piazza del Municipio, Piazza del Plebiscito and Piazza del Gesù. These scenes emphasise Naples' important status in centuries past and suggest the continuation of that legacy into the present.

Most of the films utilise several of these strategies and this combination serves two further functions. On the one hand, it helps the film simultaneously to address local audiences, who identify with the anonymous backstreets and specific micro-communities, and a wider Southern Italian or national audience,

Figure 2.2 The Neapolitan *Gemeinschaft* in *Carosello napoletano* (1954, Ettore Giannini). ©Cecchi Gori.

who experience a similar sense of recognition only at the sight of more famous monuments and views of the city. On the other, it implies a correlation between the anonymous, poor, working-class areas and the traditional sights of Naples familiar to tourists; it brings the 'gold of Naples' to those areas where 'the sea doesn't reach Naples,' to evoke the titles of two of the most important literary images of Naples from the period.[16] The pursuit of such strategies obviously necessitates a selective and partial representation of the city, and most of the films concentrate on the waterfront area from Posillipo to Santa Lucia or the historic centre. Additionally, they may feature other picturesque areas within the province of Naples, such as the Amalfi coast or the island of Capri.

Critics have typically condemned the NF's reliance on such conventionalised and stereotypical images of the city (see below). However, the combination of these strategies would seem to be indispensable to the films' discourse and to make good commercial sense. The filmmakers appear to be conscious of this fact and their use of such images is as likely to be part of a deliberate strategy as a result of laziness or a lack of originality. *Città canora* seems to foreground this fact by replicating its own folkloristic images in the stage show in which the protagonist becomes famous – a musical review also entitled *Città canora*, which celebrates the delights of Naples. The strategy is also consistent with the wider cultural and political project to promote Naples as a cultural and tourist destination, which underpinned the Lauro administration's policies to aid the post-war reconstruction of Naples.[17] Again, *Città canora* draws attention to this strategy as one character remarks, during a boat ride in which we are treated to beautiful images of the coastline accompanied by Neapolitan songs on the soundtrack, 'This is the latest discovery of the tourist industry: they've set the panorama to music. Every celebrated location has its own song: Santa Lucia, Mergellina, Posillipo, Marecchiaro.'

Closely related to the use of location shooting is the presence of Neapolitan dialect. Traditional Neapolitan dialect is sufficiently different from standard Italian as to be virtually incomprehensible to Italians from other regions. Although its use has been eroded during the twentieth century by more widely available education and the mass media, a form of dialect is still spoken by a large part of the population – particularly in popular quarters – and presents considerable difficulties for non-Neapolitans. Some films utilise dialect in their titles (*Te sto aspettanno*, *Guaglione*), others have titles in standard Italian (*Piccola santa*, *Femmina senza cuore*), while some were distributed under both Italian and Neapolitan titles (*Piscatore 'e Pusilleco/Il pescatore di Posillipo*, *Suonno d'ammore/Sogno d'amore*). Similarly, while films such as *Malaspina* utilise dialect quite extensively in their dialogue, others such as *Maruzzella* (1956, Luigi Capuano) either are entirely in standard Italian or use only a slight regional inflection and drop in the occasional well-known term in dialect. Another common approach is to use standard Italian for the protagonists and dialect for secondary characters who do not really further the narrative.[18] The reasons for these choices are not hard to grasp and clearly derive from the commercial logic underpinning the formula. While on the one hand there is a desire to exploit a niche regional market, there is also a simultaneous attention to a wider national audience for whom thick dialect would be a potential problem. Thus most of the films use dialect sparingly to give the impression of *napoletanità* and to create a sense of authenticity without compromising the comprehensibility of the narrative. This approach descends directly from the plays and films of Eduardo De Filippo, the first person to bring Neapolitan dialect to a wide national audience, albeit in a compromised, somewhat standardised form. On this level the NF of the post-war period departs from the films of the silent era, which targeted a more exclusively regional audience and used a much thicker dialect in their written intertitles. Significantly, the more marginal and regional a film's production and distribution, the greater and more uncompromising its use of dialect. For example, compare the film that re-launched the NF, *Malaspina*, with *Guaglione*, which Spinazzola describes as its point of maximum expansion (Spinazzola 1974: 185).

Stylistic excess is typically seen as a key facet of melodrama, converting the emotional intensity experienced by the characters into audience pathos. However, one of the principle characteristics of the NF is the combination of melodramatic excess at the level of plot and performance with a stylistic poverty at the cinematic level. This aspect of the NF's style is also indicative of the influence of the *sceneggiata*, with its combination of perfunctory sets and costumes and an excessive, non-naturalistic performance style. Mario Franco, for example, describes the NF as being characterised by a 'slapdash formality' (Aprà 1994: 204). Undoubtedly, such a description could be applied to *Malaspina*'s inconsistent photography and lighting, muddied dialogue, poor synchronisation, incongruous post-synched sound effects, and imperfect scene dissection. Moreover, its non-naturalistic performance style is distinct from the majority of national productions and probably derives in part from the actors' lack of experience and in part from the influence of the *sceneggiata*.[19] Nevertheless, these characteristics cannot be said to be representative of the NF as a whole and several other films like *Città canora* and *Guaglione* are much more conventionally 'well made'; scenes are more clearly articulated, camera placement is more deliberate, and camera movement is used to expressive effect. Moreover, the performances are more typical of cinematic acting styles, and the use of famous Neapolitan character actors like Tina Pica and Dante and Beniamino Maggio in supporting roles creates a successful contrast with the protagonists. *Monastero di Santa Chiara* is another interesting film that makes a far more self-consciously expressive use of the cinematic medium than the apparent lack of artifice of *Malaspina* or the self-effacing naturalism of *Città canora*. The use of oblique camera angles and the expressionistic play of light in certain scenes serve to create a sense of subjectivity, a participation in the characters' moral dilemma that is absent from the other films described. It would seem to be the case that those films that are more closely associated with the *sceneggiata* (such as the films of Mario Merola in the 1970s) tend to be characterised by greater formal imperfections than those that draw greater inspiration from film melodrama. This can perhaps be explained in terms of both their reduced budget and their increased marginality within the market place; these filmmakers do not have the means at their disposal to achieve greater technical proficiency and they see such surface gloss as largely irrelevant to the film's ability to perform its function and reach its target audience.[20] Indeed, producer Fortunato Misiano has said, 'I believe that the ingenuity and deliberate lack of artifice that you can find in my films is not only one of the reasons behind their success but also constitutes a genuine asset' (quoted in Faldini and Fofi 1979: 170).

The emphasis on location shooting, the use of dialect and the indifference to stylistic perfection should be considered key elements of the NF's approach. The canny use of locations and dialect lends an impression of immediacy to conventionalised narratives and offsets the lack of cinematic polish. It also serves to address a specific Neapolitan audience directly while allowing for the possibility of appealing to a wider national audience. The stylistic choices of the NF must be understood within the commercial logic it pursues: low-budget production, the reliance on conventions deriving from culturally specific extra-cinematic cultural forms like Neapolitan song and the *sceneggiata*, and the targeting of popular, regional audiences.

Re-Interpreting the Neapolitan Formula

Contemporary critics tended to be simply dismissive of the NF and some reviews are explicit about this fact. A review of . . . *e Napoli canta* (1953, Armando Grottini) simply describes it as 'another film set in Naples on whose story and realisation it is not worth wasting words'.[21] *Nennella* (1948, Renato May) is dismissed in similar terms because it 'belongs to those mediocre and modest Neapolitan productions which it is not worth bothering with'. This dismissive position can be explained in both aesthetic and ideological terms.

As far as aesthetic judgements are concerned, *Madunella* was described as 'a mediocre work, produced with insufficient means', and *Madonna delle rose* as 'a comic book tale, mediocrely realised'. Of *Amore e smarrimento* a critic wrote, 'the story is of little interest and its realisation is both superficial and mediocre,' and of *Piccola santa*, 'it's a conventional story, realised in a mediocre fashion.'[22] The success of these films, despite their stylistic imperfections, was seen by critics as indicative of the low level of sophistication of their intended audience. This suggests that such aesthetic judgements derive from a distinction between 'popular cinema', addressed to an 'uneducated' or 'undiscriminating' viewer, as opposed to a culturally respectable or aesthetically refined cinema directed to a better-educated, more selective viewer. For example, *Voto di marinaio* is described as 'a very modest film that could only appeal to provincial audiences'. Another critic writes of *Zappatore*, 'We realise that films of this kind and this level appeal to a certain public. However, this doesn't prevent us from deploring the fact that after half a century of cinema Italy is still producing such stuff.' *Suonno d'ammore* is dismissed with the observation, 'it is one of the usual films set in a popular setting and full of songs and dramatic and emotional scenes that only appeal to undemanding audiences.' A similar bias has also characterised responses to melodrama generally:

> One reason for the low esteem in which melodrama has been held is its identification with mass, or what has been termed 'low culture,' in contrast to 'high culture.' . . . The bias against low culture, whether of an ethical or aesthetic cast, has generally been linked to a class and gender bias. (Landy 1991: 16)

One could argue that, whereas melodrama in general has been subjected to a class and gender bias, the NF suffers from a geographical bias in which these 'undemanding audiences' are implicitly identified with Naples and the South.

Vittorio Spinazzola was the first critic to examine the phenomenon of the NF as a whole and to engage with it seriously on a thematic and stylistic level. His chapter concludes with the following judgement:

> And so [the NF] develops the highly rhetorical myth of an 'enduring *napoletanità*' in the name of which the majority of films conclude with an effusive, trivial, and apolitical homage to Naples and its inhabitants . . . It is sad to observe for how long a large portion of Italian spectators have identified with films which are inspired by a blind attachment to the past and based on a parochial mythology and – dare I say it – racism that makes them the most conservative instance of Italian popular cinema. (Spinazzola 1974: 189)

Spinazzola's criticism is ideological, rather than aesthetic, in that he considers the films' socio-political content and offers a value judgement based on comparisons with a pre-existing ideology. This approach, which is consistent with one of the dominant traditions of the Italian critical establishment of the period, derives from a desire to mount a defence of unquestionably important films (in particular Neorealism) in the face of the harsh realities of the market place and the opposition of the political establishment (specifically the policies of Giulio Andreotti).[23] Claudio Carabba is undoubtedly correct in maintaining that, within the conditions of the time, this approach was both justified and necessary (Aprà and Carabba 1976: 42). However, in terms of a historical study such as this, the ideological basis of such criticisms needs to be recognised and put to one side. Unfortunately, many of the subsequent studies of this cinema have been conducted not by film scholars but by Neapolitan specialists like Roberto Ornanni and Enzo Grano, and as such fail to engage critically with their subject. Instead, they are frequently compromised by exactly the same 'myth of an enduring *napoletanità*' that Spinazzola criticises.

What is interesting about ideological criticisms of the NF is the extent to which they re-inscribe the positions displayed by the films themselves. Thus, while books on Neapolitan cinema, such as Roberto Ornanni's *Napoli nel cinema*, often adopt a celebratory line that replicates the process of cultural affirmation evident in the films, Spinazzola's criticisms reveal an antagonism to the social and moral philosophy underpinning the films that is characteristic of the mainstream (typically left-wing) critical establishment. Stefano Masi has offered an interesting alternative interpretation of the NF of the 1970s by arguing that, rather than being the expression of provincialism and cultural stereotype, the NF constitutes a unique and valid alternative to the homogenisation of contemporary (cinematic) culture:

> The principal merit of this cinema is its rejection of a program of total consumption by producing marginal stereotypes that are entirely self-sufficient and cannot be homogenised by the great industry of culture . . . It is an admirable cinema because it is not subject to an inferiority complex and does not aim to produce beautiful sequences. It aims at the 'lowest' areas of consumption, targeting a small portion of the market. And it knows that it can do so, just as it knows that it can be grammatically incorrect, 'ugly' and 'bad'. (Masi 1979a: 278)

Adriano Aprà makes a similar observation about the popular melodramas of the 1950s in general:

> At the moment it is difficult to say to what extent the structural and commercial dimensions of Italian popular cinema of the 1950s was the last manifestation of a national, or even regional, cinema – a final, conservative act of resistance against an increasingly international industry. (Aprà and Carabba 1976: 12)

This position recalls some of the arguments about the function of regional cinema in relation to the globalisation and homogenisation of mass culture advanced in the Introduction.

As with the general discourse about Naples and the South described above, all of these criticisms construct the NF as something other, rather than seeing it as part of the wider practices of post-war Italian cinema. The principal problem of such an approach is that it ignores the relationship between the depiction of Naples, the generic structure underpinning the narratives, and the commercial function of the films. This abstraction results in criticisms of conventional narratives, stereotypical images of Naples, and the targeting of undiscriminating viewers. One is reminded of Carole Sklan's suggestion, discussed in the Introduction, that the 'core' industry sets the terms for what is critically acceptable and thus condemns the products of the 'periphery'. This chapter, on the other hand, has attempted to relate the use of specific images of Naples and the discourse around *napoletanità* to the generic conventions in which they are embedded in order to establish the function the films fulfilled within a specific social and industrial context. In an environment characterised by a conflict between the values of a traditional and modern society and by the complex of problems summed up by the term 'Southern Question', the NF articulated concerns about 'progress' by displacing the political and the social on to the emotional and personal. This process involved not so much a negation of social and political reality as an attempt to resolve tensions, reaffirm the persistence of a 'correct' social and moral order, and provide a cathartic release. The use of *napoletanità* and the mobilising of conventional stereotypes, which critics have also found problematic, played an important role within the articulation of these concerns and within the re-negotiation of cultural identity at a moment of social transition. The NF should therefore be considered an important expression of Neapolitan culture, representative of a whole range of issues that cannot be reduced to the mere 'myth of an enduring *napoletanità*'. In terms of the film industry, the NF exploited the particular characteristics of the production and exhibition sector in order to produce a low-budget product aimed primarily at a niche market that played an important role in the economic flourishing of Italian cinema during the 1950s.

This discourse around notions of *napoletanità* is one of the defining characteristics of the NF and thus serves an important commercial function, distinguishing it from the other popular formulae of the period and carving out a niche in the market. The extent to which the emphasis on (frequently stereotypical) notions of *napoletanità* is apparent in both the titles and the publicity materials associated with the films is clear evidence of its importance within the commercial logic pursued by the formula (see Fig. 2.3). However, the celebration of *napoletanità* also serves several other functions. It serves as an affirmation of Neapolitan culture in the face of its perceived decline since Unification and the consequent feelings of shame and inferiority, and thus can be associated with a range of literature and art that emerges from, and responds to, the Southern Question. In terms of the political discourse circulating at the time, it can also be seen as part of the wider cultural project to promote Naples as a cultural and tourist destination, which underpinned the Lauro administration's policies to aid the development of the area. In terms of the melodramatic structure underpinning the formula, Naples serves a crucial role, for it is identified with the benign and correct moral order that underpins the moral fantasy. Thus a whole series of values (family, love, honesty and so on) are equated with Neapolitan society, while the disruptive influences are seen to come from elsewhere. The NF's success is thus dependent on its ability to fulfil a range of functions: political (the promotion of Naples and its culture), psychological (negating problems of poverty and feelings of inferiority due to the Southern Question) and commercial (the deliberate address to a target audience, the use of popular Neapolitan singers). Furthermore, these functions are grounded within a conventional, familiar generic structure that maximises the audience's ability to assimilate these functions and to derive pleasure.

Figure 2.3   The folkloristic image of Naples marketed by the Neapolitan Formula: original poster for *Città canora* (1952, Mario Costa). ©Webphoto.

CONCLUSION

By the end of the 1950s, the 'economic boom' was well under way, yet Naples' participation in this process was limited, as industrialisation, construction and urban expansion only introduced a series of new problems to the city and further widened the gap between social classes. It is perhaps significant that the NF died out at this moment, while a single new voice with a radically different political and aesthetic agenda emerged in Neapolitan cinema: Francesco Rosi, first with *La sfida* (1957) then, more importantly, with *Le mani sulla città/ Hands over the City* (1963). Although the NF re-emerged in the 1970s with the unlikely success of Mario Merola, it had also changed, diverging, as Stefano Masi has noted, between those films contaminated with other generic models like the urban crime film and those that relied on an even more explicit reference to the *sceneggiata* (Masi 1982: 21–2). While the former included a moralising perspective, denouncing urban squalor, political corruption and rampant violence, the latter appeared increasingly anachronistic, creating an element of kitsch largely absent from the films of the 1950s. In the 1980s Mario Merola was gradually replaced by the neomelodic singer Nino D'Angelo. Ciro Ascione has convincingly argued that his films modify the conventions of the NF to reflect not the traditional values outlined above, but rather the petit-bourgeois aspirations of a new Neapolitan youth.[24] Thus, D'Angelo 'incarnated the values of cultural homogenisation that dominated the 1980s' (De Crescenzo 1995: 138), but this attempt to transform the NF into a more respectable and bourgeois genre seems to have resulted in its virtual extinction.

In recent years there has been a renewed interest in Neapolitan cinema, due to a series of major retrospectives in Naples, Paris and New York, the interest of certain intellectuals and members of the avant-garde in the *sceneggiata*, and the rediscovery of the work of Elvira Notari, which has brought Neapolitan silent cinema to the attention of the international critical community.[25] Perhaps equally important for a re-evaluation of the traditions of Neapolitan cinema is the critical success of the NNC, which by its very definition implies both a relation to such traditions and a distancing from them. These filmmakers face a range of problems; the over-representation of Naples constitutes a dilemma from which it is virtually impossible to escape,[26] while changes in the cinema industry have drastically altered the production, distribution and exhibition structures in which Neapolitan cinema operates and this has necessarily had an impact on the type of films Naples can produce. This raises a number of important questions about the relationship between these two very different instances of Neapolitan cinema. Has the renaissance in Neapolitan cinema succeeded in finding new ways of articulating Neapolitan culture? Or, alternatively, has it lost the NF's canny ability to exploit a particular commercial logic within the structures of the film industry and to address the immediate concerns of a specific, targeted audience? Does the positive critical reception of recent films reflect a shift in the aesthetic and thematic qualities of the films themselves or rather a broader shift in cultural perspectives and conceptions of the relationship between art and ideology? Such issues will be dealt with in the following chapters as we finally devote our attention to a textual analysis of the films of the NNC.

NOTES

1. The term Neapolitan Formula (*filone napoletano*) was first coined by Vittorio Spinazzola and has subsequently been adopted by a number of other critics (see Spinazzola 1974, Caprara 2006 and Goffredo Fofi in Caldiron and Della Casa 1999: 159–62).
2. For a more detailed history, see Chapter 1.
3. Several recent documentaries have examined this tradition: Paolo Santoni's feature-length *Cuore napoletano* (2002) examines Neapolitan song in all its manifestations across two continents, while Antonietta De Lillo's short *'O sole mio* (1999) considers the cultural significance of this particular song.
4. Such a performance can be seen in *The Godfather: Part 2* (1974, Francis Ford Coppola). On the social geography of the *sceneggiata* see Runcini 1989.
5. See Papa 1976, Bello and De Matteis 1977, Fofi 1977 and the aforementioned Grano 1976.
6. See, for example, Pino Mauro's more socially conscious *Cronaca nera*, Vittorio Marsiglia's parodic *Isso, essa e 'o malamente*, and the Brechtian re-readings of Gennaro Vitiello's *Padrone e sotto* and Leo De Bernardis's *King-Lacreme Lear-Napulitane*.
7. For example, *Fenesta che lucive* (1914, Roberto Troncone).
8. See Marlow-Mann, forthcoming 2011.
9. The shift in the late 1950s and early 1960s to adventure formulae like the peplum and the spaghetti western, which, unlike melodrama, promote individualism rather than a sense of community, can possibly be explained by the 'economic boom' and consequent rise of a capitalist ideology.
10. This shift in meaning is nicely embodied in the three films that take this phrase as a title (1924, Eugenio Perego; 1952, Riccardo Freda; and 2007, Enrico Caria).
11. For a more detailed discussion of *Lacrime napulitane* and the *torna* narrative, see Marlow-Mann 2009.
12. *I guappi* (1974, Pasquale Squitieri) is entirely based upon this distinction.
13. Significantly, the film also equates Maria's 'fall from grace' with guilt over Italian involvement in the Second World War and casting is crucial to this notion; Maria is played by Vera Rol, a well-known soubrette from the 1940s, who was accused of collaboration with the Germans.
14. Perhaps the most famous example of such a narrative is the 1925 *sceneggiata* by Enzo Lucio Murolo, *Guapparia*, filmed in 1984 by Stelvio Massi.
15. On the notion of *vedutismo* and the representations of Naples in the cinema, see Bruno 1993: 201–229 and Iaccio 2000: 144–57.
16. Giuseppe Marotta (1947), *L'oro di Napoli*, Milan: Bompiani and Anna Maria Ortese (1954), *Il mare non bagna Napoli*, Einaudi: Turin.
17. On the relationship between the NF and Lauro's policies, see Fusco 2006.
18. A number of character actors like Tina Pica and Beniamino Maggio have made a career from playing such comic supporting roles.
19. Vera Rol came from dialect theatre while Aldo Bufi Landi was making his film

debut after appearing in hundreds of *sceneggiate*. Most of the rest of the cast were chosen from the inhabitants of the locations where the film was shot.

20. This reaches its apotheosis in the video productions of *sceneggiate* released by Quality Sound in the late 1990s, which are shockingly amateurish and betray a complete disregard for almost any kind of aesthetic criteria.

21. This and all subsequent citations are taken from the extracts from contemporary reviews contained in Chiti and Poppi 1991.

22. Note that 'mediocre' is the adjective most frequently used to describe the NF; this betrays the fact that the critics are misguidedly seeking something exceptional from a formula product that relies on standardisation.

23. On the debates around the political function of the cinema at the time, see Aristarco 1981.

24. On this aspect of D'Angelo's work, see also Ravveduto 2007: 62–5.

25. See Bruno 1993, Troianelli 1989, Aprà and Gili 1994, and Aprà 1994.

26. With regard to this over-representation of Naples, see Bruno 1997.

3. *ESTRANEI ALLA MASSA*: THE NEW NEAPOLITAN CINEMA AND THE CRISIS OF *NAPOLETANITÀ*

Estranei alla massa (literally 'outside the crowd' or 'beyond the masses') is the title of an interesting documentary directed by Vincenzo Marra in 2001, which depicts the everyday lives of seven members of the eponymous football supporters' club and then follows them to a match in Treviso where the Neapolitan team is humiliatingly defeated. Although the club's name is intended to denote a proud independence, which as we have seen is also characteristic of the NF, it also connotes separation and isolation, rather than the sense of belonging typical of fan clubs. The documentary and its title are thus emblematic of the way in which the NNC has called into question the sense of social cohesion and communal belonging that underpinned the NF.

In actual fact this process was prefigured by three crucial but anomalous films of the late 1970s: Werner Schroeter's German-Italian co-production, *Neapolitanische Geschichten/Nel regno di Napoli/The Kingdom of Naples* (1979), Salvatore Piscicelli's *Immacolata e Concetta: l'altra gelosia* [Immacolata and Concetta: The Other Jealousy] (1980) and Massimo Troisi's *Ricomincio da tre* [I'm Starting from Three] (1980).[1] However, in these directors' later films the treatment of Neapolitan identity became less central or less problematic, while elsewhere the success of neomelodic singer-actor Nino D'Angelo gave the NF a renewed lease of life. Therefore a conventional and unproblematic image of *napoletanità* coupled with narratives that served a conciliatory function continued to prevail throughout the 1980s. Nevertheless the seeds sown by these films reached fruition in the early 1990s, paradoxically at the same time that Naples underwent a cultural and political renaissance.

This chapter will begin by examining the way in which the discourse of *napoletanità* and the functions it served in the NF are undermined by the NNC through narratives emphasising social exclusion and existential alienation. It will then focus on the way a number of films have questioned the traditional image of the *Gemeinschaft* family and critiqued its patriarchal conception. Both of these themes converge in the archetypal figure of the *scugnizzo* to which the NNC has repeatedly returned. The chapter will then conclude by considering the possible responses to this crisis in *napoletanità* that the NNC pessimistically proposes: migration or extinction.

A Period of Transition

Released shortly before the earthquake that constitutes such a watershed in the recent history of the Italian South, Salvatore Piscicelli's debut feature *Immacolata e Concetta: l'altra gelosia* was inspired by a true story of a crime of passion and is narrated through the classic triangular structure of the *sceneggiata* (see Piscicelli's comments in Ferzetti 1983: 37). The film begins with two crimes: Immacolata's prostitution of an underage girl to Ciro Pappalardo, to whom she owes money, and Concetta's shooting of her lesbian lover's husband. The two characters meet in prison and begin an affair that continues after their release, much to the dismay of Immacolata's husband, Pasquale. After Immacolata's daughter is seriously injured in a fall, she resumes her relationship with Ciro in exchange for financial assistance. When Concetta discovers Immacolata is pregnant with Ciro's child, she kills her.

Despite its narrative revolving around crimes of romantic passion, the film departs significantly from both the *sceneggiata* and the NF in several ways. Firstly, the lesbian relationship contrasts markedly with the resolutely heterosexual construction of the *sceneggiata*; one might say that it is a case of 'Essa, essa e 'o malamente' ('Her, Her and the Bad Guy') rather than 'Isso, essa e 'o malamente' ('Him, Her and the Bad Guy'). While this does not affect the course of the narrative, it does represent a challenge to the fixed gender roles on which the *sceneggiata* relies and thus anticipates both the NNC's emphasis on alternative sexualities and the subversion of the *sceneggiata* through sexual difference in the films of Corsicato (see Chapter 4). Secondly, rather than producing the emotional involvement typical of melodrama, Piscicelli distances the viewer through the use of stylistic devices more characteristic of European art cinema; the narrative pace is slow, the camera favours static shots or slow, deliberate, circular pans, and the editing elides moments of narrative significance in favour of more mundane events. The performances, moreover, are resolutely non-naturalistic, relying on artificial blocking of characters within the frame, exaggerated gestures, and dialogue delivered with excessive deliberation, emphasis and unnatural pauses. Although the *sceneggiata* also employs a somewhat non-naturalistic performance style, it is only when abstracted from its emotional context that these devices appear mannered, artificial and almost Brechtian. Similarly, the use of an impenetrable Neapolitan dialect serves not as an indicator of authenticity, as in the NF, but rather as a distancing device (see Zagarrio 1997: 451). The music, which reworks the tango popular during the 1950s through the influence of jazz, also functions in this fashion, as Piscicelli himself has observed (Ferzetti 1983: 46).

The most significant difference between *Immacolata e Concetta* and the *sceneggiata*, however, lies in the nature of the relationships between the characters, which are almost exclusively defined in terms of economic dependence. In the NF, like the *sceneggiata*, family and romantic relationships are based around love, devotion and sexual passion, and the protagonist's actions are always in defence of the family unit. While economic difficulties may act as an obstacle to romantic union, they never actually determine the basis of relationships, and while *'o malamente* may use blackmail or trickery in an attempt to seduce *Essa*, he can never win her through simple economic means alone. Yet this is precisely the nature of Immacolata's relationship to Ciro. Similarly, when Pasquale learns of his wife's affair with Concetta, he is unable to follow through on his threats (like *Isso* in a *sceneggiata*) because he is economically dependent on her. Only Concetta remains independent, refusing Immacolata's offer of financial help when she is released from prison, and it is for this reason, as much as for her homosexuality, that she constitutes such a disruptive presence within the narrative. This third difference between Piscicelli's film and the *sceneggiata* begs for a sociological explanation. If the *sceneggiata* relies on a *Gemeinschaft* social structure defined by 'primary relationships' (kinship, friendship or neighbourhood), *Immacolata e Concetta* revolves around the 'secondary relationships' (ownership, commodities, economic relations) typical of the *Gesellschaft*. Within such a society there is little room for loving relationships or crimes of passion and thus the narrative forces driving the *sceneggiata* become anachronistic and disruptive. In killing Immacolata in the film's final scene, Concetta does not avenge herself against the betrayal of a *malafemmena* and thus protect a notion of sexual propriety on which the social order rests, and her final desperate cry as she slumps next to Immacolata's body expresses not so much her grief as the meaninglessness of her gesture.

The final difference between *Immacolata e Concetta* and the NF concerns the film's socio-geographic location. Rejecting the popular quarters of Naples' historic centre favoured by the NF, *Immacolata e Concetta* is the first film to focus on the Neapolitan periphery that will become so significant in the films of the NNC; specifically, it is set in Piscicelli's home town of Pomigliano d'Arco, which is portrayed as a small rural town not yet absorbed by the urban sprawl of the metropolis. Although Piscicelli has defined the film as 'dedicated to the Neapolitan hinterland and its peasant culture' (Ferzetti 1983: 34), this is an agricultural environment drained of its traditional connotations, which emphasises deserted streets, crumbling architecture and widespread unemployment. The only character who flourishes is Ciro, a minor entrepreneur with a chain of butcher's shops that eventually reaches into the heart of Naples itself – a member of the emerging petite bourgeoisie. Significantly, Piscicelli has commented on the 'materialist' and 'resolutely anti-Catholic' qualities of this culture (Ferzetti 1983: 37). This helps explain the film's title. While invoking the Catholic notion of an immaculate conception, the characters' names are used ironically, reflecting Piscicelli's materialist, rather than religious, conception of the Neapolitan hinterland. As a lesbian, Concetta is never likely to conceive and, significantly, it is her discovery that Immacolata is pregnant with Ciro's child that leads to her decision to murder her. Equally, Immacolata is presented not as pure ('immaculate') but rather as something akin to the *malafemmena* of the *sceneggiata* – 'a slut', as Ciro's wife puts it. On one level the film's subtitle ('the other jealousy') refers to the film's modification of the triangular structure of traditional melodrama through the use of a homosexual relationship; however, it also points towards the extent to which it is not simply emotional jealousy (affective ownership) that drives the characters but rather power relationships (economic ownership).

Paolo Bertetto argues that Piscicelli's stylistic choices are antithetical to his deployment of the narrative structure of the *sceneggiata*, which requires emotional involvement, and thus the film is an 'unconvincing hybrid, full of contradictions' (Bertetto 1981: 142). However, the formal and narrative choices described above can also be explained by Piscicelli's materialist analysis of contemporary Neapolitan society; the aim is to depict the alienating effects of a materialist society based around 'secondary' relations, and this is achieved by staging a popular cultural form like the *sceneggiata* but denaturalising it, removing it from its socio-geographic context and violating its conventions with formal devices borrowed from art cinema. That Piscicelli should take such an approach is unsurprising given his background; he has stated that he was formed both by trips to the cinema with his mother as a child in the 1950s, during which he must have watched the NF and other popular melodramas, and much later by working for the Pesaro Festival of New Cinema where he was exposed to the New Waves of the 1960s and 1970s and Marxist film criticism (Bo and Cielo 1985: 174 and 180). It is not surprising, then, that his approach resembles that of Rainer Werner Fassbinder, who also reworked melodrama through Brechtian formal devices and focused on the corrupting influences of capitalism and impersonal economic relations. This fact highlights the impact that the New German Cinema had on the development of Neapolitan cinema in the late 1970s; not only did Werner Schroeter's *Nel regno di Napoli* prove as decisive an influence as Piscicelli's film on the later development of the NNC, as we shall see in the next chapter, but Mario Martone also chose to name his theatrical troupe *Falso Movimento* after Wim Wenders' *Falsche Bewegung/ False Movement* (1975).

SOCIAL AND EXISTENTIAL ALIENATION IN THE NEW NEAPOLITAN CINEMA

In the 1990s a number of films reprised Piscicelli's focus on the problems faced by the underprivileged inhabitants of a degraded, post-industrial urban periphery, and although not all the films adopted Piscicelli's explicitly Marxist perspective, it is hard not to see in them the theme of social alienation writ large.[2] The idea of social exclusion or marginalisation is not entirely new to Neapolitan cinema; indeed, the precarious nature of the Neapolitan economy is a recurrent theme in earlier films focusing on characters that struggle to find work, a house or a role in society.[3] Besides comedies like *Totò cerca casa* (1949, Steno and Mario Monicelli), it is also present in those films of the NF that focus on youngsters whose love is opposed by the parents, such as *Città canora* (1952, Mario Costa) and Ettore Maria Fizzarotti's trilogy *In ginocchio da te* (1964), *Non son degno di te* (1965) and *Se non avessi più te* (1965). However, in these films such problems are seen as external threats to the social order that Naples embodies rather than an intrinsic part of it, and thus the films articulate consolatory narratives that resolve the causes of the characters' marginalisation and unproblematically reassimilate them into a social order to which, fundamentally, they always belonged. Conversely, more recent films have emphasised the difficulty in resolving these issues, suggesting that they reflect a fundamental split between the individual and the community and a more intractable problem at the heart of Neapolitan society.

The films of Vincenzo Marra, for example, betray his formation as a lawyer specialising in civil rights in their focus on the poor, underprivileged or socially excluded, characteristics that have generated comparisons with both Neorealism and the work of Ken Loach. His second film, *Vento di terra* [Land Breeze] (2003), was inspired by an encounter with tramps on the streets of New York and his subsequent reflection on 'what happens when a series of unexpected, dramatic events strike someone who doesn't have the means to affront them, who lacks what I call a "parachute".'[4] The film tells the story of the Pacilli family, who live in the notorious district of Scampia, which has become a virtual metonym for the social alienation of contemporary Naples (see pp. 164–5 and Fig. 3.1). When his father dies, the unemployed Vincenzo briefly flirts with crime before joining the army out of desperation. His mother is driven to a suicide attempt by her landlord's (illegal) attempts to evict her and then moves in with her daughter, Marina, who has relocated to Cassino to work in a factory. She becomes increasingly lonely and depressed until Vincenzo secures her a new flat in Naples. He participates in the war in Kosovo but on his return he is struck with an illness caused by the radioactive

Figure 3.1 Scampia in *Vento di terra* (2003, Vincenzo Marra). ©Mikado.

materials to which the soldiers were needlessly exposed while on duty. He is forced to move in with his mother once more while a lawyer offers to fight for compensation.

The difficulties faced by the Pacilli family are primarily the lack of a decent job and a stable living environment, basic rights that any citizen should be able to expect. The irony that they are denied these rights is underlined in two scenes: firstly, when the cadets are taught about civil rights, which – significantly – immediately precedes the scene of Vincenzo's mother's suicide attempt, and secondly, when Vincenzo is denied a bank loan for his mother's apartment because his salary is insufficient ('I am an employee of the State,' he vainly protests, emphasising that he is contributing to a social system that should in turn support him). The only opportunity open to marginalised Southerners like Vincenzo and his Calabrian friend Francesco is to join the army, which further strips them of their rights and individuality (expertly depicted in the rigorous training scenes). Vincenzo's illness is revealed as the result of the army's negligence when, as a mere infantryman, he is needlessly exposed to radioactive materials. His near-catatonic silence when a lawyer requests his signature so that he can participate in a class action suit against the army in the film's final scene reflects both a pessimistic sense of defeat and the fact that the lawyer is part of the same socio-political structure from which the Pacilli family has consistently been excluded and thus is not a credible solution to their problems.

In those films of the NF that touch on the problem of finding a house or job the characters are never really marginalised since the institution of the family acts as their 'parachute'. However, while many of Vincenzo's and Marina's actions are performed out of a sense of obligation to the family, they only serve to break the family apart, obliging them to abandon Naples and their mother. Moreover, in Cassino Marina is a victim of sexual harassment perpetrated by her own uncle and this provokes Vincenzo's sole outburst of anger in the film (elsewhere Vincenzo Pacilli gives an understated performance that effectively conveys his alienation). It is as if his anger and frustration can only find expression in the kind of passionate, interpersonal conflict typical of the NF while he remains impotent and impassive when faced with apparently insoluble social problems.

Vincenzo's alienation is also conveyed stylistically, in particular through the extensive use of slow, deliberate camera movements that recall those of Piscicelli and create a sense of detachment, rather than the emotional engagement typical of the NF. The opening shots are an agonisingly slow 360° pan across the anonymous tower blocks of Scampia that ultimately settles on the infamous Vele, followed by another sustained shot of Vincenzo staring blankly out of the window of his flat. Thus Marra immediately creates a correlation between the ugliness and depressing anonymity of the buildings and the blankness of Vincenzo's stare, and in so doing grounds his alienation within a specific social predicament.

Vento di terra depicts the marginalisation of disenfranchised working-class characters in the post-industrial Neapolitan periphery and the destruction of the family structure on which the traditional *Gemeinschaft* society was based. It is rooted in an analysis of how social indifference affects the family and the individual, which is entirely consistent with Piscicelli's study of the social alienation sub-proletariat in the Neapolitan hinterland. Alberto Crespi is therefore undoubtedly correct in his assessment of Marra's cinema as 'materialist, in the Marxist sense of the term' (Crespi 2004). There is also a parallel to be made with the work of Marxist filmmaker Luchino Visconti, and in particular with *Rocco e i suoi fratelli/Rocco and His Brothers* (1960), which also focuses on the break-up of a Southern Italian family under the forces of social change. But in terms of style the two directors are miles apart; the contrast between the histrionics of Salvatore and Rocco, and the near-catatonia of Vincenzo at the end of the two films could not be more marked. As with Piscicelli, Marra's rejection of such a stylistic register is the formal correlative to his rejection of the thematic structures underpinning traditional melodrama.

The depiction of a disenfranchised proletariat reoccurs in Maurizio Fiume's debut, *Isotta* (1996). Here the setting is Bagnoli, the area to the west of Naples that was developed in the early part of the twentieth century as the first major industrial centre in Southern Italy but which has been in decline since the 1970s, culminating in the closure of the Italsider steelworks in 1993. This once beautiful coastal area is now blighted by environmental decay while its inhabitants suffer from unemployment and associated social ills. The credit sequence presents a series of aerial views of the city, which are reminiscent of the credits of *Le mani sulla città/Hands over the City* (1963, Francesco Rosi), but which significantly progress outwards from the historic centre to the periphery and from readily identifiable tourist spots like Piazza del Plebiscito to the Italsider steelworks and the anonymous apartment blocks in which Isotta lives. Isotta and her friends, Luisa and Caterina, work a dead-end, factory-line job as seamstresses. Isotta's obesity is at once the cause of and a metaphor for her troubled relationship with the world, and this use of a character's physicality is also characteristic of other recent Neapolitan films like *L'amore molesto* and *Il verificatore*. However, unlike Vincenzo in *Vento di terra*, Isotta's problems are not solely material, but rather derive from her tendency to indulge in fantasies that only highlight the inadequacy of reality. Maurizio Fiume has stated, 'I narrate the inner life of a person living on the margins . . . a factory worker lacking the cultural tools necessary to understand the world she lives in and to defend herself from it. Isotta responds by dreaming' (Liggeri 1996). However, Isotta eventually violates her credo that you should not confuse dreams with reality by imagining a potential romance with Aleksandros, an attractive Greek businessman she befriends, only to have her illusions shattered when he becomes involved with Luisa instead. Isotta muses in voice-over, 'I guess sooner or later everybody experiences that moment when reality hits you with all its force: for a while you see things the way you want to, and then you see them how they really are.' Although Isotta ultimately accepts her situation and reconciles with Luisa, in the final scene she retreats once more into a fantasy world in which she dances with Aleksandros: a happy ending that can exist only in her imagination.

While *Isotta* lacks an explicitly political dimension, the contrast Fiume establishes between idealised fantasy and harsh social reality is none the less similar to the way in which Piscicelli and Marra challenge the value system of traditional Neapolitan cinema by substituting its melodramatic approach to narrative with a historical materialist one. Fiume's subversion of the NF's characteristic miraculous happy ending also reveals the extent to which, like Marra and Piscicelli, he substitutes the moral fantasy of an 'enduring *napoletanità*' with a pessimistic account of social alienation.

There are several other recent Neapolitan films that also focus on alienation; however, unlike *Isotta* and *Vento di terra*, they feature characters from a different social class and point to causes that are not so explicitly material in origin. For example, in *Morte di un matematico napoletano/Death of a Neapolitan Mathematician* (1992, Mario Martone) an account of the last 7 days in the life of Renato Caccioppoli provides an opportunity to depict a milieu conspicuously absent from earlier Neapolitan cinema: a Neapolitan bourgeoisie comprised of the intellectuals, academics and political activists that constituted the mathematician's social and professional circle. Of course, such an environment has always existed, and it has occasionally been touched upon in literature, most notably in 'Il silenzio della ragione', the chapter of Anna Maria Ortese's *Il mare non bagna Napoli* (1954) in which the author returns to Naples and meets the city's literary circle. Like Ortese, Martone depicts a restricted micro-culture in which everyone seems to know everyone else. Interestingly, one of the figures depicted in Ortese's story, Raffaele La Capria, reviewed Martone's film and described it as 'a singular, even anomalous film, which does not resemble any other film on Naples' (quoted in Ranucci and Ughi 1995: 42). Nevertheless, Martone's depiction of a high-cultural tradition in Naples is actually rather ambiguous, since he depicts Caccioppoli as an alcoholic and suicidal figure whose relationship with his immediate environment is far from straightforward. The decision to focus on the last seven days of Caccioppoli's life emphasises not his significant intellectual and artistic achievements, but rather his human failings, something that led to a lengthy polemic by those who knew and admired him on the film's release (see ibid.: 41). Like Delia in Martone's subsequent *L'amore molesto*, Caccioppoli is depicted as an outsider, deeply alienated from the city and the environment in which he finds himself.[5] Martone has observed how the casting of Carlo Cecchi and Anna Bonaiuto, the only non-Neapolitans in the two films, made the protagonists 'strangers in their own town' and that this process reflected his desire to 'enter into an oblique and disorienting relationship with the city that corresponds to the state of Naples at this particular time' (quoted in Addonizio et al. 1997: 100). Caccioppoli falls asleep on the table during a university faculty meeting (and is left undisturbed by his colleagues when the meeting ends), gives lessons while drunk and awards examination marks to candidates at random, expressing his complete disregard for the academic system. Although he regularly visits the offices of the Italian Communist Party, he is not a party member. He has an ambiguous relationship with his estranged wife and a difficult one with the brother who attempts to curb his alcoholism but who, like everyone else, fails to acknowledge his fatally self-destructive tendencies. When a student who is about to marry and take up a teaching post at the university observes that he merely wants that which Caccioppoli has already achieved, Caccioppoli's reply constitutes the perfect expression of his alienation: 'it's sad to see the efforts you expend to become just like everyone else.' Instead, Caccioppoli spends his time wandering through the streets of the historic centre, interacting with people on the margins of society such as tramps and a group of *femminielli* (transvestites and transsexuals). Although he stops to talk to the *femminielli* and appears comfortable in their presence, they also recognise his difference, asking whether he is a foreigner.

In short, while focusing on a bourgeois, intellectual milieu over the popular one favoured by the Neapolitan films of Vittorio De Sica, Eduardo De Filippo and the NF, Martone chooses to focalise his account through a figure whose relationship to this environment is highly problematic. This has led several critics to interpret both the character and the film in existentialist terms; Tullio Kezich compares the film's tone to that of Jean-Pierre Melville's *Le Samouraï* (1967) while Tullio Masoni describes it as 'the tragedy of an individual crushed by the demands of the real' (quoted in Ranucci and Ughi 1995: 34, and Masoni 1992: 64). Given this existentialist dimension, the question of subjectivity assumes considerable significance. While most of the film is focalised by Caccioppoli and details his problematic relationship with the city, he is obviously absent from the final scene of his funeral, which depicts the city's relationship to him. Here speeches by people who never really understood him attempt to explain his life and death, while institutions like the university and the Italian Communist Party attempt to claim as their own this man whose participation in their affairs was partial at best. None of the speeches succeeds in assimilating this radically other figure into any one group, not even – in the case of the mayor's speech – in claiming Caccioppoli for the city itself.[6] Significantly, during this sequence Martone shifts focus from the speeches and people participating in the funeral to concentrate on two grave-diggers discussing the controversial fact that the dead man will be buried within the family tomb, even though he took his own life. One could argue that Caccioppoli's rejection of convention and intellectual dogma, his alcoholism, alienation and inability to participate fully in the world, mean that he must ultimately be expelled both from the city and from his bourgeois milieu; this, presumably, is the meaning of Áine O'Healy's description of him as 'a figure of abjection' (O'Healy 1999a: 245). However, a more provocative interpretation is that Caccioppoli is actually emblematic of the city's internal contradictions and problems; thus Aldo Schiavone suggests that 'Caccioppoli is the emblem of the suicide of a city' (paraphrased by Raffaele La Capria in Ranucci and Ughi 1995: 44). Rather than a celebration of Neapolitan culture and an expression of its renaissance, Martone's film is actually a suggestive account of the difficulty (or impossibility) of cultural life in the city.[7]

Given the importance afforded to this correlation between the protagonist and the city, it is worth saying a few words about how the film depicts Naples. The film is set in the 1950s and Martone has stated that he was neither able (given the budget) nor willing to follow the traditional route of historical reconstruction, but instead shot on location, 'cutting out' the remnants of the old Naples still present in the city (quoted in Roberti 1992b: 179–80). This process implies that several versions of Naples from different eras co-exist in the contemporary city, an idea which also forms the basis of Martone's video-documentary *Nella città barocca* (1985).[8] Moreover, this process means that 'while the film takes place in the past, it speaks of the present' (Masoni 1992: 63). Martone focuses almost exclusively on a very restricted area of the historical centre; while some scenes are set in oft-filmed areas such as the Quartieri Spagnoli, via Chiaia and via Partenope, others, such as the university district concentrated around via Mezzocannone or viale Calascione, are less common. Perhaps most significant is the use of Caccioppoli's home, Palazzo Cellamare, a building of historical importance and, significantly, the place in which Martone himself grew up and which remains his family's home (see Roberti 1992b: 173). Significantly, the film premiered not in Rome but in a single 800-seat cinema in the same university district, the Academy Astra, playing to packed audiences and earning over 15 million Lira in its opening two days of release, and then enjoying an extended run (Ranucci and Ughi 1995: 39). Thus the film both depicts and is addressed to a very specific milieu, defined both geographically and socially, with which Martone clearly identifies. Obviously, I do not mean to suggest that the film is only directed to such a minority audience; economically this would not make sense and the film did have a major impact in both film festivals and at a national level, leading Gianni Cascone to describe it as 'perhaps the most important Italian debut of the 1990s' (quoted in Argentieri 1998: 90). However, it is emblematic of Martone's approach that he chose to make the film's geography accurate so that a viewer familiar with the city could mentally extrapolate the course of Caccioppoli's amblings.[9] This approach is antithetical to the one employed by most films; even *Ladri di biciclette/Bicycle Thieves* (1948, Vittorio De Sica), which is famous for its location shooting and realism, recreates an idealised and artificial spatial geography. Consequently, the film functions differently for Neapolitan viewers of a particular cultural background, something to which Martone himself has drawn attention (Addonizio et al. 1997: 83). This dual address presents both similarities to and differences from traditional Neapolitan cinema, which also addressed a distinct portion of the Neapolitan population through its depiction of specifically local traditions, but which targeted an audience that is both socially and geographically distinct from that of Martone's film. Co-scripted by the renowned Neapolitan writer Fabrizia Ramondino and with a cast drawn from alternative theatre, *Morte di un matematico napoletano* foregrounds cultural and intellectual credentials that are far removed from the NF's emphasis on the popular. Thus the film itself comes to embody a Neapolitan high culture that is in turn explicitly associated with the environment depicted within the film's diegesis. Seen in these terms, the film is surprising, not only because its classical style departs from the director's earlier work in experimental avant-garde theatre but also because its take on the cultural milieu that produced it is so pessimistic.

These themes were later picked up by first-time director Nina Di Majo, who served as an assistant director to Martone before being given the chance to direct by her partner, producer Giorgio Magliulo. She has described how with *Autunno* [Autumn] (1999) she wanted to escape from the cliché of a baroque and decadent city in order to show that Naples also contained a 'cultured, eclectic, cosmopolitan and emancipated bourgeoisie' (Morreale and Zonta 2009: 57). However, like Martone, she portrays this environment as a troubled and alienated one. The film earned comparisons with Nanni Moretti and it is not hard to see why;[10] Di Majo casts herself as the aggressive and often unsympathetic Costanza, casts friends and family in supporting roles, and invites a (simplistic) equation between character and author.[11] Like Fellini's 8½ (1963) – another film that invites the viewer to equate the director with the protagonist – the film sets up a *mise-en-abîme* in which Costanza, like Di Majo, is writing a story about a depressed and alienated character that is a thinly veiled version of herself. Other characters criticise the way Costanza makes a 'pornographic spectacle' of her own relationships and intimate feelings, and question why readers should be interested in her story – criticisms that could also be directed at the film itself. Significantly, her university professor comments on the relentlessly downbeat quality of her writing and suggests that she should 'leave a ray of hope' at the end, and this is exactly what the film does when Costanza's story unexpectedly wins the top prize in a competition for new authors. As if to confirm this self-reflexivity, it is precisely the professor's submission of her story to the competition after she had withdrawn it that enables this ray of hope.

All of the film's characters have difficulty relating to other people and the world around them, from the mundane sentimental crises of Costanza's parents, her aunt and the professor, to the almost pathological neurosis of Costanza and Matteo, the two main protagonists. We witness Costanza's therapy sessions in which she laments her inability to relate to others and her feelings of self-loathing, and Matteo's erratic behaviour and morbid spying on his neighbour, which substitutes any real interpersonal relationship. In both cases the film suggests that their parents are a principal cause of their neuroses, and although this may seem like a rather pat Freudian explanation, the fact that the film identifies the family as a place of repression and psychological trauma aligns it with other recent Neapolitan films that question the institution of the family, as discussed below. Although the other characters' dramas and problems may be less severe than those of Matteo and Costanza, they are not that dissimilar in nature and the film clearly indicates that these problems are socially conditioned characteristics of an alienated bourgeoisie. The professor breaks off his relationship with Costanza's aunt, saying that he has had 'enough of these intellectuals who are always depressed . . . and full of the same prejudices that have always oppressed me'. Costanza's boyfriend downplays her problems, describing her as a fortunate, well-off person rather than someone who is starving to death, to which she responds by accusing him of indulging in pure rhetoric and ignoring the fact that there are different degrees of need, thus recognising how her psychological and emotional difficulties are also characteristic of her social milieu.

The suggestion of an autobiographical dimension also links *Autunno*'s diegetic reality with the cultural context of its production, as in *Morte di un matematico napoletano*. Although Di Majo suggests that the Neapolitan bourgeoisie is as much a cultural space as a geographic one (Morreale and Zonta 2009: 57), she none the less concentrates on a specific place centred on the exclusive area around via Chiaia (incidentally also the site of the offices of Teatri Uniti, which produced *Morte di un matematico napoletano*). Given that it played for 28 days in Naples and was seen by a mere 5000 people, it is likely that *Autunno* also appealed primarily to a small and specific portion of Neapolitan cinema-goers.

Similar themes recur in Mariano Lamberti's sole feature to date, *Non con un bang/Not with a Bang* (1999), which is set in Torre del Greco and focuses on a university student suffering from depression who cannot bring himself to complete his final exams and graduate. The film is dedicated to the director's father, suggesting a possible autobiographical dimension, as in *Autunno*. University is not seen here as 'a period of passage', as the protagonist's better-adjusted and more conventional friend, Antonio, puts it, but rather as an existential state of uncertainty, the moment before one enters the adult world and accepts responsibility. Cesare's reluctance to make this transition brings him into conflict with his father, the would-be *pater familias* who wants him to follow in his footsteps and become a lawyer, who cannot understand his son's state of mind, and who views him simply as a 'scrounger'.[12] Instead, Cesare retreats into a series of activities not entirely dissimilar from those of Caccioppoli: wandering aimlessly through the periphery around Torre del Greco dressed only in blood-stained pyjamas, laughing hysterically during an unsuccessful examination, throwing a fit and, above all, sleeping. The film adopts a comic stance towards its character's predicament, creating parallels between Cesare's behaviour and the family pet tortoise, and constructing a number of gags based around his venus fly trap. Whereas Caccioppoli's and Costanza's obsessions are kept obscure to the audience, Cesare's are visualised through a series of oneiric sequences, frequently employing animation,[13] such as the scene clearly inspired by the opening of *8½*, in which the flying Cesare is dragged into the crater of Vesuvius by an umbilical cord as he cries, 'I don't want to be a lawyer!' Unfortunately, the film's comedy fails to counter the fundamental bleakness of its themes or to render palatable lethargy and depression, perhaps the least cinematic of ailments. The cyclical narrative concludes where it begins, with Cesare locked in his bedroom, deaf to the wake-up call for a new day: an image of an educated Neapolitan youth too scared, demoralised and lacking in hope to affront the world and its problems, who chooses instead to turn in on himself.

Giulia, the protagonist of Nicola De Rinaldo's debut feature, *Il manoscritto di van Hecken* [Van Hecken's Manuscript] (1998), is also depressed and incapable of making the choices necessary to change her life. Trapped between a job in Naples and a relationship in Rome and unable to experience either fully, she spends much of her time on a train between the two cities and complains of 'being unable to choose, of merely submitting'. Her neurosis and unhappiness again derive from a traumatic childhood in which her father left the family to emigrate to America and her mother became a virtual recluse, abandoning Giulia in an orphanage. Giulia's soul-destroying public sector job at the Department of Architectural and Artistic Treasures constitutes a withdrawal from life, a convenient excuse to prevent her from committing to her partner in Rome, graduating from university, or fulfilling her artistic ambitions. An unexpected opportunity for change presents itself when a fifteenth-century diary by a little-known Flemish painter is requested for an exhibition but cannot be located. Giulia sets about retracing the painter's own journey through the city of Naples, where he briefly resided before being excommunicated and repatriated for his supposedly blasphemous paintings. Her efforts exceed the call of duty and the task provides her with a sense of purpose and the courage to make a choice and end her relationship with Enrico. Finally, she encounters a reclusive, elderly archivist who comments on her decision to track down this manuscript doggedly: 'Without realising it you are actually a happy person. Every now and then you are able to follow your desires. How many people can say the same?' Apparently freed by this revelation, Giulia miraculously stumbles upon the diary in the old man's archive and reads a passage clearly reminiscent of her own situation:

> It's painful to be unable to share with anyone the joy my work gives me. I no longer believe that that the visions I depict are inspired by the Devil. I realise that they are so intimately mine that I can no longer fight against them. . . . I no longer want to flee. I want to return home.

Giulia's recovery of the ancient manuscript coincides with her reconciliation with her own past and neuroses, a fact underlined by the parallels between the demonic insects in the apocalyptic, Bosch-like painting by Van Hecken she discovers and restores in the course of her research, the insects that emerge from a broken kaleidoscope in the flashbacks in which she learns that her father will not return, and the insect-themed mantra she used as a child to ward off her fears. In the final scene she returns to Piazza del Gesù nuovo – clearly also the inspiration for Van Hecken's painting – and opens the present Enrico's daughter has left her to reveal a kaleidoscope. The finale suggests that, like Van Hecken but unlike Caccioppoli, Costanza or Cesare, Giulia has accepted her demons, and perhaps no longer needs to flee the city or her past.

A less optimistic fate awaits the protagonist of *Ossidiana* [Obsidian] (2007), first-time director Silvana Maja's adaptation of her own novel about the troubled life of Neapolitan painter Maria Palliggiano, whose work was only (re-)discovered following a 1997 retrospective. The film focuses on the last decade or so of her life (1957–69) and portrays a woman who, like Caccioppoli, chafed at the confines of the society of her time. Married young to a celebrated artist and professor of fine arts many years her senior, Palliggiano struggles to reconcile the role of wife and mother with her artistic ambitions or to affirm herself independently from her husband. Significantly, she rebels against the institution of the family, which underpinned the NF, opposing and alienating her father and rejecting her mother's suggestion that, now that she is married with a child, she should be content and dedicate her attentions solely to her family. Instead, she seeks to assert her liberty and give meaning to her life through her vocation and through artistic expression. Yet the tension between these conflicting demands, the impact her choices have on her son – whom she temporarily abandons as a baby – the repeated accusations that she is a bad mother, and her failure to achieve success and recognition as an artist take their toll on her psyche. Periods of creativity alternate with neurosis, depression and self-harm, and conclude with temporary institutionalisation and, ultimately, suicide.

If Caccioppoli is presented as the 'emblem of a city on the verge of suicide', then Palliggiano can be considered a mirror that reflects the limitations of (Neapolitan) society of the period. Several conversations between the artists that constitute Maria's circle reflect on the insularity of the Neapolitan artistic scene and its inability to transcend the local or national context, while Maria's attempts to leave Naples for Berlin, Rome, Bari and America are all unsuccessful. The film's most liberating section deals with her short-lived collaboration with, and love for, an American artist, Victor Darista. Thus she is inspired by the same radical stimulus of foreign, avant-garde culture that fuelled Martone and Capuano (see pp. 96 and 100); however, the performance art they organise together (making it appear as if Vesuvius is about to erupt by setting fire to hundreds of tyres in the crater) immediately brings them into conflict with the law. When Victor returns to America, Palliggiano struggles to accept the confines of provincial culture and family life, and gradually declines. Significantly, it is with Victor's pistol that she ends her life.

The film's title refers to a volcanic rock that Palliggiano's husband defines as 'a mixture of hardness and fragility', and the film aims to investigate the psychology of a personality with similarly contradictory characteristics. Like Martone, Di Maja avoids resorting to historical reconstruction through judicious location shooting. However, she also allows access to a subjectivity denied to us by Martone through digital effects that animate Palliggiano's paintings and depict her skewed perception of reality, dreams and nightmares. In this way *Ossidiana* constructs an eloquent but ultimately pessimistic exploration of one woman's existential dilemma.

The theme of the alienation of a modern, intellectual bourgeoisie is unquestionably new to Neapolitan cinema, and completely antithetical to Naples' role as a symbol for the values of an idealised, traditional society in the NF, not to mention the stereotype of the carefree and vivacious Neapolitan that dates back at least to the Grand Tour writers of the eighteenth century. These films radically challenge the conventional cinematic function of the city. In a sense they are narratives that could take place in any modern, Western society, yet these filmmakers have deliberately chosen to set their narratives in the city and, moreover, insist on emphasising a specific geographical setting. Thus they perform a kind of normalising function, redressing the conventional difference of Naples and depicting a city that has become uniform with the rest of modern Western culture. If the NF provided a moral fantasy of immutability, then these films present us with a damning portrait of the consequences of social change. This normalising function can also be seen at work at the level of style in the reliance on an understated presentation that contrasts markedly with the melodramatic register characteristic of earlier Neapolitan cinema. As we have seen, several of these films locate the origin of their characters' alienation in a troubled family history. Let us now turn our attention to films that focus more directly on this institution.

THE CHILDREN ARE WATCHING US: THE CRISIS OF THE FAMILY

Central to the sense of community and belonging generated by the NF was its depiction of the traditional family unit as the cornerstone of society. Conversely, numerous recent Neapolitan films either have depicted the breakdown of the institution of the family, or have brought a modern *Gesellschaft* perspective to bear on the family relations of the traditional *Gemeinschaft* society in order to expose the repression, exclusion and violence on which they were often founded.

One such film is Antonietta De Lillo's *Non è giusto/It's Not Fair* (2001), whose central theme is the impact of divorce, particularly on children.[14] It tells of 11-year-old Valerio, who arrives in Naples to spend the summer with his divorced father, Matteo, who promises him an extravagant holiday in Africa that is clearly beyond his financial capabilities before abandoning him on the beach to spend time with his girlfriend. Valerio meets and befriends Sofia, whose father, Giacomo, is in the process of divorcing her mother while conducting an affair with Graziella, a young woman who lives above their flat and is already pregnant with his child. Whereas the NF explored the family under threat in order to work towards a cathartic and optimistic resolution that restores and reaffirms the family, *Non è giusto* never seriously raises such a possibility; instead the characters seek surrogates for the family they have lost in the company of other women (in the case of Matteo and Giacomo) or in mutual friendship (in the case of Valeria and Sofia). In reaffirming the primacy of the family, the NF places considerable emphasis on pregnancy out of wedlock, working towards the *figlio di nessuno*'s reabsorption into the familial unit. At one point Matteo's mother (who significantly belongs to the same generation that produced the NF) articulates a similar credo, arguing that 'family is important' and suggesting that Graziella and her new child come to live with them, an idea which does not seem to be congenial to Giacomo. This suggestion of reconstituting the family by extending it beyond the boundaries of the traditional nuclear family is later echoed by Valerio, but the more mature and perceptive Sofia replies that it does not sound like a good idea. Thus the families of *Non è giusto* are irreversibly broken 'post-families' (Avondola 2002: 43), and the film explores the impact this has on the children.

Non è giusto is notable for the mature way in which it critiques adult society and familial breakdown by focalising its tale through the eyes of young children, reprising a method that, as far as Italian cinema is concerned, dates back at least to Vittorio De Sica's *I bambini ci guardano/The Children Are Watching Us* (1943). Notable, for example, is the sequence at the Ditellandia theme park, which utilises sound effects and camera movement to replicate the children's fantasy of flight while they sit on an abandoned fairground ride, a scene that provides a brief and liberating hiatus from their immersion in the problems of the adult world. More significant is the scene that represents Valerio's fantasy of an extended family; the frame is filled by a photograph of his family that he and Sofia then manipulate in order to recompose the family unit to their satisfaction (the father miraculously appears as we hear in voice-off, 'What about your father?' 'Sorry, I forgot him.').[15] This technique makes the viewer privy to the childrens' interior world, which their parents have no access to, and serves to highlight both the parents' failure to understand their offspring and the gulf that exists between the world-view of different generations. However, despite a certain precociousness deriving from their exposure to adult relationships – as in the scene when Giacomo shouts at Sofia for not fetching him when the phone rang, oblivious to the fact that she deliberately chose not to because she realised he was having sex at the time – the children remain unable to grasp fully all that is going on around them. Thus Sofia remains ignorant of the fact that her father is responsible for Graziella's pregnancy. Her casual observation that it is unfair that the child will not have a father motivates the film's title, which pithily sums up its damning critique of the consequences of the collapse of the family structure.

Another film to employ a child's point-of-view is *La volpe a tre zampe/The Three-Legged Fox* (2002), the debut feature of Sandro Dionisio, produced by Teatri Uniti and based on the 1996 novel of the same name by Francesco Costa. Set in 1956, it tells of a boy living in the Canzanella refugee camp who becomes obsessed with the affluent wife of an American general for whom his mother works as a maid. Dionisio constructs an opposition between two social realities – the Neapolitans in the refugee camp and the affluent Americans in the NATO base – through a contrast in terms of geography (Fuorigrotta/ Posillipo), *mise-en-scène* and performance style. The film hinges on Vittorio's immature perspective as he relies on Hollywood fantasy to make sense of – or escape from – the troubled reality in which he lives. Thus he convinces himself that the American General's wife is actually an incognito Susan Hayworth and that his father is a professional dancer rather than an unemployed womaniser. Recruited to read the newspaper by Pietro Formicola, the blind communist pickpocket who lives in the camp, Vittorio soon begins supplementing the political news with his own stories – melodramatic tales of communist spies and the women they love that owe more to cinematic narrative than post-war socio-political reality. But reality constantly threatens his precarious fantasy world as the jealousies provoked by his father's infidelities provoke violence and jeopardise the future of his family. He is also witness to the tragic story of the alcoholic Sabatino, who is arrested for the murder of his wife, Lucia, after she attempts to renounce enforced prostitution, leaving their daughter no option but to follow in her mother's footsteps (events that Vittorio narrates in voice-off, like one of his stories, over the more prosaic images of the dead body of Lucia and the arrest of Sabatino). Of little consolation are Pietro's beliefs in a more socially equitable future, which seem doomed by the Monarchist victory in the elections and his own arrest and incarceration, and Vittorio is left to hope only that 'Susan Hayworth' will take him with her to Hollywood. But instead she confides in him the fable of the fox forced to chew off its own leg in order to escape a trap, implying that everyone has to give up something in order to survive. In the final scenes Vittorio abandons his impossible dream, saying that he will remain in Canzanella to ensure that his sister attends school. Thus Vittorio ultimately renounces his naïve attachment to fantasy in order to assume adult responsibilities within the troubled social landscape in which he lives.

This child's-eye view also recurs in Giuseppe Rocca's sadly little-seen sole feature *Lontano in fondo agli occhi/Pictures Deep in One's Eyes* (2000).[16] Here the setting is Frattamaggiore in the 1950s,[17] a period contemporaneous with the films of the NF; indeed, one scene takes place inside a cinema with a poster for *Tormento* (1950, Raffaello Matarazzo) on the wall, a precise cinematic reference that establishes both temporal and cultural milieu. Central to Rocca's film is an attempt to recuperate the archaic, provincial and plebeian culture characteristic of this setting, drawing on Neapolitan character actors like Nuccia Fumo, Marina Confalone and Olimpia di Maio, and the work of musicologist Pasquale Scialò who recreates songs like *Le panzè* and a performance of popular musical theatre (*La Luciana*).[18] The protagonist is an unnamed boy on the cusp of adolescence who lives in an entirely female extended family after his father abandoned them. He becomes the sole witness to the affair of a young servant girl, Rafilina, passing messages to her lover, Carmine, in the exclusively male world of the billiard hall, and in so doing experiencing the first stirrings of desire for the opposite sex. When Rafilina becomes pregnant and Carmine refuses to abandon the other woman he is involved with, the boy poisons him in a misguided attempt to help and protect Rafilina.

Although the triangular structure which the NF frequently reprised from the *sceneggiata* is in evidence here, the choice of focalising the narrative through a child who does not fully understand the implications of what he is seeing radically alters the way in which this narrative material is handled.[19] For one thing, it results in an oneiric visual style as the boy's immature perspective allows Rocca to visualise dramatically the belief systems of this archaic rural culture, as when Zia Carmela's warnings about devils lead the boy's imagination to conjure up a series of visions of the apocalypse reminiscent of the films of Ken Russell.[20] As the film moves towards its violent denouement, sexuality (and adulthood) come to be seen through the boy's eyes as dangerous and frightening. However, the discrepancy between the protagonist's understanding of events and that of the adult viewer means that we recognise that his poisoning of Carmine constitutes a tragic action on the part of a child who does not fully appreciate the consequences of his actions, rather than an honourable defence of a vulnerable and betrayed woman. By relying on an immature focaliser in this way, the film problematises the *sceneggiata*'s reliance on a final act of cathartic or redemptive violence to resolve an act of sexual transgression.

This method of problematising the *Gemeinschaft* family structure through an emphasis on violence perceived from the perspective of impressionable children achieves its fullest expression in Mario Martone's *L'amore molesto/Nasty Love* (1995), one of the best-known and most widely distributed films of the NNC.[21] Based on the novel by Elena Ferrante, it recounts the story of Delia, a woman who has chosen to leave Naples and build a new life in Bologna but who is forced to return to the city to attend her mother's funeral and resolve the mystery surrounding her death. Martone depicts the city as invasive and thus threatening; the sense of physical menace, the proximity to other people's bodies, the gaze of strangers, the ever-present noise and chaos, all threaten Delia's precarious sense of her own identity.[22] As Delia re-engages with the city and her past for the first time, we gradually discover through flashbacks the reasons for her departure; in leaving she sought to suppress part of her own identity, in particular her femininity and sexuality, as a result of having witnessed her father's physical abuse of her mother and of herself having been the victim of sexual abuse at the hands of a family friend.

The basic narrative premise, that of a young woman who has left the city to forge her own life but is forced to return in order to resolve the mystery of her mother's disappearance, recurs in a film that in all other respects is entirely different. In *Te lo leggo negli occhi/I Can See It in Your Eyes* (2004),[23] which was written and directed by Valia Santella, who acted as script supervisor on Martone's film, Chiara returns to her native city of Naples to search for her severely asthmatic daughter, who has disappeared with Chiara's irresponsible mother, Margherita. Here, too, the return to the city provides an opportunity to explore the background to this troubled mother–daughter relationship and the reasons behind the daughter's original flight from the city.

In *L'amore molesto*, Delia's encounters with her father and uncle and the flashbacks to her youth present us with a world characterised by male violence and an attempt to contain women and their sexuality, and we soon come to realise that the adult Delia has repressed her own sexuality for fear of the violence it may trigger. After Delia abandons her habitual androgynous suit for the provocative and revealing dress her mother had bought her, she too is subjected to her father's violence for the first time ('You're a whore just like your mother!') and is forced to flee once more. Similarly, *Te lo leggo negli occhi* features a key confrontation between Chiara and her father in which he accuses her of knowing about her mother's affair. However, rather than issuing a denial, Chiara instead calls into questions the assumptions underpinning his accusation and in so doing distances herself from his discourse:

> I left twenty years ago to live my own life, now let me be. You're both squalid! She carries on with other men while you play the *guappo* with another old fool. And Lucia and I are the ones who get caught in the middle.[24]

The narratives of the NF were posited on a discourse of sexual exclusivity in which the potential for (female) sexual indiscretion threatened the family unit, only for this threat to be ultimately overcome or defused. Conversely, both *L'amore molesto* and *Te lo leggo negli occhi* draw attention to the repression and violence entailed in such a process and thus problematise the patriarchal ideology underpinning such a discourse. Significantly, both of these films provide us with a woman's perspective on the family life she experienced as a child, as if to highlight the extent to which the advent of feminism has involved a rethinking of an earlier value system. In this way, the films articulate a broadly feminist challenge to the traditional narrative structure of the *sceneggiata* and the NF.[25]

Two other recent films have explored the impact of familial dysfunction through stories of characters returning to Naples, but here it is an adolescent or young adult male that takes centre-stage. In *Pater familias* [Head of the Family] (2003, Francesco Patierno), Matteo returns to Giugliano in Campania in the industrial hinterland to the north-east of Naples after a long absence and re-engages with a violent past. Adapted from the novel by Massimo

Cacciapuoti, which is based on a number of true stories, the screenplay by Cacciapuoti and Patierno applies a central narrative to unify these disparate tales; in order to visit his dying father and sign some legal papers, Matteo is granted day release from the jail where he is serving a lengthy sentence for the murder of the man responsible for the death of his cousin and the incestuous rape of his lover, Anna. During this leave Matteo also helps a friend, Rosa, to escape from the violent husband whom her father forced her to marry after she became pregnant. As in *L'amore molesto*, the sights and sounds of the city evoke memories of Matteo's past and in particular of his friends, all of whom died in various tragic circumstances (based on the true stories contained in the original novel and here narrated through fragmented flashbacks). That the film calls into question the patriarchal basis to the repression and violence charac- terising the narrative back-stories is explicitly alluded to in the film's title.[26] However, here the narrative is focalised by an adult male who himself reverted to violence to protect Anna, while the women all remain passive victims.

Filmed on location in Sant'Antimo and Aversa, Pasquale Marrazzo's debut *Malemare* (1997) tells the parallel stories of a sacristan who shelters a man wounded during an attempted robbery of his church and a cocaine-addicted prostitute who returns from Berlin because her adolescent son is now suffering from psychological problems resulting from his abandonment years earlier. The son, who alternates between silent introversion and obsessive-compulsive behaviour, is clearly subject to an oedipal crisis, desperately in need of a rela- tionship with his estranged mother and alienated from his absent father and the other clients his mother entertains in their flat. Meanwhile, delinquency and (male) violence characterise the second narrative strand centred on the sacristan. The emphasis on a degraded urban landscape and the barren, inhospitable flat shared by estranged mother and son reinforces the theme of social decay implicit in both these narratives. While one of the film's narratives (and occasionally its iconography) recall Pasolini's *Mamma Roma* (1962), the second consistently evokes a queer sensibility through its emphasis on male nudity and the obsessive physicality of the character interactions. In this way, *Malemare* problematises masculinity through an emphasis on male violence, familial dysfunction and queer aesthetics.

With its flashbacks, fragmented narrative structure and chromatically manipulated visuals, *Pater familias* combines the tropes of realism and a 'semi-visionary gaze' (Emiliani 2003: 76), which occasionally recalls the films of Capuano. Similarly *Malemare*, which was produced entirely independ- ently and without State funding for a mere 80 million Lira, turns its economic limitations into a virtue, using the lack of expensive lighting or dollies and its black-and-white 16mm cinematography to create a chiaroscuro world in which the constantly hand-held camera effectively conveys the troubled characters' subjectivity. Thus, whereas *L'amore molesto* and *Te lo leggo negli occhi* were relatively classical in terms of style and relied on a female focal-iser to carry the weight of their critique of the patriarchal basis of traditional Neapolitan narratives, both *Pater familias* and *Malemare* employ much more radical aesthetic strategies in order to enact a fracturing of the masculinity on which such narratives depended.[27]

The final film to deal with the crisis of the family is Vincenzo Terracciano's *Tris di donne & abiti nuziali/Bets and Wedding Dresses* (2009). Unlike the patriarchs of the other films discussed thus far, Franco is neither violent nor unfaithful towards his wife or children; his failing derives from an addiction to gambling, which brings the family to financial ruin and jeopardises his daughter Luisa's wedding plans. Like most gamblers, Franco believes that his problems can be resolved by a miraculous piece of good fortune at the gaming table and this recalls the *deus ex machina* that concludes so many films of the NF. This narrative convention, and the belief in miracles on which it depends, is also problematised by several other films of the NNC, as discussed in Chapter 4. However, Franco is not a talented gambler; other gamblers criticise the way in which he places bets indiscriminately rather than utilising strategy and an appreciation of the odds – in other words, the way he relies on luck rather than judgement. Although not regular gamblers, his wife, Josephine, and son, Giovanni, on the other hand, are far better at cards than he is because they are more rational. Significantly, it is a woman and a non-Neapolitan (Franco's German wife, Josephine) that holds the family together and tries to resolve the problems he creates. In the film's final scenes, when the family lacks any other means of resolving their problems, they decide to gamble their remaining money – not indiscriminately but strategically, relying on Giovanni's skill at poker. For a brief moment it looks as if they might succeed, creating an unexpected happy ending from a somewhat implausible narrative miracle. But in a moment of weakness Giovanni's judgement fails him and he loses everything; he is too much his father's son after all. In the final scenes Luisa's renunciation of marriage in favour of cohabitation represents yet another shift from the traditional family to a 'post-family', while Franco's death at the hands of the *camorrista* to whom he is indebted concludes the deconstruction of patriarchy that the film has enacted.

SCUGNIZZI AND MUSCHILLI

The two themes exhibited by the NNC explored thus far (alienation and the crisis of the family) come together in a number of films centred on the plight of the *scugnizzo*, or street-urchin. The *scugnizzo* has been a recurrent figure in Neapolitan cinema ever since Gennarino, the child star of Elvira Notari's silent films. However, until recently the *scugnizzo*, who is invariably male and typically bears a traditional Neapolitan name like Gennaro or Pasquale (or one of their diminutives), rarely took centre-stage. More often than not, he is a secondary character who acts as a surrogate child, 'adopted' by the pro-tagonist. Thus, at the conclusion of *Carcerato* (1981, Alfonso Brescia), Mario Merola's character is finally acquitted for a crime he did not commit and he invites the orphan Gennarino into the embrace he shares with his wife and daughter, in so doing completing the happy family unit and effectively resolv-ing Gennaro's status as a *figlio di nessuno*. In such films the *scugnizzo* is por-trayed in unequivocally positive terms as someone who has suffered but who maintains the joy of life stereotypically associated with Neapolitans. Although a number of films attempt to address the problems faced by the *scugnizzi*, here too the *scugnizzo* is not the centre of attention; *Proibito rubare* (1948, Luigi Comencini) focuses on the obstacles faced by a priest who attempts to set up an orphanage, while *Scugnizzi* (1989, Nanni Loy) concentrates more on the staging of a show performed by inmates of a reformatory. More recently, Wilma Labate's *Domenica* (2001) – a production of the national film industry set in Naples – has contrasted the stereotype of the independent and vivacious *scugnizzo* (for once, a girl) with a world-weary and terminally ill policeman who accompanies her through the city in an attempt to persuade her to identify a body which may belong to the man who raped her.

In 1991 Antonio Capuano's debut, *Vito e gli altri/Vito and the Others*, elevated the figure of the *scugnizzo* to centre-stage for the first time (see Fig. 3.2). It tells the story of a 12-year-old boy who lives a life on the streets after he is placed in his aunt and uncle's care when his father kills the rest of his family during a nervous breakdown. Petty crime, drugs and a spell in borstal ulti-mately lead Vito to become a hired killer for the *camorra*. Originating in the true story of a minor who was incarcerated through a miscarriage of justice, the film was rigorously based on fact (see Sesti 1991: 48). Capuano explained his choice of subject thus: 'The sight of [the *scugnizzi*] playing arcade games enchanted me . . . They fascinated me on an aesthetic level . . . I also have great respect for them. This is why I made the film. I'm not a sociologist' (Author's interview, Naples, 14 June 2003). Capuano's fascination led him to focus directly on the *scugnizzi* and their daily lives, while his respect prevented him from making them functional to a pre-existing discourse. Here, in a complete reversal of earlier films, adult characters and social institutions are depicted only in relation to the *scugnizzi*. Moreover, Capuano repeatedly allows the *scugnizzi* to speak directly for themselves (in thick dialect) through the use of voice-over and direct address to camera. These scenes are constructed as responses to a (never seen) interviewer and clearly have, in part, an anthro-pological function, elucidating the *scugnizzo*'s world.[28] Capuano's stated respect for the *scugnizzi* also leads Anton Giulio Mancino to claim that he 'has the audacity to love them and to share in their amorality', and to talk about the film's 'hazardous suspension of judgement' (Mancino 1992: 44). Many

Figure 3.2   The *scugnizzo* becomes *muschillo*. *Vito e gli altri* (1991, Antonio Capuano). ©Mikado.

viewers find this approach problematic and disturbing; confronted with such a shocking and dramatic reality, they are disconcerted by the apparent absence of moral judgement. Nevertheless, while clearly siding with the *scugnizzi*, Capuano does not present them as mere innocent victims of a brutal social reality, but rather as children who have been forced to take on adult 'responsibilities' and adapt to their situation. Thus he does not shy away from depicting the violent, criminal and anti-social elements of their behaviour; in fact, he seems to celebrate the vitality of their behaviour and lifestyle while simultaneously acknowledging the precarious and amoral nature of their existence.[29] A useful point of comparison is with Pier Paolo Pasolini and in particular with a film like *Accattone* (1961), in which we are asked to identify with a character that would usually be seen as wretched and morally reprehensible.

However, while Capuano is correct in emphasising his focus on the *scugnizzi* and their lifestyle, it is misleading to suggest that the film completely lacks a sociological dimension. The narrative is clearly structured as a series of stages in Vito's 'decline' from innocent child to streetwise *scugnizzo* and then finally *muschillo* (child assassin), a moment that is intercut with Riccardo's suicide, reinforcing the tragic nature of this finale. A sociological interpretation of this progression is not only possible but extremely enlightening; it calls into question a series of social institutions (the family, the forces of law and order, the education system, and the role of the *camorra*) that are particularly relevant to an understanding of the film's take on contemporary Neapolitan culture. By placing the *scugnizzo* centre-stage, Capuano focuses on the effects of the breakdown of the family, rather than merely using the *scugnizzo* as a symbolic element within a discursive structure that seeks to reassert the primacy of the family in the face of external social pressures, as in the NF. It is significant that the first post-credits scene deals with the literal annihilation of the family and that it is this event that precipitates Vito's journey. In contrast with earlier films, there is no surrogate family and no alternatives or potential solutions are offered. The devastating effects of the collapse of the family are highlighted throughout the film, in particular through the abuse and neglect visited on Vito by his aunt and uncle. The children are repeatedly exploited by adults; they are prostituted to paedophiles, used as drug runners and assassins by the *camorra*, held to ransom by kidnappers, and exploited as a source of income by their parents and guardians. Numerous scenes emphasise that the education system has also failed them and Anton Giulio Mancino has convincingly argued that the film opposes this failure with the efficiency and success with which the kids are 'educated' into the life of the *camorra* (Mancino 1992: 42–3). A similar opposition between the institutions of the State and those of the *camorra* is also made in relation to the legal system; it is the very fact that underage children are immune from prosecution that makes them most vulnerable to exploitation by the *camorra*. Vito is arrested, sexually and physically abused in the reformatory, and then exploited by his aunt and lawyer to obtain compensation for his incarceration. He simply says, 'the law should just leave me alone!'

Despite Capuano's affirmation, then, there is a clear sociological dimension to the film. Yet, primarily, Capuano's interest is anthropological, portraying the ordinary routine and the behaviour of the *scugnizzi*. Their world-view is articulated most clearly in six direct-to-camera statements delivered by various members of the gang, which also make explicit what is implied by the narrative arc from innocent victim to hired killer; the predicament in which the *scugnizzi* find themselves necessarily produces a particular vision of the world, and this in turn inevitably results in the propagation of the *camorra*. Immature children, denied familial support or points of social reference, exploited by adults and forced to become self-sufficient in a violent and inhospitable environment, can only aspire to being, as Vito puts it, 'the strongest', in order to alleviate their immediate suffering and obtain the most basic of gratifications. The *camorra* is thus seen not merely as a cause but as a product of the situation faced by the *scugnizzi*.[30]

In almost existentialist fashion, *Vito e gli altri* insists on the primacy of the *scugnizzo*'s experience, narrated from within. Yet its narrative arc betrays the presence of an other behind the camera who cannot help but interpret their experience.[31] The presence of an other is also apparent in the film's formal qualities. Rather than adopting a self-effacing, classical style, which would arguably permit a more direct and (apparently) unmediated representation of the *scugnizzi*'s world, Capuano chooses to fracture his film through the use of devices more characteristic of the avant-garde. Thus the realist qualities of the film (its focus on a social issue, origin in newspaper reports, location shooting, use of non-professionals, and so on) are contrasted with a barrage of radical, attention-seeking devices: the insistent substitution of the film image with a television or computer screen; the alternation of frontal, static shots and impossibly lengthy and ponderous tracking shots and circular pans; the widespread rejection of scene dissection and analytical editing (58 of the film's approximately 100 scenes comprise a single shot); the repeated use of a blank screen, frequently accompanied by a disembodied voice-over; the jarring disjunctions between sound and image; the freeze-frames, and so on. Capuano explains his stylistic choices thus:

> Whenever I noticed during editing that the film was beginning to resemble a realist account, I shuddered . . . When I was 15 I didn't read Verga, Pirandello or the Russian classics, I read Brecht and Joyce. I don't know why, but I felt a strange affinity with them even at that young age and this 'anti-narrative' imprint has remained with me. (Author's interview, Naples, 14 June 2003)

The following year Salvatore Piscicelli's similarly themed *Baby Gang* (1992) replicated Vito's narrative trajectory in the story of a young boy who wanders through the periphery of Naples in search of heroin for his older brother, who is suffering from withdrawal symptoms.[32] The film ends tragically when Luca witnesses a petty drug-dealer he has befriended, and who is only slightly older than he is, murder the wholesaler who sold their mutual friend a lethal dose of heroin. In 2004 the national film industry produced another *scugnizzo* film, which also concludes with the child being forced to commit his first murder for the *camorra*: *Certi bambini*, directed by Antonio and Andrea Frazzi, and adapted from the novel by Neapolitan author Diego De Silva. Like *Vito e gli altri*, these films focus on one central character but, beginning with their titles, stress that he is representative of a social group. All three films described so far follow a similar narrative arc, concluding with an assassination, which is seen as the moment in which the *scugnizzo* passes into the adult criminal world.[33]

In 2005, Capuano revisited this topic with *La guerra di Mario/Mario's War*, which tells the story of a 9-year-old boy from a troubled and impoverished background in the working-class district of Ponticelli, who, following neglect by his mother and her protector boyfriend, is fostered by a middle-class couple living in the affluent suburb of Posillipo. This time, Capuano chose to alternate focalisation between Mario and his middle-class adoptive parents, Giulia and Sandro, highlighting the way Mario retreats from his new parents into the company of a stray dog and a *scugnizzo* from his own background, while Sandro struggles to establish a line of communication and Giulia risks stifling him with her love. This strategy emphasises the apparently unbridgeable gap that exists between two social spheres, and Capuano expertly portrays this divergence through a studied attention to the filming of the two locations,[34] the representation of two different social environments with their respective iconographies, and the different performance styles employed by Valeria Golino and Rosaria De Cicco as his foster and birth mother respectively. Giulia attempts to bridge this gap by being open with Mario and even establishing a rapport with his birth mother, and her actions reflect Capuano's conviction that 'the city should be enlarged [to include the periphery] and not defended from it' (Tassi 2006: 24). However, Giulia's attempt ends in failure and, ultimately, *La guerra di Mario* portrays the class divisions of the city of Naples to be as polarised as relations between the two sexes, and the social fabric of the city to be as irreversibly broken as the structure of the family unit.

'Fujitevenne!': Migration and Annihilation

Since economic migration had such an impact on the social fabric of Naples and the South in the early part of the twentieth century it is not surprising that this became a recurrent theme in Neapolitan culture. However, in recent years Naples, like much of Italy, has experienced the reverse – large-scale, frequently illegal immigration from Albania and North Africa – and this too has become a key semantic element of the NNC. Within the wealth of shorts produced in the city is an interesting documentary that deals with this theme, *Africanapoli: luoghi e colori dell'interazione* (1999, Claudio Greco and Marisa Esposito). As the title suggests, this film is about the integration of these immigrants and their influence on Neapolitan culture and it features interviews with a Neapolitan woman who has married a North African immigrant and with the Neapolitan singer Maria Pia De Vito, who fuses traditional Neapolitan music with jazz and African rhythms. However, fiction filmmaking has stressed the opposite: the problems presented by a poorly integrated, stratified, multicultural society.[35] This is true of Stefano Incerti's *Il verificatore*, which takes place in the area bordering Piazza Garibaldi, the area that contains the largest immigrant population. The explicit parallels drawn between the lead character, Crescenzio, and the marginalised North African immigrants who surround him is one of the principal ways the film signals his alienation (see Fig. 3.3). The theme reoccurs in Incerti's second film, *Prima del tramonto* (1999), which

Figure 3.3   Naples as a city of alienation: the lumbering physique of Crescenzio (Antonino Iuorio) is isolated against a desolate and wintry Naples in this poster image taken from the final shot of *Il verificatore* (1995, Stefano Incerti). ©Istituto Luce.

is set in an undisclosed Southern Italian location.[36] With its multiple narrative lines, *Prima del tramonto* explores diverse aspects of the immigration problem: the exploitation of immigrants for economic gain by organised crime, the indifference or complicity of ordinary Italians, and the desperation of the marginalised immigrants themselves. Incerti's films are discussed in more detail in Chapter 4. However, in order to get a clearer picture of how the NNC has reinterpreted the theme of migration, let us first' consider a film that predates them by a over decade.

The cinematic debut of stage and television comic Massimo Troisi, who here acts as writer, director and lead actor, *Ricomincio da tre* (1980) tells the story of Gaetano's journey to Florence in order to expand his cultural horizons. He meets and falls in love with an emancipated Florentine woman, Marta, and when she becomes pregnant and is unable to determine whether the father is Gaetano or another man with whom she had a brief sexual liaison, she offers him the opportunity of becoming a father to the child but does not place any demands on him to do so. After a brief moment of doubt and hesitation that coincides with a trip back to Naples, he decides to remain in Florence and start a family with Marta.

There is a recurrent gag in the film in which everyone Gaetano meets, on discovering that he is Neapolitan, asks, 'Emigrant?' Gaetano initially insists that he intends to return to Naples, where he has a home and a regular job; however, by the end of the narrative, circumstances will have determined otherwise. The Troisi persona is largely constructed around his shyness and the awkward way he relates to those around him, something which becomes increasingly (and comically) apparent once Gaetano leaves his home town and Marta provokes a crisis in the certainties of his traditional Southern mindset. The comedy arises largely from the contrast between Gaetano's traditional Southern mentality and Marta's emancipated mindset and lifestyle. What is innovative about the film, however, is the character's willingness (despite his hesitations and reservations) to change and to embrace the values of a foreign culture, and this implies a rejection of the past, as in the sequence in which Gaetano briefly returns to Naples but has difficulty adjusting back to his old life. Such a process is antithetical to the idea of immutability and the emigrant's nostalgic attachment to Naples in the NF, and thus marks the beginning of a quantum shift in the relationship between *napoletanità* and the theme of migration. However, this process is not really developed in the director's later work, which increasingly takes place in an abstract Southern Italy, while the Troisi persona was to be unproblematically assimilated back into Neapolitan culture and the actor became – after Totò – the new symbol of *napoletanità*.

Three years after Troisi's film, the famous playwright Eduardo De Filippo suggested that educated Neapolitans should 'flee' the troubled city, provoking rancour and accusations of defeatism from both cultural commentators and ordinary Neapolitans. This utterance ('Fujitevenne!') functions as something of a watershed, drawing a line of demarcation between the utopian and dystopian images of the city; rather than a place to be dreamed of by the reluctant émigrés of the NF, Naples was now a city to escape from at all costs. That several films of the NNC should revolve around such a flight is particularly intriguing because one of the central arguments about the NNC is that the filmmakers all chose to remain in Naples, rather than relocating to Rome to join the national film industry. Even those who left Naples to gain their professional formation (Corsicato, Incerti, Terracciano) returned to shoot their first films. Interestingly, Martone has described how his early theatrical experiences constituted a rejection of Naples and its culture, something which he only returned to with his 1991 staging of Enzo Moscato's *Rasoi* and subsequent work in the cinema:

> We [the Falso Movimento group] always felt the need to escape Naples. Not literally, because we've always stayed and worked in the city . . . but with our imaginations. There are many ways to escape: for example, through alternative visual and cultural references, such as those of the American avant-garde, which we chose to draw on as opposed to the theatre of Eduardo [De Filippo] . . . I think that the first phase of our work was an escape, with all the benefits that can bring: if you want to escape, it means that there is something oppressing you, and if you are successful in escaping, then it means that thing no longer bothers you. Later I returned to the city . . . only after this flight, this assimilation of other experiences, when I felt strong enough. (Quoted in Addonizio et al. 1997: 88)

Significantly, Martone does not describe this process in terms of the desire to engage with a broader culture or gain new experiences, which is typical of many young people (like Gaetano), but rather more dramatically in terms of a need to escape. Undoubtedly, in Martone's case this need derived from impatience with traditional Neapolitan culture and its reliance on ossified conventions, stereotypical images of *napoletanità* and an insistent mythologisation of the city. When he did turn his attention back to Naples, it was first of all by way of the complex, postmodern deconstruction of such conventions and images in Enzo Moscato's play *Rasoi*, and then through films like *Morte di un matematico napoletano* and *L'amore molesto* which, as we have seen, presented a much more ambiguous and problematic image of the city and its culture.

Chapter 2 described how emigration functioned as a key *topos* in traditional Neapolitan culture; many Neapolitan songs revolve around the theme of migration and ever since the silent era numerous films have recounted the story of a Neapolitan who is forced to leave his homeland, either out of economic necessity, or to recover from a romantic delusion, or to evade the law after a *delitto d'onore*. Perhaps the most famous example is the song *Lacreme napulitane*, which inspired two film versions, *Catene* (1949, Raffaello Matarazzo) and *Lacrime napulitane* (1981, Ciro Ippolito), which are among the most significant expressions of the NF.[37] The protagonists of these films come to believe that their wives have betrayed them and thus emigrate to America to escape from the consequent sense of shame and regret. Thus the narratives involve a forced emigration and generate pathos through the protagonist's desire to return to Naples; a sense of nostalgia and the idea of Naples as a place of the imagination, memory or fantasy are central to the functioning of these works, and this is entirely in keeping with the mythologisation of Naples and *napoletanità* described above.[38] The climactic performance of the song *Lacrime napulitane* is designed to generate an emotional response in an audience that shares the film's value system and thus is complicit with and empathetic of the protagonist's situation. Conversely, both *L'amore molesto* and *Te lo leggo negli occhi* depict female characters that have deliberately chosen to emigrate in order to escape the patriarchal value system underpinning the earlier films and the repression and violence it frequently entails, and this problematises the notion of *napoletanità* and the role it played in traditional Neapolitan culture.

While the emigrations of *L'amore molesto* and *Te lo leggo negli occhi* represent an escape from the crisis in the institution of the family, the protagonists of Carlo Luglio's debut, *Capo Nord/Cape North* (2002) emigrate to escape the kind of social alienation depicted in *Isotta* and *Vento di terra*. At first glance, *Capo Nord* may appear to resemble traditional narratives dealing with emigration; scenes of migrants living together in overcrowded conditions and the emphasis on the difficulty of finding work and the consequent reliance on illegal or underpaid manual labour recall the experiences of Guglielmo in *Catene*, for example. However, there are fundamental differences. The first is that the young protagonists of *Capo Nord* deliberately choose to abandon Naples; initially, they intend to exploit a tip-off and carry out a lucrative burglary abroad, but when their plan fails they decide to forge a new life abroad anyway. The second difference is that their choice of destination is not America but Norway – no longer the symbolic land of opportunity but a country chosen arbitrarily. Thirdly, despite the hardships they encounter, there is no suggestion of nostalgia for Naples; instead, Ettore adopts fellow migrant Lawrence's utopian fantasy of Cape North: 'The only place on Earth where the sky meets the land, you feel free and the dice always show twelve.' In the film's final scenes three of the friends reluctantly return to Naples where, we are told, they never see each other again. However, Ettore does finally go to Cape North and find peace. In the final shot, as Ettore looks out to sea, Luglio provides an ironic counterpoint to the NF's visual embodiment of its idealised fantasy of *napoletanità*, the classic panorama of the Gulf of Naples. Rather than a combination of natural beauty with an urban landscape associated with an idealised sense of community, *Capo Nord* ends on an endless, empty vista. Although Ettore apparently finds peace here, it can only be the serenity of nirvana: the obliteration of the world and all of its problems in favour of emptiness.

Undoubtedly, the most interesting treatment of migration is provided by Vincenzo Marra's debut *Tornando a casa/Sailing Home* (2001), which combines the themes of immigration and emigration, as well as developing the correlation between the alienated Neapolitan and the marginalised immigrant touched upon in *Il verificatore*. At first glance, *Tornando a casa* appears to be a realist drama exploring the difficult conditions faced by Neapolitan fishermen, and this is how it has been interpreted by most critics. Just as Marra's later *Vento di terra* generated comparisons with Luchino Visconti's *Rocco e i suoi fratelli*, here the parallel is with his *La terra trema* (1948), not only because of the superficial thematic similarities but also because Marra chose to cast non-professionals who speak a thick, naturalistic dialect necessitating Italian subtitles. However, one should be careful not to over-emphasise the social realist or documentary-like qualities of the film, given that the non-professionals were encouraged to give genuine performances, rather than simply portraying themselves, and that the film relies on a carefully structured screenplay based around a completely fictitious incident. At the film's climax, young fisherman Franco briefly considers suicide before heroically rescuing a drowning illegal immigrant with wilful disregard for his own life. His actions could be interpreted as a kind of suicide in that he chooses to place his life, which he no longer values, into the hands of fate. Unexpectedly fished out of the sea by a boat full of Tunisian illegal immigrants, Franco then decides to annihilate his identity rather than his body; like David Locke in Michelangelo Antonioni's *Professione: reporter/The Passenger* (1975), he deliberately destroys his passport in order to pass himself off as someone else.[39] Significantly, this act is also an erasure of his national identity – no longer a Neapolitan fisherman he becomes yet another immigrant and is repatriated to North Africa. Through this final twist, Marra establishes an explicit parallel with Gianni Amelio's *Lamerica* (1994), in which the protagonist, Gino, is gradually stripped of the trappings of his identity and nationality, and is ultimately forced to flee Albania on board a boat full of refugees. However, whereas Amelio's film explores the conditions experienced by the Albanians by placing an Italian in their shoes, Marra focuses on Neapolitans who feel excluded from their own country by creating a parallel with the Tunisian illegal immigrants. Whereas Gino returns to Italy from Albania, Franco flees Italy for Tunisia.[40]

This fictional incident and its metaphorical implications take us to the thematic heart of the film and help explain its title. Half-way through the film it appears that the title refers to the fishermen's return to the Bay of Naples after their troubles fishing in Sicilian and African waters (significantly, it is at this point that the eponymous theme song is first heard). But the financial difficulties they experience in Naples and the opposition of the *camorra* to their independence force them to leave once again, and this raises the question of where the home that the title refers to is to be found. There is a key dialogue after a dramatic encounter with an African coastal patrol when Samir, the Tunisian illegal immigrant who works on board, says he wants to abandon the ship. Franco replies that, 'The boat is a house and a prison. It's your mother and the sea is your father. This is your life.' Paradoxically, however, it is Franco who most desires to escape from the boat. Initially, he flirts with the traditional dream of emigration to America, but Salvatore points out the limits of such a dream, asking whether he really wants to spend his life making pizzas. The only other possibility Franco entertains is based on a lie, a denial of his own identity, when he jokingly suggests to Samir that they should both go to Tunisia, where he could pretend to be a rich Italian. His final decision to reinvent himself by denying his true identity is thus motivated by a lack of alternative choices. It is this impossibility of living in Naples or of finding an alternative place abroad that keeps the characters stuck in the middle of the ocean. This idea also finds expression in a metaphorical dimension that contrasts markedly with the standard realist interpretation of the film, most explicitly in the parable of a man carrying an oar who keeps walking inland until people mistake it for a pole because he has arrived at a place where they do not even know what the sea is. Apparently about escaping from one's problems, the parable acquires an alternative interpretation in relation to the film's ending. Franco ends up in a situation where, like the oar, he is no longer recognised for what he is; thus the parable comes to signify annihilation and the loss of identity. There is a profoundly pessimistic dimension to the narrative, then, suggesting that its characters have no possibility for escape or reinvention outside of an annihilation that recalls Ettore's ultimate nirvana in *Capo Nord*.

But what is it that makes the fishermen's life in Naples so unliveable? On the one hand, it is the economic necessity of making ends meet and the difficulty of doing so without breaking the law. On the other, it is the presence of the *camorra*, which prevents the men from fishing in the local bay and forces them to accept dangerous conditions in order to obtain a loan necessary to carry on fishing. Significantly, the only character that does not share their sense of social exclusion is Rosa, Franco's girlfriend, whose job as a teacher places her within the social system and means that she does not want to leave for America because, as she tells Franco, she feels important where she is. If there is a home in the film, it is located in this character that represents an oasis of domestic bliss in a hostile society. However, the precariousness of this domesticity is revealed when she is accidentally shot by one of her students who is playing

Figure 3.4 A panorama of the new Naples: the deserted gypsy camp in Scampia. *Sotto la stessa luna* (2006, Carlo Luglio). ©Figli del Bronx.

with a gun: a tragedy which once again destroys any possibility of the creation of a family and precipitates Franco's final gesture of self-annihilation.

After *Capo Nord*, Carlo Luglio returned to the theme of migration with *Sotto la stessa luna/Under the Same Moon* (2006), which is set in and around the encampments in Scampia that are home to some 1500 gypsies[41] (see Fig. 3.4). The film explores the uneasy co-existence of the Neapolitan and gypsy populations through the stories of Franco, a reformed drug-dealer who eventually marries into the gypsy community, and Oliver, a young gypsy who falls for the girlfriend of a *camorra* boss. While Oliver dreams of having his own 'Neapolitan princess' and his friend Pavel adopts the language and behaviour of the Neapolitans in an attempt to integrate into wider society, they also find themselves the target of the hostility and racism of the indigenous community. Conversely, the disillusioned and marginalised Franco, fresh from prison and the death of his daughter through overdose, seeks solace in the sense of community offered by the gypsies. Yet the film again concludes on a pessimistic note: the shooting of two gypsies by the *camorra* and the subsequent exodus from the camp (both inspired by real events, which transpired in 1999).

In a brief but important article published in 1973, Pier Paolo Pasolini compared Neapolitans to the desert tribe of the Tuareg (Pasolini 1999: 230–1). He argued that, confronted by the homogenising forces of history and modernity, Naples and its populace were refusing to conform or change and instead would allow themselves simply to die out. Fascinated by what he saw as the authenticity of the pre-industrialist cultures he found in places like Africa, India and the popular quarters of Naples, and appalled by modern Western capitalism, Pasolini saw this act as both tragic and heroic. This provocative idea has since been echoed by Antonio Capuano, who describes the *scugnizzi* of *Vito e gli altri* as 'a tribe on the verge of extinction, like the Tuareg' (see Sesti 1991: 51), and Mario Martone, who chose to use Pasolini's text as a preface to his filmed version of Enzo Moscato's play *Rasoi*. This idea also finds expression in Franco's 'suicidal' decision to place his life in the hands of fate in *Tornando a casa* and in Caccioppoli's suicide in *Morte di un matematico napoletano*, which, as we have seen, Aldo Schiavone viewed as emblematic of the suicide of the city as a whole. Interestingly, the opening of *Certi bambini* features a scene in which, like Franco, the *scugnizzi* choose to place their lives in the hands of fate by blindly crossing a motorway – an image that Emilio Cozzi has suggested constitutes the perfect metaphor for the *scugnizzi*'s way of life (Cozzi 2004: 12). While *Certi bambini* was heavily influenced by *Vito e gli altri*, it is interesting that Capuano later chose to borrow this conceit for a key scene in *La guerra di Mario*. While, for Pasolini, death rather than conformity constitutes a form of rebellion, in these films there is no sense of rebellion, merely a pessimistic fatalism. There is, however, one recent film that is more consistent with Pasolini's view.

Set entirely in the gastroenterology department of an unidentified Neapolitan hospital, Vincenzo Terracciano's *Ribelli per caso* [Rebels by Chance] (2000) focuses on a group of patients who decide to organise, cook and eat a midnight feast, despite the restrictive diets on which the doctors have placed them.[42] In the case of Ciro, in particular, this act of rebellion could even prove fatal. As Ciro's justification for his continuing indulgence ('I want to die happy, okay?') makes clear, their actions can be considered a wilful indulgence in life's pleasures regardless of the consequences. However, they also constitute a rebellion against the authority of the doctors, the bureaucracy of the hospital and the way in which the patients are dehumanised. From the very beginning we are presented with a catalogue of flaws in the day-to-day running of the hospital, and by the time of his final dialogue with the film's protagonist, Adriano, the aloof Dr Sorvino has become the very embodiment of inhuman authoritarianism and the antithesis of the Hippocratic Oath. The patients all appear relatively healthy, yet there is no indication of when (or if) they will ever be treated or discharged; instead they are kept in the dark like helpless prisoners. Their action is therefore above all an act of rebellion against their own lack of agency within a bureaucratic and authoritarian system. The metaphorical dimension to the film and the emphasis on the character's endless waiting and unknowing, which is reminiscent of Kafka's *The Trial*, results in an existentialist dimension that explores the lengths the characters will go to in order to escape from their own mortality. Again this is developed in Adriano's final confrontation with Sorvino, when he faces up to his own fears, acknowledging that he has terminal cancer and taking control of his own life in the face of death. This ending differs from that of the NF, in which the individual is passive, a victim of forces he cannot control, and whose redemption is the product of a divine or miraculous fortune. In *Ribelli per caso* the individual rebels against the system, even if it costs him his life.

RESPONSES TO THE CRISIS IN *NAPOLETANITÀ*

The question of whether contemporary filmmakers can conceive of any options open to Neapolitans beyond suicide or emigration is an important one and there are a couple of filmmakers who have tentatively proposed remedies to the alienation described above, although their conclusions are far from unambiguously optimistic. Diego Olivares's sole feature to date, *I cinghiali di Portici* [The Wild Boars of Portici] (2003), contains a brief scene in which a character who is repairing a canoe suggests using it to sail to Africa. Significantly, however, this idea is not developed further into a discourse about migration. Similarly, the film's repeated allusions to the caging and domestication of animals are never emphasised sufficiently to become a metaphor of entrapment, and a brief instance of domestic violence is presented as merely a symptom of a character's frustration rather than being deconstructed into an analysis of patriarchal/familial repression. Thus *I cinghiali di Portici* constitutes something of an anomaly within the NNC. Although it deals with a centre for the rehabilitation of drug addicts in the Neapolitan hinterland, rather than emphasising marginalisation and alienation it focuses instead on the way the inmates bond when they are encouraged to form a rugby team. Thus the film is 'above all the story of a community' (Morreale 2006: 23). By invoking the narrative conventions of the sports film so alien to Neapolitan cinema (a group of misfits is moulded into a winning team), the film articulates a broadly positive and optimistic corrective to the films described above. Despite their problems, the *'cinghiali'* are certainly not *'estranei alla massa'*. However, the film ends at the start of the match that will decide whether or not they win the amateur championship and leaves the fates of its protagonists unresolved, thus undercutting the triumphalist finale characteristic of the sports film and retaining the kind of complexity and ambiguity typical of the NNC.

Paolo Sorrentino's *L'uomo in più*/*One Man Up* (2001) also touches on the world of sport, recounting the parallel stories of Antonio Pisapia, a successful footballer for the Neapolitan team, and Tony Pisapia, a middle-aged pop singer. Early on in the film Antonio suffers an accident and is forced to retire, while Tony's career is ruined when he is charged with the statutory rape of a minor. Although the film's theme music is Cake's *I Will Survive*, the film revolves precisely around the characters' inability to recover from these setbacks. Tony attempts to revive his musical career but his behaviour when successful has alienated so many people that he finds nobody to turn to, and his subsequent attempt to take over the management of a seafood restaurant is thwarted when it is sold to some shady individuals who may be involved with the *camorra*. Similarly, Antonio trains as a football coach but the club president turns his back on him and refuses to give him a job. Both characters find themselves suddenly marginalised, surplus to society's requirements, 'in più'.[43] Although the narrative clearly has ambitions beyond a simple tale of thwarted ambitions, the precise meaning behind Sorrentino's Premio Solinas-winning script remains deliberately elusive. For one thing, the nature of the relationship between these two characters, born on the same day, sharing the same name, and whose lives seem to follow a parallel course, is never made explicit. Despite their fame, neither character seems to be aware of the other's existence, nor does anybody else comment on this strange coincidence.[44] Yet at their nadir their paths cross and they exchange gazes pregnant with unspecified significance, apparently recognising some strange affinity with one another. Antonio subsequently appears on the TV programme, *Public Confessions*, saying, 'But this is not what I want to talk about. Today I met a person . . .' His gaze into the camera is met by Tony, watching the programme in his living room, and the phrase is left incomplete and unexplained. Antonio's subsequent suicide apparently prompts Tony's otherwise unmotivated assassination of the president of the football club who had previously betrayed Antonio. Tony then appears on the same *Public Confessions* programme, where he insists that, unlike Antonio, he will never commit suicide because he is a free man. Yet in the very next sequence he jumps into the Bay of Naples while fleeing from the police – a suicidal act that constitutes a refusal to renounce his status as 'a free man' and return to jail. As in *Ribelli per caso* and Pasolini's conception of Naples, his act constitutes both a renunciation and a rebellion. The film then presents us with a highly ambiguous coda in which an imprisoned Tony cooks fish for his cellmates, earning their approval and thus regaining the kind of public recognition that both he and Antonio craved. There are several possible interpretations of this final scene; we could either assume that Tony survived and was arrested, although there is no indication of how this might have happened, or we could read it as his fantasy at the moment of death, an interpretation possibly alluded to by the final shot in which the camera tracks out through the bars to peer down at the sea below.

The film thus tantalises us with a series of hypotheses but its ultimate meaning remains elusive. To make sense of the film, we need to consider its symbolic structure more closely. Tony clearly feels both guilt and remorse for the death of his brother during a diving expedition, shown during the credits, and the film repeatedly features fragments of a dream in which Tony's mother walks towards the sea to meet a diver emerging from the water. However, it is only after Antonio's suicide that we witness the dream's conclusion; the diver removes his mask to reveal the face of Antonio, while Tony stands on the beach clutching the diver's knife he will later use to kill the president. This sequence multiplies the film's doppelgangers to suggest that Tony's subconscious has substituted Antonio for his brother in order to create the possibility of remedying his actions and alleviating his sense of guilt by avenging Antonio and then fulfilling his disapproving mother's earlier suggestion that he should have been the one to die at the bottom of the sea. The film's coda then presents us with a fantasy of success, in which Tony gains the unconditional approval of his cellmates for a fish supper.[45] However, even this scene remains ambiguous since, as *I Will Survive* begins to play on the soundtrack once more, the camera tracks out through the prison bars, which emphasise the extent to which Tony is not free, to focus on the sea below, where his body possibly rests.

Sorrentino's subsequent film, *Le conseguenze dell'amore/The Consequences of Love* (2004), shares numerous similarities with his debut. Once again, it features a narrative about a successful man whose life is ruined by a single action; in this case an enormously successful stockbroker loses 220 billion Lira invested for the Mafia. When we are first introduced to Titta Di Girolamo he is an isolated and alienated man, estranged from his family and kept a virtual prisoner in a Swiss hotel by the Mafia for whom, we gradually learn, he regularly delivers large sums of money to a Swiss bank. Once again, the character attempts to rebel against his situation, to 'survive', only for the film to conclude with an ambiguous 'suicide'. Having fallen in love with the hotel barmaid, Titta appropriates a large sum of money, which two of the Mafia's hit men had unsuccessfully tried to steal from him, presumably with the intention of escaping and starting a new life with her. However, erroneously believing that she has rejected him, he anonymously donates the money to his neighbour, an elderly gambling addict who dreams of doing something 'spectacular' to end his life rather than merely growing old and dying in a hotel room. Then, in retaliation for the life that has been stolen from him, he refuses to reveal the money's whereabouts to the Mafia and instead allows them to execute him. Like Tony in *L'uomo in più*, he performs a 'spectacular' action for the sake of a virtual stranger in the name of freedom and in so doing renounces his life. Both films thus hinge on what André Gide termed an 'acte gratuit', an unmotivated action performed, in true existentialist fashion, to assert one's liberty in the face of a destiny over which one has no control. Like *L'uomo in più*, *Le conseguenze dell'amore* also ends with a coda; Dino Giuffrè, the man Titta insists on referring to as his best friend, despite the fact that he has not seen him for over 20 years, pauses to look pensively into the distance while the dying Titta proclaims in voice-over that he is certain that Dino Giuffrè occasionally stops to think of his best friend, Titta di Girolamo.

There is an implicit parallel between the NF's assuaging of concerns about Naples' loss of status since Unification and Sorrentino's fascination with the idea of a fall from grace and the possibility of second chances. However, whereas the NF used Naples symbolically to structure the film's discourse, Sorrentino refuses to employ the city explicitly as part of his thematic structure. Indeed, *L'uomo in più* virtually effaces the city from the screen through its choice of anonymous locations and partial views, while *Le conseguenze dell'amore* is set in Switzerland and features a character that resolutely refuses to be identified as Neapolitan, insisting that he comes from Salerno. Significantly, *L'uomo in più* is set on the cusp of the 1980s, and a number of critics have drawn attention to the film's emphasis on this historical setting through its careful use of *mise-en-scène* (for example, see Zanetti 2001: 64). Sorrentino depicts this historical juncture as a moment of transition when the hopes of the hedonistic 1970s were dashed and replaced by a cultural vacuum and ruthless capitalism, an idea also featured in several recent American films.[46] It is worth recalling that 1980 was also a significant moment for Naples and the South of Italy; a devastating earthquake not only caused widespread damage but the subsequent mishandling and embezzlement of relief funds threw into sharp relief the corruption that had underpinned Neapolitan politics and society over the past decades, as well as providing vital funds that helped transform the *camorra* into a global criminal enterprise. It could also be argued that this crisis laid the foundations for the Neapolitan renaissance since Bassolino's rise can also be understood as a consequence of the widespread anger and dissatisfaction over the corruption and mismanagement of the post-earthquake years.

Sorrentino's films provide us with an (implicit) metaphor for the decline of Naples and its current alienation. His characters' reconciliation and liberation are achieved only through death and a mysterious connection with a virtual stranger, and thus the films' resolution entails the introduction of a metaphysical dimension that arguably recalls the *deus ex machina* of the NF. Thus, while his films represent the search for a solution to the pessimism that has characterised so many of the films discussed here, it could be argued that the metaphysical solutions they offer constitute a retrograde step – albeit a brilliant, fascinating and flamboyant one – in comparison with the historical materialist or existential analyses described earlier.

CONCLUSION

The pessimism inherent in the image of an alienated Naples is in sharp contrast with the idea of a supposed 'Neapolitan renaissance', which dominated discourse on the city in the 1990s and of which the NNC is supposedly one expression. This relationship will be analysed in more depth in Chapter 5. However, given the NNC's thematic revisionism and rejection of *napoletanità*, we should first ask what legacy the NF has left contemporary filmmakers. The next chapter will therefore examine the way in which the narrative, generic and stylistic conventions of a popular form rooted firmly in the society and culture of post-war Naples have been revisited and reworked by filmmakers for a modern, twenty-first-century audience.

NOTES

1. Dario Minutolo has also identified these films as a point of transition (see Argentieri 1998: 17–19).
2. The heirs of Piscicelli's other innovation (the reinterpretation of the conventions of the *sceneggiata*) will be investigated more fully in the next chapter.
3. The Italian expression 'trovare una sistemazione' (literally, 'find a settlement') encompasses all three of these into a general, almost existential, category.
4. Quoted in the director's notes on Dolmen Home Video's DVD of the film.
5. On this subject see also O'Healy 1999a, Rascaroli 2003 and Roberti 1992a.
6. Although the title appears to do just that, the same cannot be said for the film itself.
7. This idea is clarified and developed in *Teatro di guerra*, which is analysed in Chapter 5, while Schiavone's metaphor of suicide is discussed further on pp. 104–5.
8. Antonietta De Lillo used an analogous technique for the eighteenth century in *Il resto di niente*, as described in Chapter 5.
9. This method recurs in his next film, *L'amore molesto*, whose published screenplay even contains a map of the course its protagonist takes through the city (Martone 1996: 24).
10. Her earlier short, *Spalle al muro* (1997), also won Moretti's Sacher prize. *Autunno* even contains a scene in which Costanza randomly stops a passer-by to ask him if he is happy in his marriage, just as Nanni assails passers-by with idiosyncratic questions in *Caro diario* (1993, Nanni Moretti).
11. Di Majo has described her characters as 'emanations' of herself or the 'materialisation of persecutory fantasies' (Morreale and Zonta 2009: 60).
12. The fantasy sequence in which he appears as a hotel receptionist who hands Cesare a bill for 26 years of lodging is particularly amusing. Significantly, the only business we see Cesare's father conclude is helping a local landowner prevent a motorway passing through his property, an action which inevitably hints at corruption.
13. In an economising move typical of the NNC's mode of production these animations are borrowed from a film school short, *Vesuvio*, by Rosario Lamberti. In their deliberate naïveté, these sequences anticipate the historical animations of *Il resto di niente* (see p. 172).
14. Although autobiographical interpretations of films can be reductive, it is none the less worth noting in passing that *Non è giusto* was made shortly after the director's separation from long-term partner, producer Giorgio Magliulo, who subsequently became involved both professionally and romantically with Nina Di Majo, and that the film is dedicated to her children.
15. It is an unusual instance of a diegetic character ostensibly taking control of the image track, which is just one indication that De Lillo is more attuned to the possibilities offered by the medium of cinema and by recent technological advances than is often conceded. Not only was her company Megaris among the first in Italy to offer online editing facilities, but *Non è giusto* was the first Neapolitan feature shot entirely on digital video. Later, *Il resto di niente* made use of digital technology as part of its process of historical reconstruction (see p. 172).
16. Shown at Venice in 2000, the film had only the briefest of theatrical releases in early 2001 and remains unseen on home video or TV.

17. The film was shot in Sant'Agata dei Goti due to the dramatic changes to the urban landscape of Frattamaggiore since the 1950s.
18. Scialò is an expert on Neapolitan song and the *sceneggiata*, the author of several books on the subject (Scialò 1995 and Scialò 2002) and musical supervisor of Paolo Santoni's documentary *Cuore napoletano* (2002) and Giuseppe Bertolucci's adaptation of Enzo Moscato's *Luparella* (2002). Anton Giulio Mancino complains that 'the excessive urgency to recreate the image of a particular historical period and popular setting . . . grates with the narrative progression and emotional dynamics' (Mancino 2000: 49). However, aside from being one of the principal pleasures offered the spectator, this aspect of the film actually plays a fundamental role in the development of the film's discourse, as will become clear below.
19. It also raises the theme of the emergence of sexuality and the passage into the adult world and Rocca seems to have had a psychoanalytic conception in mind when developing these ideas. See, for example, the Freudian 'primal scene' when he witnesses Carmine and Rafilina have sex, the depiction of the cinema as Metzian 'imaginary signifier', and the play with the Lacanian motif of mirrors that gives the film its title. Such a theory-inflected approach to narrative conventions is also a significant departure from traditional Neapolitan cinema.
20. This fantastic dimension is hinted at in the opening scene depicting a ball rolling though an attic out of frame. Although the scene's significance becomes clear only at the end, the image explicitly recalls both Mario Bava's *Operazione paura* (1966) and Fellini's 'Toby Dammit' episode of *Histoires Extraordinaires* (1968, Roger Vadim, Federico Fellini and Louis Malle).
21. There are already several excellent analyses of this film and I will therefore limit myself to saying less here than the film would otherwise deserve, reserving the additional space for less well-known, but equally valid, films. On the film's treatment of identity, see O'Healy 1999a. On the treatment of sexuality in the film, see Gianfranco Cercone's 'Appunti per uno studio sull'erotismo in alcuni film napoletani', in Pellegrini et al. 1996: 27–31. On the film's use of genre conventions and on its depiction of femininity, see Small 1999. For a more sustained discussion of the way the film reworks Neapolitan convention, and in particular of its relationship to *Lacrime napulitane* (1981, Ciro Ippolito), see Marlow-Mann 2009.
22. All of the aforementioned articles contain more sustained analyses of Martone's unconventional treatment of the city.
23. The mention of eyes in the titles *Te lo leggo negli occhi* and *Lontano in fondo agli occhi* is interesting, given the crucial role played by focalisation and point-of-view in the films under discussion.
24. Significantly, in this conversation Chiara momentarily abandons standard Italian and reverts to Neapolitan dialect, just as Delia did in her encounter with her father.
25. For a more detailed exposition of this process, see Marlow-Mann 2009.
26. On the function of this Latin title, see Mauro 2003.
27. See also the discussion of Corsicato's approach to gender and the *sceneggiata* in Chapter 4.
28. There are interesting similarities to and differences from Larry Clarke's *Kids* (1995), which also presents an almost apocalyptic view of contemporary urban youth, narrated from within. While Clarke never uses such radical stylistic devices as Capuano's direct address to camera, he does use voice-over to allow us access to the children's thoughts and belief system and also had the film scripted by a street-kid, Harmony Korine. Korine would later become a scriptwriter and filmmaker in his own right, unlike the non-professional actors in Capuano's film whose fate was more tragic – several of them ended up dead or in jail.

29. Dario Minutolo sees this dialectic between an inherent vitality and a constant awareness of one's own mortality as characteristic of recent Neapolitan cinema (see Pellegrini et al. 1996: 23–6). A reflection on mortality also constitutes the subject of Antonietta De Lillo's unconventional anthology feature, *Racconti di Vittoria*.
30. This reflects, of course, one of the traditional interpretations of the 'Southern Question': that the State's absence or ineffectiveness in the South creates a void in which the Mafia can flourish.
31. For a more detailed exploration of this idea, see Marlow-Mann, forthcoming 2012.
32. The two films were conceived more or less simultaneously and independently; Capuano's script won the Premio Solinas in 1988, while Piscicelli's was developed from his own short story published in 1992.
33. Whereas Capuano favours a complex regime of focalisation to place the viewer in an ambiguous relationship with his protagonist, Piscicelli utilises a more straightforward *pedinamento* (the 'following camera' theorised by Cesare Zavattini).
34. On the distinction between the 'two Naples', see Ravveduto 2007: 53.
35. On the 'Balkanization of Italy' and its relation to images of the South in Italian cinema in general, see Wood 2003.
36. It was shot in a variety of locations including Naples, Aversa and Foggia.
37. The former is the most successful national production influenced by the NF, while the latter is considered by many to be the quintessential film-*sceneggiata* and is undoubtedly the key film of Mario Merola's œuvre.
38. On the theme of emigration, see also Marlow-Mann 2009, Bruno 1997 and Aprà 1994: 75–90. On the idea of Naples as an imagined city, see pp. 149–50 and Fofi 1990: 95–104.
39. Similarly, Delia also defaces her passport at the end of *L'amore molesto*, cancelling her own identity and assuming that of her mother.
40. Marra's first documentary short, *Una rosa, prego* (1998), also explores the relationship between Neapolitans and a marginalised immigrant population in the form of the gypsy children who sell flowers on the streets of Naples.
41. The film also screened at festivals under the title *Sotto la luna di Scampia*.
42. The use of a hospital as a metaphor for wider society is not new; both *One Flew Over the Cuckoo's Nest* (1975, Milos Foreman) and *Britannia Hospital* (1982, Lindsay Anderson) use a similar location to explore issues of conformity and rebellion.
43. The title, like the film, is actually open to multiple interpretations; it refers to the football tactic pioneered by Antonio Pisapia, the fact that they both suddenly find themselves superfluous, and the fact that they are two people who, on some level, share the same identity.
44. The film was conceived when, fearing that he might never get the opportunity to make a second feature, Sorrentino decided to combine two separate stories he was developing.
45. Fish also play an important symbolic function and for Tony his skill at cooking, which he learned in prison, represents the possibility of a second chance. The only fish he refuses to cook is octopus, since an octopus was responsible for his brother's death. Significantly, it is when he violates this rule, effectively confronting his past, that he encounters Antonio.
46. For example, Martin Scorsese's *Goodfellas* (1990), a film that Sorrentino professes to admire and which also revolves around a rise-and-fall narrative. Moreover, Tony's entrance to a disco during his post-concert celebrations recalls Henry Hill's queue-jumping nightclub entrance in Scorsese's film; both scenes are choreographed to music and shot with a steadycam in an extended long take that follows the protagonist's movement through a series of spaces and encounters in order to

emphasise a sense of mastery over his environment. Interestingly, Paul Thomas Anderson's *Boogie Nights* (1997) also hinges on this same historical juncture, relies on a rise-and-fall structure, and features a scene shot in a similar fashion to similar effect.

4. GOLD AND DUST: HYBRIDITY, POSTMODERNISM AND THE LEGACY OF NEAPOLITAN NARRATIVE

The films discussed in Chapter 3 invoked the themes and motifs of traditional Neapolitan culture only implicitly, and in practice their rejection of the underlying assumptions on which these were founded was complete and unequivocal. Conversely, Antonio Capuano's *Polvere di Napoli* [The Dust of Naples] (1998) explicitly invites interpretation in relation to one of the key representations of Naples – Giuseppe Marotta's collection of stories, *L'oro di Napoli/ The Gold of Naples* and Vittorio De Sica's 1954 film adaptation of the same name. Indeed, the opening caption deliberately enters into dialogue with De Sica's uncritical celebration of *napoletanità*: 'That which you see in films, even if it sometimes shines, is not always gold. It more closely resembles silver and, more often than not, is merely dust.' However, contrary to this statement, and unlike his earlier *Vito e gli altri*, Capuano does not attempt to reveal the harsh reality behind the stereotype. Instead, he pursues a vein of surreal comedy that has little at all to do with questions of realism and betrays a much more ambivalent relationship to his source of inspiration.

Only the first episode explicitly reworks a situation from De Sica's film, reprising the central character of an impoverished habitual gambler from 'I giocatori' and being set in the same building overlooking Piazza del Gesù nuovo. Capuano draws our attention to this parallel when the episode's protagonist, Bibberò, observes a mural depicting the square and asks, 'Do you think it's the same square?' Throughout the episode there is a deliberate comic play between (filmic) representation and reality. When Bibberò returns a football to the square below, a ball simultaneously comes into play on the game broadcast on television as if he had returned the ball to the televised match; Bibberò challenges the butcher who questions his prices, stating, 'We are the film's protagonists'; and at one point a *posteggiatore* ends his rendition by breaking the fourth wall and requesting a donation from the audience. As it progresses, the episode becomes increasingly surreal and any semblance of realism is stripped away; visions are conjured up by the stifling heat and Bibberò momentarily sees giraffes strolling through the *piazza* below and his opponents as pigs ready for the slaughter. This surrealism and self-reflexivity are reprised by the third episode, in which 'Pasquale the Shark' sprouts a fin and duels with an Argentinian soap-opera star in a Pompeian amphitheatre reminiscent of Sergio Leone's circular arenas to the accompaniment of a Morricone-esque soundtrack. Conversely, the second episode, which depicts the journey of two newlyweds from the periphery to the historic centre, subverts the traditional iconography of Naples by depicting it as an almost post-apocalyptic waste-land with deserted, dust-blown streets. An opening caption emphasises this transformation, stating, 'When they arrived they didn't recognise anything, neither the city nor its inhabitants.' As the episode progresses, the characters discover that they cannot even find the Chiesa di Santa Chiara, one of the most famous landmarks of the city. In the final episode two musicians nicknamed after Charlie Parker and Gerry Mulligan play at Cancello Jazz, a less prestigious version of Umbria Jazz in the Neapolitan hinterland. On discovering that their instruments have been stolen, they are forced to don masks of Totò and Peppino De Filippo and improvise a comic double act, which enjoys the resounding success denied their jazz performances. Ciarli and Gerri's attempt to import a foreign, elitist musical culture fails because this is an inward-looking culture that responds positively only to their absurd re-proposal of a local popular cultural matrix. But it is not only the intended audience that is mocked here, but also the pretensions of the protagonists themselves. In the early hours of the morning a group of North African immigrants offers them tomatoes in exchange for the opportunity to play their saxophones and the scene is soon transformed into a frantic jam session as the incredulous Ciarli and Gerri discover that these low-paid immigrant farm workers are far more gifted musicians than they are. In the Neapolitan hinterland, the marginalisa-tion of an elite foreign culture such as jazz is paralleled by the marginalisation of these North African immigrants.

If the final episode's invocation of marginalisation and immigration recalls the crisis of *napoletanità* explored by the films in Chapter 3, then its emphasis on the gulf that exists between popular Neapolitan cultural forms and elite foreign ones is characteristic of the films to be discussed in this chapter. These films address the legacy of traditional Neapolitan culture by evoking the conventions of the *sceneggiata* and the NF, and by posing the question of what relevance such cultural forms could possibly have for a modern audience. Just as the former tendency was prefigured by *Immacolata e Concetta*, the latter is anticipated by a more or less contemporaneous film, the German–Italian co-production *Nel regno di Napoli/Neapolitanische Geschichten/The Kingdom of Naples* (1979, Werner Schroeter).

HYBRID NARRATIVES

History and the Individual

Nel regno di Napoli narrates thirty years of Neapolitan history from 1943 to the mid-1970s by focusing on the inhabitants of via Marinella in the popular quarter by the port. There is a parallel between this approach and the epic historical narratives of Bernardo Bertolucci's *1900* (1976) and Marco Tullio Giordana's *La meglio gioventù/The Best of Youth* (2003). However, whereas they use a (melodramatic) fictional story to illustrate the social and political changes in Italy over time, here the relationship between these two narrative regimes is more complex as the historical narrative (conveyed by a series of date captions presented against still images and accompanied by a voice-over describing significant events) is problematised by the interceding fictional narrative sequences. One could describe this approach as a hybrid between a documentary narrative mode and an extremely stylised and rhetorical fictional one. The captions create a conventional narrative of the principal events of post-war Italian history, from liberation and reconstruction, through the ideological battles between communism and Catholicism, to the economic boom and the embracing of capitalism, the 1968 protests, and the political and social uncertainties of the early 1970s. However, the fictional narrative problematises the convenience of this history by showing that such a broad narrative has more dramatic and frequently divergent implications for individuals. The opening sequences are emblematic in this regard. A voice-over that tells us that 'this is the first city in Italy to free itself from Fascism' is followed by a father's anguish at the news that the Germans have slaughtered a group of Neapolitans. He then transposes his political hopes for a new Italy on to a personal level by naming his daughter Vittoria. The credits then scroll over a shot of a child walking through an empty, ruined apartment, which evokes the ending of *Germania anno zero/Germany Year Zero* (1948) – the only one of Rossellini's films to paint an entirely nihilistic picture of the destruction of war – while the soundtrack plays *Simme 'e Napule paisà*, a song that simultaneously expresses the hope for a re-birth of the city with the shock of a Neapolitan returning to discover the city destroyed and his family gone. Then a documentary sequence describing 'the reconstruction of Naples' is followed by a fictional scene in which the adolescent Rosa is prostituted to a black American sailor (accompanied, of course, by *Tammuriata nera* on the soundtrack).[1] Thus, in the space of the film's opening 15 minutes, a narrative of liberation and reconstruction in the 'documentary' sequences is repeatedly undercut by the fictional narrative's emphasis on the death and suffering visited upon the inhabitants of via Marinella.

As the film proceeds, the fictional narrative calls into question the values inherent in each of the conflicting ideologies that drive the forces of history. While left-wing critics attacked the illusory and escapist qualities of the NF's underlying Catholic ideology, Schroeter here paints an equally bleak picture of the way in which communist ideology is comprised of empty phrases that do little to alleviate the suffering of the fictional characters. In the extraordinary 1964 sequence Valeria blames her communist husband Simonetti for her daughter's death, since he opposed the black market that provided the only source of the penicillin that could have saved her. This death – paralleled by the exporting of Michelangelo's *Pietà*, the archetypal image of a mother's suffering over her dead child – is followed by repeated shots of Simonetti's speech. The repetition of these shots, which recalls Eisenstein's method of ridiculing Kerensky in *Oktyabr/October* (1928), reinforces the conventionality of his discourse and the extent to which he acts as a vehicle for the passive transmission of ideology. Capitalism, on the other hand, is embodied by the figures of Pupetta Ferrante, who is characterised as a psychologically unbalanced lesbian vamp, and the lawyer Palombo, a stereotypical mother's boy and predatory homosexual. As they prey on the working-class Vittoria and Massimo, the 'deviance' of their sexuality parallels the exploitation of the proletariat by the bourgeois and industrialist classes. Towards the end of the film, after Valeria has killed Simonetti and gone insane, Vittoria remarks to Massimo, 'Now that you have seen Valeria you can understand the sadness that characterises our community in via Marinella.' This comment, which seems addressed more to the audience than Massimo, highlights the extent to which the film's focus is on the local close-knit community described in Chapter 2, the suffering of its members, its dissolution under the forces of history, and the failure of the various ideological solutions proposed to offer any kind of individual salvation.

The two 1970s sequences towards the end of the film paint a picture of an uncertain present. Abandoning the historic centre for the beach at Bagnoli, they establish an ironic counterpoint between the use of the song *Santa Lucia luntana*, in which an emigrant experiences nostalgia for this beautiful waterfront area, and the bleak, overcast beach in the Neapolitan periphery with its ugly industrial backdrop. Vittoria – in keeping with her name – succeeds in educating herself and gaining her independence by accepting a job as an air stewardess. However, as Massimo observes while melancholically reflecting on his own loneliness and sense of despair, 'I felt affection for my sister, but even she left. I don't think that she is happy, even if she now wears a uniform. She no longer seems like herself.' If this statement reflects two of the pessimistic proposals exhibited by the films discussed in Chapter 3 (emigration and the erasure of one's identity), then the third is mirrored by the death of Rosaria with which the film ends. This is staged in a highly stylised manner under the porticoes flanking the Galleria Umberto and is paralleled by a dance to a frantic *tammuriata* in which Pulcinella (the quintessential symbol of *napoletanità*) seems to be performing his own death throes. Meanwhile, Massimo's repeated cries for help, delivered as he disappears into the night, apparently apply as much to himself and the city as they do to Rosaria. A more desperate ending is hard to imagine. The film's final scenes thus present us with the death throes of 'the Kingdom of Naples' – a title that becomes bitterly ironic – death throes that no ideology (Marxist, Capitalist, Catholic) seems able to remedy.

One could argue that Schroeter's approach is postmodern, specifically in the way in which he problematises ideology and historical narratives – Lyotard would say 'meta-narratives' (Lyotard 1984) – through an emphasis on their contingency and irrelevance to the individual. Formally, the film also reflects the influence of postmodernism through its mixing of different styles; indeed, Serge Daney wonders whether the film is 'left-wing fiction, kitsch melodrama, decadent *fotoromanzo*, the history of a city, an opera in a minor key, or simply Schroeter's first "realist" and "narrative" film?' (Daney 1980: 28). In addition to the contrast between documentary and fictional modes of narration, there is also a wide variance of style and tone within the fictional sequences. Some exterior sequences echo Neorealism's emphasis on concrete social environments, while others recall Schroeter's avant-garde past in their emphasis on theatricality, non-naturalistic performance style, garish lighting and kitsch décor. The domestic conflicts and Pupella Ferrante scenes recall the *sceneggiata* and anticipate *Immacolata e Concetta*, not only through the casting of Ida Di Benedetto as a woman who tries to prostitute a young girl, but also through the emphasis on the commodification of personal relations. However, whereas Piscicelli deliberately uses Brechtian devices to undercut the *sceneggiata* narrative and undermine its ideology, Schroeter's postmodern pastiche creates a contrast between different styles and modes of narration; no single narrative or ideology is privileged or affirmed.

A similar approach to problematising historical narratives recurs in Giuseppe M. Gaudino's *Giro di lune tra terra e mare* [Moon Orbits Between Land and Sea] (1997). In interview Gaudino has repeatedly stressed his independence from the NNC (see Argentieri 1998: 78 and Zagarrio 1999: 195). However, like the other directors considered here, he works independently at regional level, subverts stereotypes of Naples – or more precisely Pozzuoli in the Province of Naples – and poses questions and reaches conclusions not that dissimilar from the other films under discussion here. Gaudino should thus be considered as both autonomous and yet following a parallel trajectory to the

NNC. *Giro di lune* is his sole feature film to date, although it elaborates on a number of his earlier shorts and documentaries and reutilises some of the same footage.[2] Such reworking is a constant of Gaudino's career and *Giro di lune* exists in at least three different versions, each of which exhibits both additions and subtractions; there is no single and definitive text but rather a series of stages of a work in progress.

Like *Nel regno di Napoli* the film works on several diegetic levels characterised by different stylistic approaches. One narrative revolves around the Gioia family who live in the Rione Terra district of Pozzuoli and are repeatedly forced to move house due to the devastating effects of *bradisismo*.[3] The daughter, Assuntina, has been estranged since she reported her older brother, Carmine, to the police for his alleged part in the death of her husband. Her brother, Tonino, who gave up university in order to help in the family fishing business, is in conflict with their father, Salvatore, over the direction the family business should take, and this comes to a head when an outbreak of cholera results in the loss of the mussels on which their livelihood depends. Gennaro, the youngest member of the family, dreams of becoming a professional footballer and spends his time wandering around Pozzuoli with a group of friends. He also acts as the film's narrator. The Gioia's story is then intercut with the histories of Pozzuoli that Gennaro narrates: the Emperor Nero's murder of his mother, Agrippina; the arrival of Saint Paul and the murder of a young Christian by his classmates; the female warrior Maria la pazza, who defeats the Saracens only to be abandoned by her own people and then go insane; the Sibilla Cumana, a visionary who becomes convinced she is the mother of the new Messiah; and the death of the musician Giovanni Pergolesi.

As in *Nel regno di Napoli*, then, a melodramatic narrative revolving around the break-up of a family under the pressures of social change is intercut with a series of historical narratives. The melodramatic narrative, which exhibits clear parallels with Visconti's *La terra trema* (1948), concerns itself with the breakdown of the traditional family (see La Penna 2005: 180). The patriarch Salvatore is responsible for exiling Assuntina because her 'betrayal' of Carmine violated the *Gemeinschaft* code and was thus seen as 'dishonouring the whole family', and he continues to affirm his authority, refusing to give up their boat and enter into a collective venture or to abandon their old home even as it collapses around them. Following in his sister's footsteps, Tonino ultimately rebels against his father over his refusal to join the collective and his decision to harvest the infected mussels despite the orders of the local mayor, actions that can be interpreted as the expression of the *Gemeinschaft*'s rejection of the law of the State and a refusal to embrace *Gesellschaft* social relations. Salvatore then resigns himself, returning to the old house by the sea and dying shortly thereafter, the symbol of a moribund social order.

Like Schroeter, Gaudino uses a series of stylistic operations very different from those of classical cinema. The first of these is the cutting between various time periods – an intervention in the temporal structure at the level of order, to borrow Gérard Genette's terminology (see Genette 1980: 33–85). Although technically appropriate, the term flashback does not fit very comfortably with Gaudino's film, for rather than flashbacks within one single narrative we essentially have a series of narratives from different time periods between which Gaudino cuts. The stylistic devices used for each of these temporal levels are different:

1. The 1970s Gioia sequences are shot on 35mm with naturalistic lighting, hand-held cameras and a relatively classical editing style. The actors speak in thick Putolean dialect and are recorded in direct sound. These sequences respond to a broadly realist aesthetic.
2. The effects of the earthquakes on the people of Pozzuoli are shown in black and white documentary footage shot by Gaudino and others over ten years previously. These scenes contribute to the realist dimension of the contemporary sequences.
3. Brief passages that Gaudino refers to as 'image-clots' (Argentieri 1998: 78) are comprised of time-lapse sequences and fragmented images of the city, shot silent on video or super-8, accelerated and accompanied by music.
4. The Pergolesi sequences are shot silent on 35mm in fluid long takes and accompanied by music. Interestingly, these are the only historical sequences that are consistently not shot in the style described below.
5. The historical sequences are shot on old 35mm stock bearing evident signs of wear and tear, often in stop motion. Sections of footage are frequently removed, creating micro-ellipses, while on other occasions frames are printed more than once. There is also use of accelerated and slow motion. The moving images are also subjected to freeze-frames, optical zooms and re-framing achieved during post-production. These sequences were shot mute and the Roman sequences were then post-synched with dialogue in Latin.

As Gaudino has suggested, these devices assure that the different levels of diegetic reality are not confused (Petitti 1998: 33). The most radical of Gaudino's devices (time-lapse, slow- and fast-motion, stop-motion, and the subtraction or addition of frames) constitute an intervention at the level of duration, in Genette's terminology, through which narrative time is either compressed or expanded (Genette 1980: 86–112). Again, Genette's terminology does not really do justice to these devices, which result in an effect of 'stuttering linearity' (La Penna 2005: 186).

What are the effects of these aesthetic strategies? It could be argued that intercutting the various narratives collapses the notion of linear temporality so that past and present co-exist. Undoubtedly, the syntactic organisation creates thematic parallels between past and present, but although certain moments suggest that the modern-day characters 'step back in time', in general it is the historical figures that exist like phantoms in the present. Francesco Crispino argues that:

> The film constantly frustrates traditional cinematic chronology and cause-effect logic . . . so that the story is articulated 'vertically' across the narrative's time structure. Thus *Giro di lune* (also) expresses the idea of . . . the cyclical nature of History, the unchanging nature of the human condition and its binding relationship with the surrounding environment. (Zagarrio 2000: 374)

Crispino's description of Gaudino's style is accurate but I would take issue with his interpretation of this style as an expression of the cyclical notion of time, for not only do the stylistic choices applied to the various temporal levels emphasise their difference but the entire film is also structured to convey a process of decay resulting from the effects of time and change. Indeed, Gaudino has called the film 'a story of the "ruins" of space and time' (Argentieri 1998: 78). This notion of decay is embodied in the film's style, as Gaudino's interventions in the historical sequences (the use of outdated stock, the subtraction of frames and the preservation of obvious splices) are indicative of the effects of age on a film. Tassi argues for a mythic interpretation of the film (Tassi 1998: 31), something that is partly embodied by the film's use of a voice-over and which corresponds to Crispino's idea of 'the cyclical nature of History'. However, of this voice-over Gaudino has stated that, 'They are like inserts of oral history reconstructed from the personal lives of ordinary people of the area rather than literary recollections, and are therefore fallible. I wasn't aiming for a philologically accurate reconstruction' (Argentieri 1998: 77). Rather than an accurate presentation of historical reality or an unchanging mythic archetype, Gaudino presents us with popular legends that have become degraded through repetition and have, to some extent, lost their significance.

Throughout the film the 'decay' of the Gioia family and the institution of the patriarchal-*Gemeinschaft* family unit – which contrasts starkly with the NF's emphasis on an enduring *napoletanità* and the melodramatic re-composition and re-affirmation of the *Gemeinschaft* – is paralleled by the emphasis on the material decay of the city of Pozzuoli. In the film's closing scenes we are presented with time-lapse sequences showing the decay of the Gioia house and boat, and a lengthy final montage of tracking shots along the facades of the old decaying buildings of Pozzuoli and then the bleak facades of the modern housing projects into which the Gioias are forced to move. The ending thus presents a progression from the centre to the periphery, from the sea to the hinterland, and from the traditional home to the anonymous, modern spaces of urban alienation. As the family breaks up and fishing no longer proves viable, Luigi applies for jobs in Pomigliano d'Arco, the industrial setting of the films of Piscicelli, while Salvatore dies and his sons move away. In other words, the film ends in the same locations and by emphasising the same marginalisation, alienation and loss of identity as the films described in Chapter 3.

The film takes place in the 1970s, at the same time as Schroeter and Piscicelli explored the transformations that would lead to the society depicted by the NNC, and it narrates retrospectively the process of change and decay that took place during this period. Tassi suggests that the film is 'above all the story of the search for a sense of identity' (Tassi 1998: 31) and one could rephrase this as the attempt to recover the sense of identity that the Gioia family have lost. Indeed, Gaudino himself is explicit about this dimension to the film:

> It's as if they had lost their archaic tribal nature.[4] . . . The film recounts this apocalyptic sense that 'there is nothing behind us' . . . We inhabitants of Pozzuoli failed to notice the passage of time that affected our land. We isolated ourselves in our homes thinking that the world stood still. But time actually went on. This is why the new popular housing buildings were welcomed as beautiful and modern . . . because we didn't realise that this sudden development would necessarily have brought about a cancellation of memory. (Argentieri 1998: 75)

While the Gioia sequences reconfigure the melodramatic narrative matrix of the NF into the discourse on marginalisation, alienation and the loss of identity described in Chapter 3, what really distinguishes Gaudino's film from traditional Neapolitan cinema is its use of historical narratives characterised by stylistic devices reminiscent of the avant-garde. These devices are never experimental, but rather serve to relate the implosion of the Gioia family to the city of Pozzuoli and its history as a whole. If, on one level, Gaudino's film recalls Visconti's *La terra trema*, its parallel between the death of an individual and the death and decay of a city is also reminiscent of the same director's *Morte a Venezia/Death in Venice* (1971). Yet stylistically the film is radically different from any other film in cinema history. It is undoubtedly a hybrid. Indeed, Vito Zagarrio has described it as 'schizophrenic' (Zagarrio 1999: 193), while Gaudino terms it 'stratified' (Petitti 1998: 34). Despite, or because of, the various levels on which the film works, Crispino is right to describe it as '(undoubtedly) one of the more interesting debuts and (probably) one of the most significant [Italian] films of the decade' (Zagarrio 2000: 373).

Neapolitan Noir

Stefano Incerti's debut *Il verificatore/The Meter Reader* (1995) tells the story of Crescenzio, an overweight and introverted man who works as a gas-meter reader and lives with his brother, Beniamino, and a friend, Giuliana, with whom he is secretly in love. Both Beniamino and Giuliana work for a shady individual identified solely as 'the Owner', whose electrical repairs business operates on the margins of legality. Tensions come to a head when Giuliana rebuffs Crescenzio's advances only to be raped by her boss. Crescenzio exacts revenge by blowing up the building with the Owner inside, only to discover that he has accidentally killed his brother in the explosion as well.

When asked about the parallels between this narrative and the *sceneggiata*, Incerti replied:

> I am not a connoisseur of the *sceneggiata*, but clearly the character played by Renato Carpentieri [the Owner] is the classic bad-guy, the despicable *guappo* . . . So, yes, in a sense the mechanism of the romantic triangle is present, but on an unconscious level. If I had a point of reference then it was the American independent cinema of the seventies. (Author's interview, Rome, 17 June 2003)

This statement is revealing of the way in which the originality of *Il verificatore* lies in its fusion of two culturally distinct narrative forms. The Owner displays a kind of self-reflexive awareness that the events he is participating in correspond to a clichéd and outmoded narrative, suggesting that Crescenzio is playing the role of a '*guappo*' in a 'tale of jealousy' of his own invention. However, Crescenzio is diametrically opposed to the classic *guappo* and has different motivations. Rather than being good-looking, confident and arrogant, he is overweight, shy and introverted; rather than being the master of his environment, he is the victim of it; and rather than defending his honour and that of 'his' woman, he appears to be seeking revenge or relieving his frustration over the fact that the Owner has taken that which he was consistently denied. Furthermore, while the actions of the *guappo* in the classic *sceneggiata* are designed to safeguard not only his honour but also his family, Crescenzio's actions result in the death of his own brother. Thus the dramatic final explosion destroys not only *'o malamente*, but also, metaphorically, the very foundations of the *sceneggiata* structure.

However, simply to reduce the film to this narrative is misleading; indeed, Incerti has defined *Il verificatore* as primarily 'a film about loneliness' (Causo 1995: 64). It is obvious that Crescenzio's solitude is inextricably bound up with a complex about his weight, and his obsession with physical form is made manifestly clear, particularly through the film's emphasis on reflections. Incerti claims that he exploited the actor's physique during the film's production, risking giving Antonino Iuorio a genuine complex in the pursuit of psychological resonance (Author's interview, Rome, 17 June 2003). The film's unconventional depiction of Naples also has important ramifications for the treatment of this theme. Apart from two brief sequences, the film is set around Piazza Garibaldi, the area that contains the highest density of immigrants in the city, and, as in *Tornando a casa*, Incerti emphasises the parallel between Crescenzio and these immigrants as a way of stressing his alienation. Moreover, Massimo Causo states that:

> Christmas weighs heavily on the unusually cold, grey, wintry streets of Naples in *Il verificatore*, like the threat of a futile happiness. The simple fact of seeing a film about solitude emerge from the streets of Naples demonstrates how much the cinematic image of this city, and the South in general, has changed in recent years. (Causo 1995: 64)

Comparisons were instantly made with Martone's reinvention of the city in *Morte di un matematico napoletano* – unsurprising, given that Incerti served as production manager on that film. Indeed, Crescenzio's alienation from his environment, like Caccioppoli's, is conveyed through his physical relationship to the city. While Caccioppoli wraps himself in an ubiquitous dirty overcoat, which both serves to protect him from his environment and expresses his exclusion from it, Crescenzio's obesity, like that of the protagonist of *Isotta*, is simultaneously a material cause for his sense of difference and symbolic of it. At one point a metaphoric link between city and character is developed when the camera performs a circular pan around Crescenzio, beginning with a medium close-up of his face and ending with an over-the-shoulder shot of a painting of a volcano erupting. The two extremes of this shot are similar to a point-glance and point-object, linking the character's rage and frustration to the eruption in the painting and depicting him objectively while simultaneously conveying his inner state. As Incerti himself has observed, 'They say that Vesuvius will erupt again sooner or later and I wanted to include this . . . as if to suggest that Crescenzio's sense of rebellion derived from seeing this image of the volcano' (Author's interview, Rome, 17 June 2003).

Despite its superficial resemblance to the narrative conventions of the *sceneggiata*, then, the film has more in common with the narratives of alienation of the NNC than it does with the NF. As in *Nel regno di Napoli* and *Giro di lune*, this difference is also manifest on a formal level. The camera adheres closely to the central character; it is frequently mobile and the most recurrent stylistic device is the use of a hand-held camera, providing either subjective shots from Crescenzio's point-of-view or long takes that follow – Zavattini would say 'shadow' ('pedinare') – the character. Of his choice of film style, Incerti has stated:

I wasn't afraid of the overheated melodramatic qualities of the script because I was already thinking of a *mise-en-scène* which would cool it down. I wanted to step back from the characters and narrate them without the kind of participation that would have turned the film into a soap opera. If the story is told with detachment . . . then the exasperated tone of the *sceneggiata* dissolves, transforming it into this strange story which . . . could have been set in Naples, Milan or Glasgow and it wouldn't have changed anything. (Addonizio et al. 1997: 73)

The theme of solitude, the relationship between the protagonist and a decaying urban landscape, and the use of stylistic devices that force the viewer to identify with a character with which they cannot easily fully align themselves betray the influence of the New Hollywood of the 1970s mentioned by Incerti. In particular there are numerous affinities with *Taxi Driver* (1976, Martin Scorsese), on which, to my knowledge, no critic has ever picked up. Both films feature characters defined by a job that involves travelling and encountering strangers and which provides the film's title. Both are introverted loners who ultimately commit an act of violence against a criminal figure responsible for abusing a young woman. In both cases their superficial motivation is to make amends for this crime but their real motivation is more ambiguous and closely bound up with their pathological psychology. Both films are character studies of troubled individuals living in difficult urban environments and both films end with their protagonists heading off, fundamentally unchanged (see Fig. 3.3). Significantly, they take place in the twin cities of New York and Naples,[5] can be considered key works in a new cinematic movement, and utilise narratives of alienated loners to reveal something about the character of the cities and their inhabitants.

Incerti's second film, *Prima del tramonto* [Before Sunset] (1999), also borrows from recent American independent cinema. On its release several critics compared the film to Tarantino's work and it is easy to see why; the interlocking narrative structure and idle banter between two *camorristi* about everyday issues like swimsuits and tailoring recall *Pulp Fiction* (1994), while the bloody violence and triangular Mexican stand-off in the denouement recall *Reservoir Dogs* (1992). Stylistically the film also owes more to contemporary American cinema than the stylistic models adopted by other films of the NNC: cinemascope composition, cross-cutting between parallel narratives, fluid steadycam tracking shots, use of slow motion, action deliberately cut to music, and so on. Perhaps the most noticeable difference from contemporary American films is the slower pacing, which can be explained by the fact that the film also has other concerns besides its generic crime narrative: in other words, exploring the issues of immigration and marginalisation (as discussed on pp. 97–9).

Another example of a crime genre hybrid is Carla Apuzzo's *Rose e pistole/ Guns and Roses* (1998). The film begins after Rosa has eloped with her lover, Angelo, whose child she is carrying. Pursued by her ex-husband, Pappalardo, and the hit man he has hired, Rosa takes refuge in a phone-sex company where she used to work, while Angelo unsuccessfully attempts a bank robbery in order to secure the funds that they need to escape. Although this narrative set-up is reminiscent of the classic romantic triangle, the husband's response to his wife's infidelity is constructed not as a *delitto d'onore* but as a purely criminal revenge delegated to a psychotic hit man. Moreover, the narrative foregoes the conventional development that this set-up implies in order to explore different generic territory. If Incerti constructs a modern noir in which parallel narratives and cross-cutting permit digressions into thematically rich but narratively irrelevant topics such as migration, then Apuzzo achieves a similar result by embedding a series of micro-narratives in the form of the stories recounted by a myriad of secondary characters. These digressions depict criminal or socially marginal subcultures such as burglars and bank-robbers, phone-sex workers and porno actresses, drug-addled dentists and fetishist mathematicians. These marginal cultures are also constructed, as in so many other films of the NNC, both geographically, through the intriguing use of the post-industrial landscape of Bagnoli and the Campi flegrei, and through the introduction of immigrant characters, such as the Serbian hit man (see Wood 2003). But Apuzzo is not really interested in articulating a discourse of social marginalisation as in *Immacolata e Concetta* or *Le occasioni di Rosa* (1981), both of which were co-written by Apuzzo and directed by her husband Salvatore Piscicelli, who here returns the favour by co-writing, producing and editing. Rather her aim is to create what Marangi defines as 'Neapolitan Pulp' (Marangi 2000: 50). As in *Prima del tramonto*, the influence of Tarantino is apparent in the three-way Mexican stand-off, the ironic chapter headings, the verbal digressions into cultural fads and urban legends about coke deals gone wrong, and the undercutting of audience expectations by unexpected narra-tive twists, as in Marcello's tale of a robbery thwarted when his target turned out to be a serial killer. Unfortunately, this is the least successful aspect of the film since, like *Prima del tramonto*, it lacks the narrative drive of its American models or the verbal inspiration and innovative generic pastiche of Tarantino to which it clearly aspires. A more productive instance of generic revisionism, however, can be found in a number of contemporary tales of the *camorra*.

Camorra Tales

Antonio Capuano's *Luna rossa/Red Moon* (2001) is a transposition of Aeschylus' Greek tragedy *Oresteia* to the world of the Neapolitan *camorra*. It tells of a powerful *camorra* family, the Cammarano,[6] which gradually self-destructs through betrayal, internal power struggles and the vengeful actions of its youngest member, Oreste. If Capuano's earlier films invite comparison with Pasolini, here, as with Gaudino, the obvious parallel is with Visconti; the implosion of a corrupt family system based around sex and power relations recalls *La caduta degli Dei/The Damned* (1969), while the invocation of Greek tragedy and the theme of incest link it to *Vaghe stelle dell'Orsa . . ./Sandra* (1965). All of the characters in the film are members of an extended family based in an isolated and heavily guarded fortress on the outskirts of Naples. The family is headed by the elderly Toni, who we later learn gained that position by murdering his brother. His son-in-law, Amerigo, is his right-hand man but eventually murders him in order to assume power. Egidio, Toni's nephew, has for many years been having an affair with Amerigo's wife, Irene, and plots against Amerigo, eventually persuading the weak Libero, Toni's grandson, to murder him in order to assume a position which Egidio argues should be his birthright. Egidio betrays and murders Libero and power shifts back to the other side of the family bloodline, Toni's nephew, Antonino. Ultimately, Amerigo's son, Oreste, who had abandoned the family, returns to exact his revenge on Egidio and annihilate the entire family. Irene reveals that Egidio was actually Oreste's biological father before trying to seduce him. Oreste kills her before handing himself over to the police and turning State's witness.

For the Cammarano the family is the most important element to which both individual and social needs and desires must be sacrificed; when members of the family are killed, their immediate relatives must subsume their grief for the good of the family as a whole, while society at large is perceived as either something hostile or a resource to be exploited. Thus the *camorra* is portrayed as the logical extension of Edward Banfield's amoral familism and its consequences are aptly symbolised in the fortified walls that surround the Cammarano home.[7] Amerigo is the first to suggest changing this system, opening up to the outside world and abandoning violence to embrace legal business enterprises, but Oreste is the one who ultimately brings change, stepping into the outside world and then returning to bring destruction. This destruction is shown as a natural consequence of the family's own rules, a literal implosion brought about by the natural product of this society – the angry, rebellious and vengeful Oreste.

The film problematises not only amoral familism, but also the patriarchal values underpinning traditional Southern Italian society. The irony is that *Luna rossa* challenges this patriarchal system through a narrative about a young man who commits an act of violence in order to avenge his father. Sexuality in this world is inextricably linked to power and this is evident in the web of shared sexual relationships through which the characters seek to manipulate one another. The extent to which sexuality becomes a weapon used by the women, just as the men use guns, is made explicit by Irene: 'Even if she doesn't come back, Orsola isn't dangerous until she becomes a woman.' At one point Amerigo also attempts to use sexuality in this way by raping Irene; however, this only provokes contempt when he fails to complete the act. In keeping with his role as the figure of rebellion, Oreste is the most sexually ambiguous character, and the perversion of sexuality within the family is transcribed on to his body in the form of scars resulting from self-harm inflicted for sexual gratification.[8] At one point he wears women's underwear and indulges in incest with his sister under the watchful eye of his mother; a scene more transgressive to notions of sexual propriety and patriarchal values is hard to imagine.

After the surreal postmodernism of *Polvere di Napoli*, *Luna rossa* re-establishes a link with Capuano's earlier films through its focus on children who reflect the flaws and corruption of the adult society of which they are a product. However, while Vito and Nunzio were impotent victims, Oreste is able to rebel against this corruption and the film revels in this rebellion, most obviously in the liberating moments in which Oreste races through the fields on his motorbike to the sounds of Raiz's music (Raiz is the lead singer of Almamegretta). In this way, *Luna rossa* celebrates the implosion of a rigid social structure based around patriarchal values and amoral familism. That this implosion is the result of an attachment to an anachronistic system in a modern society in which sexual mores are changing and global capitalism has become a major shaping force is made explicit in Oreste's deposition, the very first words of the film: 'We represented the barbarity of a pre-historical society in the heart of the modern age.' This celebration of destructive rebellion and social collapse is clearly diametrically opposed to the idea of an ahistorical, unchanging value system on which the NF relies.

Although the narrative structure does not mirror the *sceneggiata* like *Il verificatore*, Capuano draws attention to his film's relation to – and distance from – this traditional Neapolitan form as explicitly as he signals his relationship to De Sica in *Polvere di Napoli* by naming the film after a famous Neapolitan song and featuring that song at a key moment in the narrative. Significantly, however, the song is not used as a catharsis at the film's climax, but rather mid-way through during the murder of Toni. Nor is the narrative an illustration of the song's lyrics, which tell of a man's anguish over his lover's betrayal; instead Rita Cammarano defines it as 'a song about betrayal', creating a parallel with the treacherous murder of Toni. The song is, in a sense, 'misused', which itself suggests the distance that Capuano is taking from the *sceneggiata*. The title is perhaps best explained by Toni Cammarano's statement that, 'The sky is tinged red. This is my dream . . . a red sky and the family's shirts soaked with blood.' Capuano's choice of Greek tragedy also derives from his recognition of the common cultural roots that link Greek tragedy to popular Neapolitan melodrama, something that he had already explored in his 1993 stage version of *Medea*, which he chose to adapt as if it were a *sceneggiata* (see Capuano 1994). In translating Greek tragedy into a narrative about the break-up of a *camorra* family, *Luna rossa* provides an important corrective to the way in which the *camorra* has traditionally been depicted on screen.

Crucial to this project, as in *Il verificatore*, is Capuano's choice of style – an extremely rigorous and anti-naturalistic style also characteristic of Greek tragedy. Capuano has said, 'When I wrote *Luna rossa* I already knew that I wanted to make a tough, claustrophobic film . . . I knew that few people would want to sit through such a film' (author's interview, Naples, 14 June 2003). He thus abandons his habitual naturalistic use of thick dialect in favour of an artificial, almost poetic form of dialogue in which the characters frequently express themselves through metaphor and in which interactions are characterised less by a dialogue than by a series of disconnected monologues. The performance style reinforces this approach through the use of deliberately artificial, theatrical performances in which excessive emotions are carried over into an emphatic, mannered performance style. The film also uses a number of highly stylised theatrical devices, the most obvious of which is Irene's costume, hair and make-up, which change in every scene, reflecting the falsity of her character and creating a radically denaturalising effect for the viewer. Metaphor and symbolism abound, particularly in the repeated and explicit parallels established between the characters and animals. The film makes few concessions to its audience and on a first viewing the plot is difficult to follow due to the large number of characters and the film's complete disinterest in identifying the characters and their relationships at the start of the action, as one would expect in a more classical film. As in Greek tragedy, many of the key events do not happen on screen but rather are related after the fact, and this can be considered a form of subtraction; rather than emphasising key dramatic moments or encouraging the audience's emotional involvement in the film, Capuano downplays these moments and distances the audience. Significantly, Capuano initially intended to make the film without music, a choice that would have radically differentiated the film from almost any commercial feature film and which was only abandoned during post-production because Raiz wrote an unsolicited piece of music that greatly pleased Capuano.

Through these stylistic choices and the use of the structure of Greek tragedy Capuano avoids both stereotype and melodramatic extremes and instead creates a more brutal portrait of the *camorra*. As Capuano puts it,

> I wanted to talk about the *camorra*, but not in the conventional American way of dealing with gangsters. Instead I wanted the *camorristi* to be really repulsive, to live shitty lives and direct their cruelty first and foremost towards themselves. The audience had to think, 'You are repugnant – a real piece of shit'. (Author's interview, Naples, 14 June 2003)

This approach is diametrically opposed not only to the *camorra* films of Squitieri, Brescia and others but also to a more recent film like Tornatore's *Il camorrista/The Professor* (1986), which looks towards the Hollywood gangster film for its narrative and stylistic model.[9] The motivation behind Capuano's approach – although not the actual stylistic devices he chooses – is thus similar to that of *Il verificatore*.

Nicola De Rinaldo's *La vita degli altri/Other People's Lives* (2001) contains two parallel yet interwoven narrative strands; one deals with the threat of a potential volcanic eruption and focuses on Luisa, a young researcher at the Vesuvius Observatory, while the other deals with Mariano, an ageing *camorra* boss who, following the death of his wife and brother, has attempted to put his past behind him but is troubled by an investigative judge trying to persuade him to turn State's witness and by Cenamo, the *camorra* hit man who wants to assume the now vacant position of local boss. The film draws an explicit parallel between the threat posed by Cenamo to Mariano and his estranged daughter, Silvia, and the threat posed by Vesuvius to the local population. This parallel is made visually (through shots showing Vesuvius towering over the isolated villa where Mariano is holed up), through montage (we repeatedly cut from the threats made to Mariano to increasingly violent earth tremors) and through dialogue (Luisa suggests that Mariano 'lives in one of the highest-risk areas'). However, the film is more interested in exploring the characters' reactions to these threats and the reasons behind their attitude than in the threats themselves. In a scene that explicitly cites the opening sequence of Francesco Rosi's tale of political corruption and building speculation in Naples, *Le mani sulla città/Hands over the City* (1963), local politicians and businessmen attempt to exploit the situation for their own gain, downplaying the imminent danger and trying to gain advance warning of an eruption so that they can buy land cheaply, which will later be needed for reconstruction. They involve Marco, Luisa's senior partner and lover, in this process but the more idealistic Luisa refuses to be corrupted. However, while Luisa and Marco both choose sides, at the start of the film Mariano is simply biding his time, hoping he will be left in peace in his isolated villa. Like Giulia in De Rinaldo's previous film, *Il manoscritto di Van Hecken*, he has deliberately chosen to withdraw from society and when asked about his life of crime he repeatedly affirms, 'I'm retired.'[10] Like Giulia, however, he eventually overcomes his inertia, helping his daughter escape to safety and a new identity, and in so doing finally convincing her that the distance he put between them during her childhood was in the interests of her safety, not a result of indifference. Like Giulia, he is reconciled with his troubled family past, yet he refuses to flee himself, preferring to confront Cenamo. But the expected showdown never arrives; instead the final shot has Mariano face to face with his sister (a fierce exponent of the need to remain *camorristi*) underneath the imposing volcano. As the screen fades to black we hear the sound of either an explosion or an eruption, and a caption appears: 'The volcano suddenly re-awoke and for three or four days it did nothing but emit huge clouds of smoke. There was plenty of time to escape but the inhabitants did not move. – Pompeii, 79AD.' Unlike the inhabitants of Pompeii, Mariano's refusal to flee does not derive from ignorance but rather the need to face up to his past and the violence it involves. Having already criticised the local priest for absolving him when he was a criminal and having refused the State's pardon offered by the investigative judge, there is an unmistakable sense of sacrifice and atonement to Mariano's final actions.

Through this narrative De Rinaldo, like Capuano, advances a critique of the traditional *camorra* narrative. On one level the story of a *camorrista* who has decided to abandon a life of crime but who is forced to confront his criminal associates reprises a narrative familiar from countless earlier genre films. For example, in *L'ultimo guappo* [The Last *Guappo*] (1978, Alfonso Brescia), Francesco's son is knocked down by a car while he is on his way to a duel to defend his honour. He makes a vow to the Madonna to give up the *camorra* way of life if the boy is spared and the rest of the film deals with his attempts to acquiesce to humiliation and offences when his request is granted. However, when his now adult son gets involved with his old rival Don Pasquale and is killed, Francesco is forced to resurrect his true nature as a 'man of honour' and exact revenge. The film ends when Francesco, wounded, without family and on the run – but with his honour once more intact – tearfully abandons Naples. The questionable morality and *camorra* ideology implicit in this narrative are called into question by *La vita degli altri*. Although Mariano faces a similar situation – he has withdrawn from crime but his life and that of his child are in danger – his actions are different. His right-hand man Michele suggests that they should reform the gang and go to war to eliminate Cenamo but Mariano declines, despite the fact that Cenamo was responsible for placing the bomb that killed his wife, recognising that he himself had been responsible for even worse crimes. In the final scenes we learn that Mariano killed his mentor because he believed it was he, rather than Cenamo, who was responsible for his wife's death. Michele suggests that Mariano had been 'like a son' to him, something that Mariano emphatically denies: 'There was never honour or rules, even when we were in charge – only blood and betrayal. What counts [in the *camorra*] is this: who possesses power and money.' The film thus undercuts the distinction that earlier Neapolitan films made between the honourable *guappi* of the past and the immoral and criminal *camorristi* of today. It recognises that the two are indistinguishable and that the only way to break the chain of violence is 'to retire'. Although Mariano continues to refuse to turn State's witness, it is not out of *omertà*, but rather because 'I no longer want to make decisions about other people's lives.'

POSTMODERN PARODY AND PASTICHE

Gender and the Post-*Sceneggiata*

Inspired by the fact that Pappi Corsicato served as an uncredited assistant to Pedro Almodóvar on *¡Átame!/Tie Me Up! Tie Me Down!* (1990), many critics have drawn parallels between the two men's work (for example, Garofalo 1993 and Catelli 1993), while *I buchi neri* was even advertised as 'the new film by the Italian Almodóvar'. However, while admitting to his love of Almodóvar's work, Corsicato has denied any direct influence (Addonizio et al. 1997: 42 and Salvi 1993: 60), while other critics have also resisted what they see as too simplistic an equation (Scarlini 1996 and Bolzoni 1993). Yet this association is far from meaningless, deriving not merely from a superficial aesthetic similarity but rather from both filmmakers' reliance on culturally specific generic matrices. Furthermore, their emphasis on strong female protagonists and on characters who collapse traditional gender boundaries undermines the way in which these traditional melodramatic frameworks function.[11] Whereas Almodóvar's reference is Spanish and Hollywood melodrama of the 1950s, Corsicato's is that of the *sceneggiata* and the films of the NF (Addonizio et al. 1997: 42 and Salvi 1993: 60).

Corsicato's first film, *Libera* [Free] (1993), began as a low-budget short shot over five days. Its success at the Palazzo delle Esposizioni in Rome permitted Corsicato to raise the finance to complete a further two episodes ('Aurora' and 'Carmela') and release it as an anthology feature. The positioning of the original episode at the end of the film and the fact that its title has been applied to the film as a whole run the risk of privileging its significance over the other two and thus distorting any analysis of the film. I will begin by discussing this episode only to show how the other two episodes subsequently revise our interpretation of it. The episode 'Libera' begins by depicting the life of drudgery experienced by a woman totally subservient to her husband. As she runs their news-stand, he stays home, claiming to suffer from exhaustion, and entertains prostitutes. Libera's emancipation comes not from uncovering his infidelity but rather from the accidental discovery that she can exploit it to her own economic advantage by filming his exploits and selling the cassettes as pornographic tapes at the news-stand. Whereas certain feminists have suggested that female sexuality can be used as a tool for emancipation,[12] Libera instead turns her husband's sexuality against him. Such a narrative, combined with the use of the name Libera ('Free'), invites us to read this episode in terms of feminist emancipation, an interpretation that has indeed been picked up by a number of critics. However, a closer analysis of the film's ending, in which Libera removes the furs, jewellery and make-up indicative of her newfound 'emancipation' with a weary and unhappy expression, undercuts such a positive interpretation. Libera remains economically dependent on her husband, and her newfound wealth is achieved only at the expense of sacrificing any possibility of an emotional relationship in her personal life.[13] As Gianfranco Cercone observes, 'the woman's liberation to which the title explicitly refers . . . degenerates into an emotional vacuum, a cynical commercial operation and a proud but bitter solitude' (Pellegrini et al. 1996: 29). Rather than a story of liberation, 'Libera' presents us with a vicious circle in which Libera's situation at the end of the final episode echoes that of Aurora's at the beginning of the first.

Libera obtains economic advancement by accepting her husband's betrayal and commodifying it. Similarly, Aurora has obtained economic and social advancement through marriage to a wealthy man and remains wilfully ignorant of her husband's infidelities. When Pistoletta, a lover from before her marriage, resurfaces and attempts to rekindle their affair, Aurora initially resists his advances. It is only when her husband abandons her, taking his money with him, that she returns to Pistoletta, but by then it is too late and she finds herself alone once more. Although the final shot invites us to share Aurora's pain at being abandoned, as with the final episode only a superficial reading could result in a feminist interpretation of this narrative; indeed, there is a discursive strand that seems to place the blame for her situation squarely at her own feet. Early on in the film Don Arcangelo says: 'You were smart to listen to me and marry your husband. Now you are a rich, satisfied and free woman.' His sentiments are echoed by Aurora's friends, who are brutally caricatured in order to emphasise the erroneous nature of their views: 'What do you care if he's always out? At least he lets you live the life of a lady.' Thus it becomes clear that Aurora has chosen to marry her husband rather than Pistoletta for economic stability rather than for love and it is clear that she has got what she wanted in the comically absurd gadgets that adorn her kitsch ultra-modern apartment and in her regular shopping trips.[14] Significantly, it is not infidelity but the loss of her bank account that leads her to return to Pistoletta.

At this point it is worth highlighting how the narrative runs perilously close to the conventions of traditional Neapolitan melodrama only to subvert these conventions through the way the events are focalised by its female protagonist. The return of an old lover who threatens a marriage is the basis of the 'torna' narrative of films like *Catene* (1949, Raffaello Matarazzo) and *Torna* (1984, Stelvio Massi) discussed on pp. 54–5. Yet this narrative is drained of its usual melodramatic associations because the marriage is already a farce; what Pistoletta threatens is not a loving relationship but the economic stability of the bourgeois life that Aurora has bought into through marriage. Similarly, the story of a woman who abandons the man she loves to marry a richer man, which forms the back-story to this episode, is one of the fundamental narrative archetypes of the NF. Yet by telling the story from the woman's point-of-view and focusing on her joyless marriage rather than on the suffering of the abandoned lover, the film resists presenting her in the stereotypical guise of the *malafemmena*. This proximity to traditional Neapolitan melodrama is highlighted by the inclusion of two musical numbers. In the first Don Arcangelo performs *Angeli neri* [Black Angels], in a scene which both makes reference to and distances itself from Nicolardi and Mario's classic song *Tammuriata nera* (also featured in *Nel regno di Napoli*); here the child in question is a product of a mistake during artificial insemination rather than of rape or prostitution and the routine is absurdly performed by an effeminate and sexually ambivalent priest to an audience of workmen. In the second Corsicato offers a comic parody of the serenade in which the classic Neapolitan song is replaced by Tommy Riccio's *Tutta 'na storia*, a tacky example of neomelodic music set to a disco beat. Moreover, rather than singing, Pistoletta merely mimes to playback, while Aurora stands on a balcony of the eighteenth floor with Pistoletta appearing as little more than a dot below. The episode can thus be seen as a kind of 'post-*sceneggiata*' in two senses. On one level, it constitutes a 'sequel' to the traditional *malafemmena* narrative, describing the consequences for a woman who chooses to abandon true love for money. This does not, of course, call into question the moral and ethical assumptions on which such a narrative is based, and it is on this level that the film fails to fit the feminist framework that has sometimes been applied to it. On another level, it functions as a postmodern re-appropriation and reworking of the conventions of the 'torna' narrative and of the aesthetic of the *sceneggiata*. However, it is not that Corsicato ridicules the *sceneggiata* or the traditional melodramatic matrix *per se*; rather he points out the extent to which they are anachronistic and out of place in the contemporary social milieu. As Gianfranco Cercone says:

> Corsicato has an ambiguous relationship with his story, treading a fine line between participation and ironic detachment . . . It is as if he wanted to show us that the Naples of today has been transformed to such an extent that it is no longer a suitable context for a popular melodrama. (Pellegrini et al. 1996: 28)

As in earlier Neapolitan cinema, the use of specific locations is particularly significant to this process. 'Aurora' is set in the Centro Direzionale, a location that is emblematic of the bad administration of the post-earthquake 1980s and which also features in Corsicato's most recent film, *Il seme della discordia* (see Fig. 4.1). With its space-saving skyscrapers, concrete open spaces and subterranean road infrastructure, the Centro Direzionale was designed to alleviate urban congestion in the chaotic and run-down area around the station. Yet its failure (many of its offices and apartments remain empty) is due largely to its separation from the surrounding area, and it is precisely this aspect that the film accentuates, associating its sterility and isolation with Aurora's emotional

Figure 4.1   The hyper-modern Centro Direzionale of *Il seme della discordia* (2008, Pappi Corsicato). ©Medusa.

predicament.[15] Until she is abandoned by her husband, Aurora barely ventures out of this environment; yet even the local TV with its adverts in Arabic suggests the multicultural chaos that lies just beyond the Centro Direzionale's confines. Finally, as her carefully constructed nouveau riche life collapses around her, Aurora returns to her home town of Brusciano to the north-east of Naples during the *Festa dei gigli* celebrations, only to discover that Pistoletta has stolen all of her remaining possessions and abandoned her. This return home thus lacks the reconciliatory qualities of earlier films that opposed the corruption of the city with the purity of traditional local communities, such as *Zappatore* (1950, Rate Furlan, and 1980, Alfonso Brescia) or *Rosalba, la fanciulla di Pompei* (1952, Natale Montillo). The crowded environment is both invasive and threatening and Aurora is swept away by the crowds. However, unlike Alexander and Catherine at the end of *Viaggio in Italia/Voyage to Italy* (1954, Roberto Rossellini),[16] there is nobody for her to be miraculously united with and she must depart alone; the emotional annihilation induced by her pursuit of the capitalist dream is now complete.

If 'Aurora' draws on the traditional 'torna' narrative, then the remaining episode, 'Carmela', draws on the 'figlio di nessuno' narrative matrix typified by *I figli di nessuno/Nobody's Children* (1921, Ubaldo Maria del Colle and 1951, Raffaello Matarazzo). Yet here, too, the approach is that of the post-*sceneggiata*, describing the events that transpire when a young man returns from the orphanage to meet the mother he barely knows. If in 'Aurora' and 'Libera' it is the ambivalent invocation of feminism that has ruptured the traditional melodramatic narrative, then here it is gay liberation and queer theory. Not only does the episode have an explicit queer aesthetic that reflects Bastiano's homosexuality, but the whole narrative also turns on the revelation that his mother, Carmela, is actually Carmelo, his father, who underwent gender reassignment surgery when Bastiano was little. The classic orphan narrative revolved around a lack – either of a mother's affection or a legitimising paternity – and in 'Carmela' it is Carmelo/a's fear of the effect this lack will have on Bastiano that motivates his gender reassignment. Yet this merely creates a new lack, the lack of a father, and Bastiano ends up in an orphanage anyway. Rather than infidelity, death, or the interference of a third party, as in the classic melodramatic narrative, it is the lack of gender certainties that sparks off the narrative drama; Carmelo's bisexuality provokes his wife's suicide when she catches him with another man and this in turn – we must infer – leads to Bastiano's homosexuality. If 'Libera' and 'Aurora' are troubling from the point of view of feminism, then 'Carmela' is so from that of queer theory. Indeed, throughout the episode runs a fear of emasculation that leads to a rejection of sexuality and the episode abounds with blatant castration symbols that reinforce the fact that Carmelo/a's transsexuality is the result of trauma rather than a rational choice.[17] This fear of emasculation is also bound up with the emphasis on virginity typical of traditional Catholic culture and central to so many traditional Neapolitan narratives. The film's recurrent use of the term 'intact' is clearly significant here; after his surgery Carmelo is no longer intact, while Miriam remains intact (i.e. a virgin) because she cannot persuade anyone to sleep with her, and it is Bastiano's refusal of her advances (his 'failure to be a man', as it were) that leads to his downfall. Thus within the film's internal logic it makes perfect sense that the episode ends with Italia accidentally deflowering herself on her own high heels when she falls down the stairs; in the gender confusion of Corsicato's world, this is the only phallus available!

Let us now consider the episode's opening sequence – a genuine tour-de-force of signification and one of the finest sequences Corsicato has ever filmed. It begins with a shot of the Procida coastline – an image almost indistinguishable from the folkloristic depiction of Naples in the credit sequences of films like *Città canora*. We later discover that the family lived in Procida until the traumatic events of the narrative back-story took place, thus associating this image with the plenitude of an idealised past. However, the image freezes, the title 'Carmela' appears and the camera pulls back to reveal that we are actually looking at a postcard; Corsicato thus confronts us with the fact that such images are fixed, idealised and unreal. The camera pulls back further still to reveal a mirror to which the postcard is attached, reflecting both a television set playing Hitchcock's *Vertigo* (1958) and Carmelo who is visibly moved to tears while watching the film.[18] The choice of scene – in which Scotty confronts Judy about her true identity, having discovered Carlotta's necklace, and she explains why she allowed him to refashion her in Madeleine's image – is significant, creating a parallel with Bastiano's discovery of Carmelo/a's true identity and with Carmelo/a's refashioning himself into the mother's role. But the manner in which the scene is shot means that Scotty and Judy's drama is essentially thrice removed from reality: firstly, because it is fictional; secondly, because it is mediated by the television; and thirdly, because it is reflected in the mirror. Yet despite (because of?) this distance, it speaks a profound emotional truth to Carmelo/a. The camera continues to pull back further still, emerging from the *basso* on to a rainy street as Bastiano enters and looks at Carmelo/a. Suddenly, the rain stops unexpectedly, revealing once again the artificiality of what we are watching. Carmelo/a recognises Bastiano and wipes away her tears (echoing the rain ceasing). Thus in the space of one camera movement we move from an idealised memory (the postcard), through a fictional metaphor of the narrative back-story (*Vertigo*), to the diegetic reality of the narrative proper. But the status of each of these is in turn revealed to be artificial. The postmodernist implications of this sequence are significant and will be discussed further below.

Libera could be interpreted, then, as a film by a gay director, who reinterprets the extremely rigid gender positions of traditional Neapolitan culture in the light of feminism and gay liberation. But the film's translation of earlier conventions into modern terms is more ambiguous than this interpretation suggests;[19] instead there is a fundamental discomfort about issues of sexuality, which is also clearly coded in relation to *napoletanità* and which becomes increasingly problematic in Corsicato's next film, *I buchi neri*, discussed below.[20]

More problematic still is Massimo Andrei's sole feature, *Mater Natura* [Mother Nature] (2005), a transgender comedy that is among the least successful films of the NNC. It is a somewhat schizophrenic film that develops along dual narrative lines. The first tells a tragic love story between the transgender prostitute Desiderio and Andrea, who claims to love her but whose ambivalence leads him to marry a 'normal' woman before being killed shortly after she becomes pregnant. The second revolves around Desiderio's companions in the transgender community; Lana Turner is attempting to stage a transgender play, Massimino is helping to elect the Government's first transgender MP, and Mother Europe aims to become a 'universal mother', ultimately opening a new-age commune on the slopes of Vesuvius to which all the characters gravitate. In keeping with other films of the NNC, *Mater Natura* touches on the theme of social marginalisation; it also features several scenes characterised by a postmodern irony reminiscent of Corsicato, most notably the incongruous car-wash scene with its eroticisation of the male body and deliberate music-video aesthetic. However, these elements lack the 'political' dimension of a film like *Libera*. Instead, Andrei associates the postmodern kitsch that characterises the film's aesthetic with the 'performative' nature of transgenderism, a quality that is ultimately resolved by Desiderio's decision to reject the 'falsity' of her lifestyle, if not her chosen gender.[21] Turning her back on a lifestyle of prostitution, she chooses to retire to the fittingly named 'Mother Nature' commune, where all of the protagonists seem to realise their true nature. However, this resolution necessitates a withdrawal from the society that marginalised her to the slopes of Vesuvius, and this constitutes not a political act but a renouncing of politics, something that is rendered explicit by Massimino's rejection of the MP, when he reneges on the promises he made to the transgender community. One of these promises was the need to 'destroy the traditional family', yet the film achieves its resolution through the reconstitution of an alternative 'post-family'. Although the idealised depiction of the Mater Natura community is undoubtedly more optimistic than the 'post-family' of a film like *Non è giusto*, the fact that it is predicated on a withdrawal from society means that they have merely traded an urban ghetto for an (admittedly more attractive) rural one. Such an ending is thus reminiscent of those films of the NF in which the *malafemmena* found peace and atonement for her 'sins' by retiring to the sorority of a convent.[22] That *Mater Natura* is far from the progressive film it might at first appear is nowhere more clear than in the almost unthinkable (ideologically, if not commercially) decision to cast a woman in the role of Desiderio rather than a trans-gender actress. If *Libera* used feminism and alternative sexualities to subvert the ideology of traditional Neapolitan melodrama, then *Mater Natura* seems to do the exact opposite; it falls back on to the conventions of melodrama and thus undermines the supposedly progressive intent behind the film's project.

These limitations also apply, albeit to a lesser extent, to 'Maruzzella', Antonietta De Lillo's contribution to the collective film *I vesuviani*. It is the story of a transvestite played by Enzo Moscato (who also played Mother Europa and the sexually ambivalent priest in *Libera*), who works as a prostitute in a hardcore cinema. While nowhere near as ideologically compromised as *Mater Natura* – and undoubtedly less 'political' in its initial intent – the episode none the less concludes along conventional lines as Maruzzella unexpectedly finds love and marries a young woman who is an unlikely habitual client of the cinema.[23] Before 'Maruzzella', however, De Lillo directed a film together with then-partner Giorgio Magliulo that made a much more interesting use of postmodernism by playing not with gender but with the idea of the miraculous.

50-Point Miracles

Perhaps the biggest difficulty that traditional Neapolitan narratives present for the average modern viewer is not their conventionality or their arguably dubious sociological message (both of which are undercut by the films discussed thus far), but rather their implausibility. This implausibility is most evident in the *deus ex machina*, which is not only typical of melodrama in general but which also constitutes the perfect expression of a culture in which the annual liquification (or not) of San Gennaro's blood is commonly held to govern the city's fortunes for that year, or in which the winning lottery numbers can be divined from dreams or from the interpretation of signs in every day life (*la smorfia*).[24]

There is a delightful gag at the start of Massimo Troisi's comedy, *Ricomincio da tre* (1981), when Gaetano mocks his father for going to church to pray for the re-growth of the right hand which he lost in an accident.[25] Gaetano argues that there is nothing similar in all the biblical miracles. Jesus made the blind see and the lame walk, but at least they already had their eyes and legs; it would be absurd to expect a limb to grow back spontaneously. His friend, Lello, argues that that is why his father has to pray so hard – because it is a difficult miracle. Gaetano rejects the distinction between a difficult and an easy miracle, and the conversation degenerates into a hilarious argument about the difference between a 'MIRACLE! MIRACLE!' and 'a miracle' – or, as Gaetano pithily puts it, 'a 50-point miracle'. The joke essentially revolves around the attempt to apply a rational framework to the explanation of miracles, quantifying them in terms of their difficulty.[26] The conflict between such rationality, typical of modern Western beliefs, and the superstition inherent in traditional Neapolitan culture is picked up in *Matilda* (1990), Antonietta De Lillo and Giorgio Magliulo's second feature, their first to take place in Naples and chronologically the first film of the NNC. The film is a fairly sophisticated comedy exploring such superstitions, which Paolo Vecchi defines as 'a brilliant comic variation on the typically Neapolitan theme of the *jettatura* [curse]' (Vecchi 2002: 38).

Following the accidental deaths of three consecutive fiancés, Matilda becomes convinced that she is cursed. After a period of depression she meets Torquato through a lonely hearts ad but when he learns about her past and falls victim to a series of accidents, he breaks off the relationship. It is only when Matilda intervenes in his lonely life, bringing him fame for the paintings that had been a mere hobby, that he decides to take her back. It is ultimately revealed that it was actually Matilda's psychologically unbalanced brother, Alex, who was responsible for the deaths; he had arranged the 'accidents' in a misguided attempt to prevent Matilda from marrying and leaving the family. Significantly, this explanation shifts the blame from the metaphysical to a psychotic pathology deriving from the brother's excessive attachment to the family unit so central to the NF. However, *Matilda* does not take place in the kind of popular quarters in which one might expect a story revolving around a belief in *jettatura* to be set; Matilda's bourgeois family live somewhere above Posillipo while Torquato lives next to the lago Miseno in Bacoli and works in a cultural institute (actually the Biblioteca di Storia Patria). Thus both characters have difficulty in accepting what they fear to be the truth, but superstition is so deep-rooted in their cultural background that they cannot entirely dismiss the possibility. The head of the institute where Torquato works is the figure who most clearly articulates this dilemma when Torquato asks him if he believes in superstitions: 'No. It's nonsense . . . Superstitions are mere phantoms generated by ignorance. However, I think that they have put a curse on the Institute. In short, it's not true, but I believe it [*non è vero ma ci credo*].'

The Head's comments explicitly invoke one of the most famous of Neapolitan plays, Peppino De Filippo's 1942 *Non è vero ma ci credo*,[27] which tells of a superstitious businessman, Gervasio Savastano, who hires the hunchback Alberto Sammaria because of the Neapolitan belief that hunchbacks bring good luck – a belief that seems to be confirmed by subsequent events. He even goes as far as coercing his daughter, Rosina, into marrying the man, only to become obsessed on the wedding day with the fear that the couple might have deformed children. Sammaria ultimately reveals that he is not actually a hunchback after all, but rather the young man with whom Rosina was in love but whom Gervasio refused to let her marry. The idea of the hunchback disguise was a trick played by the couple, with the complicity of Gervasio's wife, in order to persuade him to change his mind. In the film's closing scene Sammaria asks Gervasio, 'Are you convinced now that it was all in your head? . . . There's no such thing as a curse. You were delusional, but now you are cured.' However, as the couple set off on their honeymoon, Gervasio asks Sammaria to don the fake hump once more, just in case they should meet misfortune on their travels. The title of Peppino's play thus applies to Gervasio's ultimate reluctance to abandon his beliefs – beliefs that the narrative treats as unfounded. However, in *Matilda* this 'it's not true, but I believe it' extends beyond the characters to the narrative resolution. When the institute's financial problems finally become too great and it is forced to close, the head says, 'We need a miracle, but my secular beliefs, my Enlightenment philosophy deny me even this consolation, this hope for a supernatural intervention. We don't believe in superstition, right, Torquato?' The film immediately cuts to the opening of the exhibition of Torquato's paintings, which improbably brings him fame and fortune – money that the head appropriates to ensure the institute's survival. The deliberately provocative placing of this scene transition invites the audience to reflect on the absurdity and artificiality of this narrative device. Indeed, in a subsequent speech the head defines it as 'one of those unexpected reversals that you think only happens in bad literature'. It foregrounds the improbability of the *deus ex machina*, and in so doing invites the audience to accept or reject it depending on their own 'secular beliefs' and 'Enlightenment philosophy'. In the film's final scene Torquato is finally reconciled with Matilda in a classic happy ending. But as Matilda leaves the hospital room to which Torquato is confined following Alex's attempt on his life we hear the wires supporting his leg brace begin to creak and then an ago-nised scream. The final shot of the film depicts Matilda, walking away through the hospital corridor and laughing as we (and she) hear this accident. The final scene thus undercuts the psychological explanation of Matilda's curse, acceptable to the 'secular beliefs' and 'Enlightenment philosophy' of a modern twentieth-century audience, suggesting that the *jettatura* may be true after all. Furthermore, Matilda now seems (rather improbably) to accept and even find amusement in this revelation.

The film's elevation of the credo of 'it's not true, but I believe it' to a textual strategy in the final scenes is a prime example of the double coding that Linda Hutcheon sees as characteristic of postmodern parody.[28] Hutcheon takes issue with Frederic Jameson's characterisation of postmodern pastiche as offering a 'value-free, decorative, de-historicised quotation of past forms', proposing instead the idea of parody as 'a value-problematising, de-naturalizing form of acknowledging the history (and through irony, the politics) of representation' (Hutcheon 1989: 90). She argues that, 'as [a] form of ironic representation, parody is doubly coded in political terms: it both legitimises and subverts that which it parodies' (ibid.: 97). *Matilda* simultaneously acknowledges and legitimises Neapolitan superstitions and undercuts them. And, like the head, the modern, cultured audience is able to participate ironically in this paradoxi-cal process. Such an ironic, postmodern take on the miraculous reoccurs in Corsicato's second film.

In the opening scene of *I buchi neri/Black Holes* (1995) Adamo abandons his gay lover and returns to his home town to attend his mother's funeral. Accepting a job from a childhood friend, Adelmo, disposing of rotten fruit from the market, he encounters a young prostitute, Angela. They begin a rela-tionship of sorts, and although Adamo is unable to consummate their relation-ship, they both gain sexual pleasure from him spying on her with her clients. Eventually, Angela confesses that she has fallen in love with him but Adamo remains indifferent. After his pay is stolen at the beach, Adamo kills one of the perpetrators. He then abandons Angela for Adelmo's pregnant sister, Adelaide. On discovering this betrayal and being questioned by the police, Angela, like Contessa Livia Serpieri in *Senso* (1954, Luchino Visconti), denounces Adamo and he is arrested.

Corsicato's film borrows, more or less explicitly, from Albert Camus' absurdist novel *L'Étranger*. Both film and novel begin with the line 'Mother died today. Or maybe yesterday.' Like Meursault, Adamo shows no grief at his mother's funeral nor forms any emotional ties with any of the other characters; again like Mersault, he ultimately stabs a young man on the beach, a crime apparently motivated as much by the blazing sun as it is by revenge. However, while the second half of Camus' novel deals with Meursault's introspection while awaiting execution, Corsicato abandons Adamo completely in order to focus on Angela. Camus' novel embodies a philosophy of non-determinism in which Meursault resolutely refuses to embrace religion in order to save himself from execution, remaining true to his atheist beliefs and accepting responsibility for his own actions. His crime is, at least in part, the result of a kind of sensory disorientation from the influence of the sun on the beach and we are not meant to read the sun in symbolic or cosmological terms. Conversely, *I buchi neri* repeatedly shows us television screens that apparently play nothing but 1950s sci-fi b-movies and strange documentaries on the universe, and their persistent references to cosmology, together with the rest of the film's symbolism, invite us to interpret the image of the sun and indeed the 'philosophy' of the film as a whole rather differently. It is through this obscure invocation of cosmology, which is so different from Camus, that the film raises the question of the miraculous.

One of these documentaries states, 'If you were to enter into a black hole, you would return to a state of absolute purity,' and the narrative itself works towards a return to such a mythic state of purity. The film's opening scene, clearly inspired by the final psychedelic trip of *2001: A Space Odyssey* (1968, Stanley Kubrick), has the camera apparently emerging out of a black hole. The spectacular visuals and cosmic implications of this shot are immediately undercut, however, when the camera unexpectedly emerges from a toilet, into which Adamo begins to urinate. As in the opening of the 'Carmela' episode of *Libera*, Corsicato pulls the rug out from under the viewer and visually sets up the film's themes; the universe in its 'state of absolute purity' is contrasted with an abject and degraded present reality. As in Corsicato's other films, *I buchi neri* presents us with a world of emotional sterility and alienation, which is embodied in material terms through the depiction of a degraded Neapolitan society and landscape. Angela works on isolated and desolate streets that appear to come from nowhere and lead nowhere. Several of her colleagues suffer grotesque deformities; la Muta cannot speak but only utters bird-like squawks, Favorita has no hands and la Graia is only 18 years old but has aged rapidly ever since she was raped by her father, causing her menstrual cycle to block. Only Stella and Angela appear normal, but Stella is desperately in love with an imprisoned murderer whom she met only once, while Angela claims not to believe in love. Adamo is an impotent voyeur apparently incapable of establishing any kind of emotional relationship; he works shovelling decomposing fruit. The town is a desolate periphery typical of the NNC, its sole attraction is the bar on the central square, but even this is not the site of a *Gemeinschaft* community, for every time that Angela asks the barman if he has seen someone, he replies that he does not know them.

Yet on to this degraded present the narrative attempts to impose some meaning, some wider cosmological significance. It is telling that Corsicato

Figure 4.2   Favorita (Anna Avitabile) following her '50-point miracle' in *I buchi neri* (1995, Pappi Corsicato). ©Filmauro.

attempts this through a shift in focalisation, abandoning Adamo to concentrate once more on an almost archetypal woman played by Iaia Forte. After Adamo's arrest Angela is visited by an (apparently) extraterrestrial being which simply states, 'Now that you have learned to love you are no longer the same person. Love is like a little miracle that transforms you . . . Angela, you are an angel.' Whereas in the NF it is the consecration of a romantic relationship that brings about transformation and closure, here the relationship fails but Angela gains some sort of (self-)knowledge anyway. At this very moment Angela's friends are also healed; Stella finally receives a letter from the prisoner with whom she is in love, la Muta regains her voice, Favorita's hands re-grow, and la Graia's menstrual cycle starts up again and she is rejuvenated. However, this ending constitutes a resolutely unconventional and ironic treatment of the miraculous. Indeed, as Favorita cries 'Miracle!', she turns to look at her new hands, one of which has re-grown deformed with grotesquely webbed digits; she grimaces in horror then turns her attention back to the good hand and cries 'Miracle!' once more (see Fig. 4.2). As if in response to the Troisi anecdote quoted above, here we really do have a '50-point miracle', which Corsicato has described as 'a cheap miracle that doesn't resolve anything' (Addonizio et al. 1997: 43). Yet the mocking of the miraculous goes still further. The extraterrestrial which precipitates this miracle appears in the form of a giant silver egg that is both absurd and unconvincing; Corsicato himself has described the film's 'crappy special effects', arguing that these were 'functional to the film's aesthetic' (Addonizio et al. 1997: 40). It is not insignificant that this image takes the form of an egg either, for Corsicato plays with the symbolic value of eggs throughout the film, while Angela's inexplicable fear of chickens is also cured by the final miracle. The documentary Angela watches on television banally frames its cosmological questions thus: 'Which came first, the chicken or the egg? Where did the universe come from and where is it headed?' Eggs can obviously be read as symbolic of reproduction; however, they can also be taken to represent infertility (given that the eggs we eat are, essentially, unfertilised ova), and at one point the impotent Adamo accidentally crushes a box of eggs when he kisses Angela and the broken eggs run down her skirt and legs (an image mirrored in la Graia's 'miraculous' final menstruation). Significantly, Adamo abandons Angela for a virgin who has become pregnant through an immaculate conception. Her parthenogenesis makes her the perfect mate for the asexual Adamo and thus he abandons Angela with the same words he used to his gay lover at the beginning ('There was nothing between us anyway').

As in the director's first film, *I buchi neri*'s relationship to sexuality is undoubtedly problematic. While the narrative superficially revolves around the 'miracle of reproduction', there is an insistence on the woman's body as, to borrow Julia Kristeva's term, a site of abjection through the images of menstruation, the deformity of Favorita and the bride that Adamo's lover is about to marry and even through the casual observation that they had to move Adamo's mother's body 'because she stank'. Instead the homo-erotic gaze of Corsicato's camera repeatedly lingers on Adamo's semi-nude body and this sits uncomfortably – even within Corsicato's ironic postmodernism – with a narrative that associates its male character with death and sterility and its female characters with life, love and reproduction.

Many of these themes are reprised in Corsicato's latest film, *Il seme della discordia* [The Seed of Discord] (2008), which unofficially reworks Heinrich von Kleist's *Die Marquise von O.* (also filmed by Eric Rohmer in 1976) into a narrative about a marital crisis provoked by Veronica's apparently inexplicable pregnancy immediately after her husband Mario has been diagnosed as infertile. The antinomy of fertility–sterility present in both of Corsicato's first two films takes centre stage here;[29] not only is Mario a salesman touting a super-fertiliser but his lover (again played by Iaia Forte) believes that she has only avoided pregnancy because of the lack of synchronicity of their orgasms. The miraculous also recurs when Veronica begins to believe that she may have been touched by an immaculate conception, a sub-plot that concludes with a hilarious encounter with a woman dressed as a nun, who rejects her idea by retorting, 'What a load of crap! Who ever heard of such a thing!' before hastily adding, 'Apart from the case of the Holy Virgin, of course.' Once again the miraculous is negated when it becomes clear that Veronica was actually raped while unconscious by the security guard who rescued her from an aborted robbery. Significantly, Veronica's mistaken belief first arises when she comes across a kitsch picture representing the Immaculate Conception, whose effect itself relies on an optical illusion.

A number of other films of the NNC have reprised this treatment of the miraculous. In 1994 Mario Martone contributed the short 'Antonio Mastronunzio pittore sannita' to the portmanteau film *Miracoli, storie per corti* [Miracles, Stories as Shorts] (1994).[30] His episode deals with the miracle of artistic creation though the story of a painter who unsuccessfully attempts to recreate one of his earlier works, only for the sought-after image to appear miraculously when he tosses the abandoned painting into a river. The brief given to the directors of *I vesuviani* to produce a series of short 'fantasy' films also led both Capuano and Incerti to deliver films that deal with this theme. The postmodern comedy of Capuano's episode 'Sofialòren' [Sophia Loren] associates the miraculous with the delusion of romantic fantasy in its tale of an octopus that is transformed into a princess at night. However, it ultimately becomes clear that the octopus's night-time transformations may in fact be an expression of its protagonist's sublimation of homosexual desires, a psychological explanation that undercuts the idea of the miraculous entirely (see Argentieri 1998: 44). The episode resolves itself when the protagonists' prosaic hunger gets the better of their higher aspirations and they eat the octopus. Similarly, Incerti's 'Il diavolo in bottiglia' [The Devil in a Bottle] creates a parallel between the belief in miracles and the alcoholic who cures his troubles with the fleeting happiness of intoxication in the Faustian tale of a homeless man given a bottle granting three wishes. Like De Lillo, however, he ultimately undercuts the miraculous altogether by revealing this was a ruse before utilising a narrative 'miracle' of his own to generate the episode's happy ending.

Neapolitan Simulacra

Although directed by the Torinese Tonino De Bernardi and produced by the Rome-based A.S.P., who also produced *I cinghiali di Portici*, *Appassionate* [The Passionate Ones] (1999) demonstrates a revisionist approach to *napoletanità* that has more in common with the films discussed here than with Neapolitan-set national productions. Moreover, it utilises numerous actors, technicians and creative personnel closely associated with the NNC and thus it would seem legitimate to include it in a survey of the NNC. *Appassionate* is a film based entirely around Neapolitan song, yet it differs fundamentally from the traditional model of the *sceneggiata*; rather than constructing a narrative from the text of a popular song and then using musical numbers to punctuate the dramatic highlights of that narrative, here Neapolitan song is an almost constant presence that unifies a number of disparate narrative threads, and in this respect the film more closely resembles the anomalous *Carosello napoletano/Neapolitan Carousel* (1954, Ettore Giannini). This is not to say that the film does not make use of the kinds of conventional narrative situation that one finds in the *sceneggiata* and the NF, but rather that it uses them in a fundamentally different fashion. Essentially, it narrates a number of separate but interwoven stories that contain all of the central *topoi* of the *sceneggiata*, such as the crime of passion, the woman who renounces life and enters a convent, and the forced emigration. Yet the film does not articulate these events as a coherent narrative moving from an initiating event to the re-establishment of order; nor does it offer a dramatic crescendo leading to emotional catharsis, as in the NF. Rather these narratives are interwoven into a patchwork that prevents the viewer from becoming fully engaged emotionally in any one of them. De Bernardi is essentially quoting a set of conventional narrative situations. Paradoxically, given the fact that *Appassionate* contains more songs (22) and devotes more screen time to them than any film of the NF, here the songs are subservient to the narrative rather than vice versa.[31] It thus becomes clear that De Bernardi is not interested in offering us a slice of popular Neapolitan culture, and this should not come as a surprise, given his background and career history. Rather he is deliberately using popular Neapolitan culture, citing it as part of a wider project that can be best described as postmodernist.

De Bernardi's postmodernist intent is signalled in the film's opening sequence, which is constructed around the song *Cinematografo*. Written by E. A. Mario in 1927 and staged as a *sceneggiata* the following year by E. L. Murolo, *Cinematografo* tells of a young man who kills his unfaithful wife during a film screening, imitating the protagonist's crime of passion when he recognises that the melodramatic story on the screen mirrors his own situation. Similarly, *Appassionate*'s black and white pre-credit sequence shows Michele taking his wife Rosa to the (fictional) film, *L'amore tragico* [Tragic Love], killing her during the performance, and then leaping on to the stage and interrupting the projection to announce that he has performed the film's denouement in the auditorium. In many respects this opening sequence is the most complex of the film and makes explicit what the rest of the film is trying to achieve. The original *sceneggiata*, *Cinematografo*, tells of a man who recognises that a staged fictional world resembles his own situation and therefore takes the events of that drama as a model for his actions. Represented as a conventional *sceneggiata* in one of the popular theatres of Naples, this blurring of two levels of diegetic reality would have implicated a third – the real audience, who would have shared the value system of both the *sceneggiata* and the film within the *sceneggiata*, and thus identified with the protagonist's drama (see p. 48). Playing to a twenty-first-century audience of first-run cinéphiles and intellectuals, *Appassionate* clearly lacks this third dimension of an audience's unquestioning identification with a representation and thus the decision to open the film with *Cinematografo*, the most self-reflexive of *sceneggiate*, is a significant one.[32] But De Bernardi goes one step further, exploiting the fact that he is making a film rather than a *sceneggiata* to emphasise the self-reflexivity of the text to the point of creating a fundamental distance between the audience and the events on screen. No longer does the cinema audience get caught up in the emotional drama, as the protagonist of the *sceneggiata*, *Cinematografo*, is caught up in the drama he is watching, but rather they are invited to assume a certain distance and reflect critically on what they are witnessing. Thus Michele's imitation of *Tragic Love* is not presented in a straightforward fashion; instead it is continually qualified by radical shifts between three levels of diegetic reality (the film-within-the-film, the story of Michele and Rosa, and the narrator telling their story). Furthermore, these levels of diegetic reality are not always maintained as distinct, as the narrator also appears in Michele and Rosa's world. Moreover, the abrupt shifts between spoken and sung dialogue, direct speech and narration, first and third person, and music and silence create a quite radical and disorienting effect. Thus De Bernardi substitutes the direct involvement in a (melo)dramatic fiction typical of the *sceneggiata* with a kind of fascination with textual play.

This approach can best be explained through Umberto Eco's description of postmodern discourse:

> The postmodern reply to the modern consists of recognizing that the past, since it cannot really be destroyed, because its destruction leads to silence, must be revisited: but with irony, not innocently. I think of the postmodern attitude as that of a man who loves a very cultivated woman and knows he cannot say to her, 'I love you madly', because he knows that she knows (and that she knows that he knows) that these words have already been written by Barbara Cartland. Still, there is a solution. He can say, 'As Barbara Cartland would put it, I love you madly.' At this point, having avoided false innocence, having said clearly that it is no longer possible to speak innocently, he will nevertheless have said what he wanted to say to the woman: that he loves her, but he loves her in an age of lost innocence. If the woman goes along with this, she will have received a declaration of love all the same. Neither of the two speakers will feel innocent, both will have accepted the challenge of the past, of the already said, which cannot be eliminated; both will consciously and with pleasure play the game of irony . . . But both will have succeeded, once again, in speaking of love. (Eco 1983: 67–8)

Having established this approach in the *mise-en-abîme* of this brief pre-credit sequence, De Bernardi is free to put his melodramatic narratives on stage, 'quoting' popular Neapolitan culture of the late nineteenth to early twentieth centuries for a postmodern twenty-first-century audience. The use of

Figure 4.3 The postmodern citation of Neapolitan culture: Rosa (Iaia Forte) performs against a painted backdrop of the Bay of Naples. *Appassionate* (1999, Tonino De Bernardi). ©Universal Pictures Italia.

distanciation devices continues throughout the film. Extra-diegetic figures (defined as 'the singers on stage') appear on realistic street corners, singing Neapolitan songs; sometimes their songs are echoed by the characters within the drama, sometimes they themselves echo the characters' dialogue. Red theatrical curtains covering the screen part to reveal real exteriors in Neapolitan alleyways or the beaches of the Bay of Naples. Diegetic characters pause to make direct-to-camera address, or step out of character and on to an artificial stage to perform for the audience (see Fig. 4.3). Shot-reverse-shot sequences create an artificial geography and a fake audience in the local inhabitants for these spectacles. Such devices radically break the traditional relationship between audience and representation upon which traditional Neapolitan culture relied and this inevitably has implications for the film's discourse about Naples.

Central to all of the stories within *Appassionate* is the play between reality and fantasy; the characters of Michele and Caterina interact with the ghosts of their victims, just as Teresa and Rosa do with their lost loves, and the film is careful to reinforce the distinction between reality and fantasy as brutal cuts suddenly remove phantoms from the screen, leaving us with the characters interacting with thin air. Central, too, is the play between past and present, signalled by the film's use of 'Naples, 1929' and 'Naples, 1999' captions and the shifts between black and white and colour. Fantasy, phantoms and the past invade the present, and the 'realism' that one normally associates with the depiction of the popular quarters of Naples that we see here is repeatedly contaminated by this fantasy reality, not only in the form of such individual fantasies but also in the collective vision of the 'suffering Madonna' who wanders the Neapolitan hinterland. How does De Bernardi reconcile this with his twenty-first-century viewer's postmodernist perspective? This becomes clear in the final scene when Rosa meets a foreign sailor, who admits that, 'I dreamed of Naples. For years in my house there was talk only of Naples.' It becomes clear that he is the grandson of Michele, who was forced to emigrate in 1929 to avoid arrest for the murder that opened the film, and Rosa decides to depart with him for America. The film thus finds its resolution in the sudden, arbitrary appearance of this figure, a foreigner who has never seen Naples but has always dreamt it. As Rosa leaves, she looks back at Naples, fixing its coastline in her memory as so many emigrants must have done while *'O paese d'o sole* plays on the soundtrack. For her, Naples will become a memory, a phantom in her mind, just as it must have become for Michele, or is for the Piemontese De Bernardi. For Naples in the film is never a real entity – it is a fantasy, something to be dreamed of, a signifier to be played with. One wonders whether De Bernardi had ever read Goffredo Fofi's article, 'The Screen's Most Beautiful Naples', in which he argues that the greatest Neapolitan film ever made is Frank Borzage's *Street Angel* (1928) – a film shot entirely in Hollywood studios by people who had never been to the city and which Fofi himself has never seen because it is now lost.

> The most beautiful Naples in films is probably this one, which is totally, absolutely imaginary. The real Naples is so much more difficult to portray and few have succeeded in doing so . . . because Naples is a site of the imaginary, even to the shrewdest of Neapolitans; Naples is a capital composed of many Naples, of many images and ideas of Naples that are hopelessly unreconciled, or, at most, can be pieced together like a puzzle, a collage made of details and superimpositions. (Aprà 1994: 259)

For Fofi and De Bernardi, Naples is the postmodern city *par excellence*, a city of strata in which the modern never cancels the past but is merely superimposed on top of it; it is a city of contradictions in which reality and fantasy co-exist because there is no such thing as reality and no such thing as fantasy. This idea is also articulated by Iain Chambers in his brief but extremely provocative discussion of the city:

> The value of Naples, both socially and aesthetically . . . may lie not in its pretended uniqueness but in its capacity for dispersal, for losing itself

and thereby escaping the predictable. Here the city does not stand for a unique, rational, firm referent, but slips through predictable schemata to become a floating signifier, drifting through a hundred interpretations, a thousand stories . . . Naples, witnessed from elsewhere, also becomes the dream-site of an imaginary city. (Chambers 1994: 106–7)

One could argue that the traditional *sceneggiata* can be considered an example of what Jean Baudrillard terms second-order simulation; it translates a concrete social reality (the Neapolitan *Gemeinschaft*) into a highly conventionalised narrative form, but such is the relationship between the audience and text that the events on stage are frequently mistaken for the real. The viewer described in Chapter 2 who responded to *Malaspina* saying, 'Watching this film, it felt as if I were in my own home' would be one example of this confusion; the numerous cases in which the audience would actively heckle *'o malamente* would be another; the protagonist's imitation of the murderous events of *Cinematografo* would be a third.[33] Conversely, *Appassionate* does not make direct reference to Naples or Neapolitan society but rather quotes existing narratives and iconography. It is an example of what Baudrillard terms 'third-order simulation' resulting in 'hyperrealism':

> Simulation is no longer that of a territory, a referential being or a substance. It is the generation by models of a real without origin or reality: a hyperreal. The territory no longer precedes the map, nor survives it. Henceforth, it is the map that precedes the territory . . . it is the map that engenders the territory. (Baudrillard 1983: 2)

This hyperrealism is also characteristic of the opening sequence of the 'Carmela' episode of *Libera* described above. It also re-occurs in Corsicato's third film, *Chimera* (2001).

Like the first episode of *Libera*, *Chimera* tells the story of an estranged bourgeois couple. Early in the film, Franco Nero's unnamed businessman says,

> We are never satisfied with what we have. We always want more. And the strange thing is that everyone seems ready to lend a hand. But as soon as you need something, even if you are desperate, a void opens up around you and nobody – I mean nobody – is willing to help you unless you give them something in return. How disgusting!

Taken in isolation, this quotation could lead us to believe that we are simply going to witness another materialist analysis of the alienation of the *Gesellschaft* society. However, we immediately discover that he is going to do exactly that – demand sex from Emma in exchange for the money she desperately needs to save her husband Sal's life. Yet he is not simply being hypocritical, for we then discover that both she and her husband are also complicit in this act; the whole charade is a *mise-en-scène*. Rather than the infidelities and commodification of relationships of *Libera*, here we have a couple who attempt to keep their love alive by role-playing, living an illusion in which, every day, they play strangers who meet and fall in love again.[34] It is tempting to interpret this narrative in self-reflexive terms, and in particular as a commentary on the kinds of melodramatic narrative typical of the NF. For what are such narratives if not the real world, distorted through a fictional lens and then repeated over and over as a way of interpreting or reflecting on reality? Corsicato is explicit about this, offering us a credit sequence that implicitly recalls the iconography of classic Hollywood melodrama.[35] He even gives us a woman-in-peril scene, in which Emma is tied to a railway siding, echoing the archetypal image of silent melodrama, a scene now so familiar as to appear comic. The film also recycles the title of Ettore Maria Fizzarotti's 1968 musical-melodrama and ends with its characters silhouetted against a patently fake *luna rossa*. However, perhaps the most interesting thing about the film is the character of the illusionist Tomas. Tomas is introduced to us as the film's narrator; indeed, the film opens with a pre-credit sequence in which he tells his wife Desirée, 'Lots of people live according to illusions. I could tell you the story of a couple who live like this.' However, as the film progresses, it becomes clear that Tomas is not simply a narrator but also a participant in the action; indeed, he is one of its driving forces since he is the one to whom Sal becomes indebted. Tomas not only narrates the events (impossibly, as they occur) but also manipulates the characters. Significantly, he is not only an illusionist but also a hypnotist who is able to control the characters' actions and alter their perception of reality.

At one point Tomas responds to Desirée's questioning of his magic by saying,

> Why do you want to know the trick? If I told you there wouldn't be any magic anymore. We only believe what we want to and for this reason we are ready to believe a lie if it is more congenial to us. That's the trick: it's just an illusion.

Similarly, for the narrative-illusion to work, it requires a willing suspension of disbelief. But here, as in Corsicato's other films, the excessively kitsch aesthetic and instances of deliberate narrative absurdity repeatedly force us to transcend this suspension of disbelief; for example, in one scene Corsicato pulls the rug out from under us by presenting an apparently real striptease, which is then revealed to be an act performed on a stage for an audience. However, unlike in his other films, in *Chimera* we are also forced to take a step back in order to make sense of the narrative itself, for the film does not generate the illusion of the classic realist text but rather constructs the impossibly labyrinthine narrative of a *nouveau roman* in which the status of events and characters is never clear.[36] Many of the early sequences are punctuated by fades to black, which we at first read in conventional terms as signifiers of temporal ellipsis. However, it soon becomes clear that not all of these devices can be read this way and thus we begin to question the significance of these moments, which then appear more like narrative 'black holes',[37] the embodiment of narrative uncertainty and inconsistency which deliberately undermine the viewer's ability to engage unproblematically with the narrative.[38] Thus far one could argue that Corsicato's film is an example of the modernist problematising of the process of representation (as the mention of the *nouveau roman* suggests).[39] However, the more one attempts to make sense of the narrative, the more inconsistencies begin to arise. Even Tomas, who initially appears as the narrator-manipulator typical of certain modernist works – and thus potential alter ego to Corsicato himself – is revealed to be a victim of such illusions; when Max persuades him to hypnotise Desirée to find out whether she is faithful or not, he hypnotises her and instead asks, 'Was it you who let the doves out of the cage?' Here the narrator himself is a victim of the illusions of his own making. What we have, then, is not so much a narrative about illusions, but a narrative of illusions. The whole film is constructed on a void, an absence of meaning.[40] Significantly, after being knocked out, Emma claims that she has 'a void in her head'.[41]

Chimera represents the apotheosis of the postmodern tendency of the NNC. Significantly, we can also trace the development of this tendency across Corsicato's films in terms of their approach to Neapolitan geography. *Libera* takes place in deliberately chosen, concrete locations within Naples itself (the Centro Direzionale, the historic centre and Scampia); *I buchi neri* moves out into the provinces – although its exactly location remains unspecified, one has a clear impression of the Neapolitan hinterland;[42] and *Chimera* takes place in entirely anonymous locations that could be anywhere in Italy or, indeed, the modern Western world.[43] As Emiliano Morreale argues:

> The setting is also significant from a geographic point of view – it's a post-Mezzogiorno. It reflects a curious evolution in the image of the South in the work of the youngest and brightest of directors, a further displacement, after the transition from rural to urban South in the mid-sixties, towards a South that we could term 'diffuse periphery'. The most figuratively striking South is no longer the urban South . . . but rather a single, uninterrupted hinterland in which memories and decay overlap, without centre or periphery . . . The model is that of the mega-cities in Campania and Salento which grow into one another like cancerous cells.

This is the image of the South which Corsicato anticipates, and which is here only alluded to. *Chimera*'s South is unrecognisable: chosen, according to the director, for mere convenience and then drained of its life-blood . . . We never see a city. Cities don't exist in Corsicato's limbo; virtually everything takes place in interiors . . . The death of the South goes hand in hand with the death of emotions that he narrates. (Morreale 2001: 33)

This gradual erasure of Naples in Corsicato's cinema, this 'death of the South', is clearly emblematic of Baudrillard's idea of the death of the real in postmodern society (Baudrillard 1983: 142). If *Appassionate* presents us with a virtual Naples, then *Chimera* does not really present us with Naples at all. It is a metaphoric death of the city that parallels the deaths and suicides pursued by the protagonists of the films described in Chapter 3.

CONCLUSION

The hybrid and postmodern approaches to Neapolitan narrative discussed in this chapter share certain superficial similarities, such as the mixing of 'foreign' narrative and stylistic forms which contrast with traditional Neapolitan narrative; however, in intent and result they are diametrically opposed. In *Luna rossa* Capuano seeks to give a harsher, more brutal and 'realistic' portrait of the *camorra* through his combination of the *sceneggiata* and the apocalyptic family narrative of the *Oresteia*. In *Il verificatore* Incerti re-configures the traditional melodramatic narrative through his borrowings from the New Hollywood and in so doing makes an original comment on the alienation of contemporary Naples. Both Schroeter and Gaudino combine discourses on history and the personal in order to undercut 'meta-narratives' in the former and to illustrate the decay of Neapolitan culture and society in the latter. In each of these cases hybridity is used in a search for 'realism' in the sense of a deeper, more accurate truth about Naples and the world. In *Libera* and *Matilda* postmodern parody (in Hutcheon's sense of the term) creates a paradoxical participation/separation of the audience, which also provides a useful commentary on Naples and its culture: the problematic attachment to a 'sentimental masochism' (Pellegrini et al. 1996: 29) and the continuing crisis in gender roles in the former and the reliance on an illusory and escapist belief in the miraculous in the latter. However, by the time of *I buchi neri*, the 'critical' edge of Corsicato's ironic parody begins to dissipate and we are left with mere pastiche (in the Lyotardian sense of the term). In the case of *Appassionate* and *Chimera* all pretence at a critical engagement with the city and its culture is lost and we are left with hyperrealism, mere textual play. In a review of *Chimera*, Alberto Pezzotta perceptively unpicks a number of Corsicato's references but then asks:

But once we have unpacked the references . . . what are we to do with them? . . . My impression is that this whole apparatus of aesthetics and citations is absolutely essential to the film: if you removed the little games typical of top-of-the-class screenwriters and the ultra-cool music, not much would remain. If in the Italian cinema of the Seventies these para-avant-garde games served to depict a society in crisis, then of what society does *Chimera* speak? How can you take seriously a character that ends up in debt because he buys too many shirts? (Pezzotta 2001: 37)

Such postmodern games obviously have a certain entertainment value, particularly for the educated, cinéphile audience to whom, in part, the films of the NNC are addressed. The viewer challenges himself to decode the film's intertextuality, derives satisfaction from his ability to do so, and enters into an amused and ironic participation with the film. However, one does have a sneaking suspicion that the film offers little more substance than that.

The influence of this postmodern tendency is evident in the fact that even Nino D'Angelo makes use of it in his effective second directorial effort, *Aitanic* (2000), a parody of *Titanic* (1997, James Cameron) which takes place on a stolen ferry to Capri and ends with the sinking of the famous stack rather than the ship. D'Angelo even ironically quotes his own past in a series of kitsch slow-motion sequences from his earlier films that are clearly intended to highlight the film's greater sophistication – a sophistication embodied by a self-reflexivity that reflects a greater self-awareness.[44] The reworking of traditional Neapolitan narrative can, then, be a very fruitful course for contemporary Neapolitan filmmakers to follow, but it is also a dangerous one. Just as the critical re-examination of Naples described in Chapter 3 runs the risk of an unproductive pessimism, so too the recycling of the Neapolitan narrative can result in an entertaining but ultimately meaningless re-shuffling of cliché. This argument invites questions about the politics of representation, and a number of contemporary Neapolitan filmmakers have engaged in a more directly political investigation of Naples and its culture, or at least raised questions about the possibility of such an operation. Let us now turn our attention to these films and to an analysis of the links between the NNC and the supposed socio-political renaissance of the 1990s.

NOTES

1. Composed in 1945, Nicolardi and Mario's classic song expresses horror at Neapolitan women giving birth to black babies, having had intercourse with black American soldiers.
2. *00580 – Annotazioni per un documentario su Pozzuoli* (1988), *Per il rione Terra* (1990) and *Calcinacci* (1990).
3. Peculiar to the region, 'bradisismo' is the rapid rising and sinking of the land due to volcanic activity.

4. The terminology recalls Pasolini's ideas discussed in Chapter 3.
5. On the relationship between these two cities, see Giuliana Bruno's essay in Aprà 1994: 72–90.
6. The name Cammarano is etymologically close to *camorra*, as if to suggest the archetypal nature of the characters.
7. In America the upper class often isolates and defends itself from the ghetto through the construction of secure 'fortresses' but in Naples the reverse is true, creating a kind of 'criminal apartheid' (see Ravveduto 2007: 77).
8. I use the term perversion here in its literal sense; sex has now assumed a new function – power and manipulation.
9. *Il camorrista* is reportedly much loved and imitated by *camorristi* (see Ravveduto 2007: 190); the same is unlikely to be true of *Luna rossa*.
10. Significantly, the Italian 'ritirarsi' means both to retire and to withdraw.
11. A similar reformulation was more recently applied to Hollywood melodrama, and in particular Douglas Sirk's *All That Heaven Allows* (1955), through the use of homosexuality and inter-racial romance in Todd Haynes's *Far from Heaven* (2002).
12. This is not the image that the film's 'working girls' create. Indeed, Libera's only friend, Immacolata, seems more like one of the victims of socio-economic forces that we find in the early films of Salvatore Piscicelli. This association, reinforced by the film's social and geographical setting (the sub-proletariat of Scampia) and the use of the name Immacolata, is far from casual and the two directors' radically different aesthetics should not obscure this fact. Indeed, there are undoubtedly similarities between Piscicelli's materialist analysis and the one that, as I suggest below, Corsicato puts forward.
13. Corsicato confirms this interpretation in Padovan 1996: 62.
14. Patrizia La Trecchia states that, 'Aurora is seen as a victim of the male universe and at the same time also of the universe that, nonetheless, she represents: the *parvenus*, the exponents of the *camorra*, whose culture is non-existent and limited to the possession of commodities most often in bad taste . . . Aurora, as her name suggests, is the birth of a new component of Neapolitan culture incarnating and representing the apotheosis of *kitsch*' (La Trecchia 2003: 116–17). Similarly, Corsicato has claimed that, 'My film originates in an undeniable fact: in Naples there is no longer a bourgeoisie, only kitsch and ostentatious opulence. The nouveau riche parades its affluence while the contradictions and conflicts between the classes have assumed new forms' (Castellano 1993: 106).
15. This episode bears a certain superficial similarity to the films of Antonioni in terms of theme – the 'malady of the emotions' in a modern, bourgeois environment – while the choice of location is analogous to the use of the EUR (Esposizione Universale Roma) in *L'eclisse/The Eclipse* (1962).
16. A film for which Corsicato has expressed his admiration – see Pellegrini et al. 1996: 39.
17. Antonietta De Lillo's short interview film, *Promessi sposi* (1993), also hinges on the unexpected revelation halfway through that the man has undergone gender reassignment surgery. However, her film is a very different one that attempts to understand and sympathetically portray the reasons behind such a decision and the problems that such an individual may face within a popular, working-class district of Naples.
18. If Corsicato is sometimes seen as an imitator of Almodóvar, this episode suggests, if not necessarily the reverse, then at least a mutual affinity between the two. Almodóvar's *Todo sobre mi madre/All About My Mother* (1999) also hinges on a man's discovery that his father is a transsexual; furthermore it makes use of

All About Eve (1950, Joseph L. Mankiewicz) and the stage version of Tennessee Williams's *A Streetcar Named Desire* in a manner that recalls Corsicato's invocation of *Vertigo*.

19. Corsicato agrees: 'It is not a queer or a feminist film as some have claimed. It's a film about solitude, malaise' (Catelli and Boscaino 1993: 11).
20. Corsicato has stated, 'I think the Neapolitan male is very feminine' (Salvi 1993: 60).
21. This is rendered explicit in Veronica's conversation with Andrea's wife, in which she announces that her whole being is merely 'acting' and reliant on 'falsehoods'.
22. It is interesting that the Mater Natura community appears to be entirely asexual.
23. 'La stirpe di Iana' [Iana's Progeny], Corsicato's episode from the same film, again proposes a feminist postmodernism in its tale of a kung fu-fighting, all-female biker gang who wreak havoc on the men who capture their leader's sister.
24. See also the discussion of the fatalism inherent in the Neapolitan world-view and the way in which it is reflected in the NF on p. 50.
25. Incidentally, the cabaret group in which Troisi earned his fame was also called *La smorfia*.
26. The application of rationalism to miracles continues in the subsequent scene in which Gaetano's father concludes his prayer to the Madonna with the suggestion that it would be better if the miracle happened at night, so as not to frighten him, and that tonight would be ideal as he needs to move furniture the next day. He then helpfully provides a detailed description of how to get to the house in case the Madonna should get confused with next door's apartment as the postman clearly does.
27. The play was filmed for RAI by Fernanda Turvani in 1959 and a film version was directed by Sergio Grieco in 1952.
28. We are first introduced to the head as Torquato talks to him through a TV monitor. Having invited him for lunch, Torquato waits for a response and the head 'miraculously' appears standing behind him. This deliberate play between the mediated, virtual image of the head and his real self is a clear indicator of the film's postmodern intent.
29. These are referenced by a reversal of the fantasy sequence from *I buchi neri* in which Adamo imagines being smothered by rotten fruit during intercourse in the similarly oneiric scene in which Veronica is covered by petals while masturbating and, more explicitly, by Mario watching the Don Arcangelo artificial insemination scene from *Libera* on a television set.
30. Appropriately, Corsicato was originally also to have contributed an episode but funding difficulties prevented him from doing so.
31. Significantly, in a total reversal of the NF's reliance on casting famous singers, here many of the songs are performed by the actors themselves.
32. Equally significant is the fact that this particular *sceneggiata* was never adapted by the NF.
33. In his pioneering work on the *sceneggiata* Enzo Grano argues that, 'The real protagonist of this enormous theatrical machine is the public, which identifies itself with these narrative situations typical of its social condition' (Grano 1976: 201). Interestingly, *Fondali notturni* (discussed in the next chapter) provides an alternative interpretation of this process when its protagonist suggests that such a spectator was merely 'acting the part of someone going to the *sceneggiata* . . . and doing so more for the sake of others than himself: it was a social duty.' This difference reveals the gulf between the postmodernist conception of the films discussed in this chapter and the more politically oriented films discussed in the next.
34. Corsicato's subsequent *Il seme della discordia* also concludes – after the breakdown of a relationship the husband defines as 'imperfect, but sincere' – with the couple

discussing the need to be honest with one another, only for Mario to question the very nature of truth and respond to his wife's question with a small white lie.

35. Here I am referring to the use of a dramatic orchestral score and a crane shot that sweeps down through the trees; Morreale compares the camera movement to the work of Delmer Daves (Morreale 2001: 33).

36. Parallels could be made with the Robbe-Grillet-scripted *L'Année dernière à Marienbad/Last Year at Marienbad* (1961, Alain Resnais).

37. In *Il seme della discordia* Corsicato uses a similar 'black hole' in a more conventional fashion, utilising restricted narration to suppress the truth about Veronica's rape and construct a mystery narrative.

38. David Lynch is a clear influence on this use of fade to black and above all on the superimpositions used to convey the disorientation Emma experiences as she loses consciousness, having been hit on the head. The way the characters embody multiple identities also recalls Lynch's *Lost Highway* (1997). Perhaps the greatest similarity is *Mulholland Dr.* (2001), in which the entire narrative almost literally falls into a black hole mid-way through, only for the characters to re-emerge in a new guise. The scene in which Tomas has the hypnotised Sal dance backwards on a stage in front of a blue curtain also recalls *Blue Velvet* (1986) in terms of the setting and *Twin Peaks* (1990–1) in terms of the dancing backwards. Corsicato has, in fact, acknowledged his liking for Lynch's work (Castellano 1993: 109). One could also cite a similarity with Brian De Palma's penchant for repeatedly changing the diegetic status of the events and the course of the narrative in a film like *Raising Cain* (1992). All of these films have been described as postmodernist.

39. Even in his first film Corsicato plays with such metacinematic devices, at one point deliberately revealing the film's crew reflected in a mirror and breaking the illusion of reality.

40. At one point Franco Nero's businessman opens his desk drawer, presumably to reveal the money that it is going to motivate the *mise-en-scène* that they are enacting, but the drawer is empty. Similarly, the 'drawer' from which Corsicato pulls his narrative is also empty.

41. Marcello Garofalo defines Corsicato's cinema as a 'cinema-mirror, in the sense of absence of depth, of superficial abyss'. He goes on to argue that 'Corsicato makes films as if he were painting a *trompe-l'œil*, mimicking a "third dimension" and going beyond the effect of reality. It is as though he casts grave doubts on the principle of cinematic reality, transforming it into an ironic simulacrum' (Garofalo 1995: 92–3).

42. It was mostly shot in Bassolino's home town of Afragola but the town's apparent proximity to the sea suggests it is supposed to be elsewhere.

43. The return to the Centro Direzionale in *Il seme della discordia* only apparently represents a reversal of this progression, as once again we are presented with a world in which the antinomy artifice–reality no longer has any meaning. This is rendered most explicit in the character of Nike, who is introduced standing next to a mannequin she closely resembles and who later performs as part of a group appropriately named 'Les Clonettes'. 'What can you expect from someone who shares a name with a shoe?' observes one character pithily. Here the artificial world of the Centro Direzionale is not opposed with an external reality, as in *Libera*, and thus functions as a 'no-place', much like the one in *Chimera*. Indeed, Morreale compares it to the sci-fi *La decima vittima/The 10th Victim* (1965, Elio Petri) (Morreale 2008: 33).

44. Admittedly, D'Angelo's choice of direction was probably influenced as much by *Tano da morire* (1997, Roberta Torre), for which he composed the music, as it

was by the other Neapolitan films here, but even this film has significant links to the NNC since it was produced by A.S.P., who produced both *Appassionate* and *I cinghiali di Portici*, and its post-production was carried out at Megaris in Naples with Giogiò Franchini acting as editor.

5. SYMBOLIC POLITICS: THE NEAPOLITAN RENAISSANCE AND THE POLITICS OF THE NEW NEAPOLITAN CINEMA

Antonio Bassolino and the Neapolitan Renaissance

Following the crisis of the Italian party system precipitated by the *tangentopoli* scandals of the late 1980s, proposals were made for electoral reforms to move away from a party system based on proportional representation towards a majoritarian, presidential system. Although not followed through at a national level, these proposals were applied to the election of city mayors in 1993 and then regional presidents in 1999. In Naples the 1993 elections saw a closely fought battle between Antonio Bassolino of the left-wing Partito Democratico della Sinistra (PdS) and Alessandra Mussolini of the right-wing Movimento Sociale Italiano (MSI), from which Bassolino emerged victorious to embark on a series of reforms. Bassolino's impact on the city was seen as nothing short of miraculous and the idea of a sudden and unexpected 'Neapolitan renaissance' rapidly took hold. Four years later he was re-elected with a landslide victory, winning 73% of the vote. In 2000 Bassolino ran for President of the Region of Campania and thus stepped down as Mayor, an action that generated great consternation, particularly in Naples where it was seen as a betrayal. Bassolino was replaced by his vice-mayor, Riccardo Marone, and went on to victory in the regional elections, albeit with a much smaller majority of 54%, while Rosa Russo Iervolino took over as Mayor in the 2001 elections with 53% of the vote.[1] As Bassolino's popularity began to wane, the efficacy of his policies and the legitimacy of the Neapolitan renaissance were called into question for the first time.

The seven-year period of Bassolino's governance roughly coincides with the rise of the NNC, inviting the question as to the relationship between these two phenomena. Indeed, the NNC has often been seen as an expression of this wider Neapolitan renaissance, despite the fact that it slightly predates Bassolino's election. The extent to which the re-affirmation of Neapolitan culture in the 1990s is a product of Bassolino's policies or, conversely, to which Bassolino is the political expression of a wider cultural process is a contentious issue. Eduardo Cicelyn and Goffredo Fofi sensibly argue that:

> It is neither interesting nor productive to debate which came first, Bassolino or the new Naples. No sensible person can believe that the mayor is responsible for the cinema, theatre, music and art produced in recent years. Vice versa, neither should we underestimate the importance of the new political climate in giving certain aesthetic practices . . . an increased profile. (Bassolino et al. 1996: 8)

It is undeniably true that Bassolino's policies and the wider Neapolitan renaissance form an important context for understanding the NNC, and Martone's cinema, in particular, contains several references to this context.

Central to Bassolino's policies was an attempt to 'make the city work' by challenging bureaucratic corruption and inefficiency, and altering both the population's reluctance to obey the law and conform to social norms and their lack of faith in the political system. Contrary to past experience, and much to everybody's surprise, this appeared to work. Bill Clinton's visit to the city for the G7 summit in 1994 provided a remarkable demonstration on the international stage of the apparent change in Naples. Concurrently, there was a dramatic recovery of the tourist trade, Bassolino was successful in attracting private investment to the city, and Naples became the first Italian city to launch a bond on Wall Street, a sign of the city's financial recovery from virtual bankruptcy when Bassolino took over. Such policies were perhaps surprising from a long-standing representative of the Italian Communist Party and reflect Bassolino's part in the changing role of the European left-wing parties in the 1990s.

In Chapter 2 we saw how, according to Percy Allum, Neapolitans have traditionally felt estranged from the political process and the institutions of government. An essential part of Bassolino's policy was an attempt to reverse this process, encouraging Neapolitans to take both social and political responsibility for the state of the city and to participate in the political process: in short, to make Neapolitans into 'citizens'. Bassolino is explicit on this point: 'There is no doubt that left to its own devices the city tends not to respect these rules [of social cohabitation], but if it is involved and recognises a positive value in the individual proposals, then the people of Naples will participate' (Becchi and Bevilacqua 1996: 232–3). In 1996, shortly before Bassolino's re-election, it seemed that such a process had already been largely successful:

> The most difficult challenge has already been overcome; there has been a revolution in the collective beliefs of the Neapolitan populace . . . resulting in a newfound recognition that the political process is capable of alleviating the difficulties of everyday living and proposing solutions to the problems . . . of urban life. (Becchi and Bevilacqua 1996: 204)

One of the principal ways in which Bassolino aimed to generate this participation in both the social and political affairs of the city was through a re-articulation of the notion of *napoletanità* and a harnessing of a sense of civic pride by emphasising the city's cultural patrimony.[2] Such a 're-branding' of the city's sense of identity placed considerable emphasis on the media, and Bassolino's considerable charisma and his ability to 'manipulate' the press undoubtedly played a key part in the success – both perceived and actual – of the renaissance. Renato Nicolini, who filled the new position of 'Councillor Responsible for Identity' during Bassolino's first term, described four potential avenues through which this cultural patrimony could be exploited: literature, theatre and staged events, television, and the cinema, in order to 'encourage the surge in production which in just a few years has made Naples Italy's cinematic capital' (quoted in Palestino 2003: 84). Furthermore, emphasis was placed on 'revisiting and reformulating Naples' historical and artistic patrimony in a modern light': for example, by utilising the locations of the soap *Un posto al sole* or staging concerts in historic public spaces (ibid.: 84).

Murray Edelman's notion of 'symbolic politics' has been evoked by a number of commentators in relation to these policies. Edelman argues that political actions contain both an instrumental dimension (the policies' practical impact on society) and an expressive dimension (their perceived value), and that certain politicians or policies place considerable emphasis on this latter, symbolic dimension (Edelman 1985). Ceci and Lepore provide a positive interpretation of this process, to which Bassolino would undoubtedly subscribe: 'Symbolic measures can serve to kick-start the motor of a damaged city which lacks the strength to rebuild itself alone' (Bassolino et al. 1996: 41). However, Bassolino's government has not been immune from the more negative interpretation of 'political spin', as in the claim by the right-wing party Forza Italia that 'the pro-Bassolino mass-media apparatus has even managed to create an image of a Neapolitan renaissance lacking any basis in reality' (Aristofane 2005). During Bassolino's second mandate the optimism and enthusiasm surrounding his project began to wane and the emphasis shifted to this second side to his symbolic politics:

A sense of dissatisfaction was first felt in early 1997 after heavy rains caused the collapse of buildings and roads and following the famous 'revolt of the parish priests' who used angry sermons to expose the conditions of life in the periphery. In January *La stampa* wrote that 'The city awoke in the rain to find that behind the so-called Neapolitan renaissance was a broken-down city marked by deaths, landslides and decay in the periphery . . . Is the dream over?' (Cappelli 2003: 29)

However, it was really after Bassolino's transition from city mayor to regional president in 2000 that a significant shift in the perception of both the state of the city and the impact of its Mayor's policies took place. The principal complaints regarded the state of the periphery, the continued rise of crime and the *camorra*, and the fact that Bassolino's government had focused more on the image of the city – in order to stimulate tourism and private investment – than on tackling social problems. Significantly, these are the problems that are also most evident in the films of the NNC. Capuano's films, in particular, have focused on the periphery, the neglect of its populace and the *camorra*. *Pianese Nunzio: 14 anni a Maggio* even features a 'revolt of the parish priests' in the figure of Father Lorenzo Borelli (see p. 182).

URBAN SPACE AND *NAPOLETANITÀ*

A central part of Bassolino's symbolic politics was the way in which urban space was articulated. Concerns over urban planning have long been a key facet of political discourse in Naples; however, under Bassolino, a newfound emphasis was placed on the re-qualification and valorisation of historical or cultural locations. The clearest example of this is Piazza del Plebiscito, which since the 1970s had been scandalously used as a bus terminal and car park. In 1994 the *piazza* was repaved and pedestrianised, and from 1996 came to function as 'the symbol of the Neapolitan renaissance' (Palestino 2003: 72) and the site of a New Year's celebration that quickly became an established ritual. Significantly, it is a new symbol rather than a traditional image of the city that has assumed such a central role in the politics of the 1990s. Bassolino's promotion of such symbolic locations, or 'sites of identity', as he terms them (Bassolino et al. 1996: 59), aimed to harness civic pride, creating a sense of community that would be applicable to the entire populace, be they inhabitants of the historic centre or the periphery.[3] Bassolino claimed that,

We are trying to extend the feeling of civic identity to include those who until now have not felt involved. The feeling of belonging that the symbol of Piazza del Plebiscito has provoked in recent years is not so important for citizens that live in the posh districts and have an extraordinary panorama before their eyes every day . . . but above all for those who come from the tough and difficult periphery, places like Secondigliano or San Giovanni. (Becchi and Bevilacqua 1996: 228)

Although schemes like 'Il maggio dei monumenti' and 'La scuola adotta un monumento', which aimed to create a rapport between these 'sites of iden- tity' and the population of both the city and the provinces, were enormously successful, one criticism levied against Bassolino was that the emphasis on locations in the historic centre was conducted at the expense of run-down peripheral areas. His interventions here revolved primarily around cancelling the evidence of the disastrous changes made by previous administrations. Two key examples are the as yet uncompleted demolition of the Vele in Scampia and the dismantling of the industrial complexes at Bagnoli.

Chapter 2 suggested that the NF's emphasis on the beauty of Naples, with its folkloristic images of the alleys and *bassi* of the historic centre and panoramas over the bay, was entirely consistent with Mayor Achille Lauro's attempts to revive the war-torn city and re-brand it as a tourist destination. One could hypothesise that the NNC played a similar role in articulating Bassolino's vision of the city, particularly since, as we have seen, Councillor Nicolini identi- fied the cinema as one of four ways of valorising the city's heritage. However, this is not the case. Appendices 6 and 7 illustrate the sheer diversity of loca- tions featured in the NNC, as opposed to the NF, which concentrated almost exclusively on the historic centre and the picturesque seafront area around Santa Lucia, Chiaia, Posillipo, the island of Capri and the Amalfi coast. While Bassolino concentrated on sites of architectural and historical significance within the historic centre, comparatively few recent Neapolitan films have been set primarily or exclusively in this area or have emphasised such sites.[4] One significant exception is *Appassionate* which, although it features isolated sequences in the hinterland, remains rooted primarily in the historic centre and in particular the area around the port and the Quartiere di Sant'Antonio ai Monti. No other film of the NNC devotes as much screen time to location shooting on the streets of the historic centre as does *Appassionate*, and this is central to the film's 'quotation' of popular Neapolitan culture (see p. 146). Even more significant than the reduced emphasis on the historic centre is the virtual absence of the locations promoted in Bassolino's policies, and in particular Piazza del Plebiscito. Pappi Corsicato shot four short documentaries on the art installations established there,[5] and there is an interesting short film that also takes place in (or rather above) the *piazza*, *Angeli* [Angels] (2001, Domenico Ciruzzi).[6] However, no feature films utilise this key location. In fact, in discuss- ing *Morte di un matematico napoletano*, Dario Minutolo talks about 'the *tour de force* that Martone imposes on the camera . . . in the "repressed" dolly-shot that prevents Piazza del Plebiscito from being visible' (Zagarrio 2000: 335).

Figure 5.1   The infamous Vele of Scampia in *Gomorra* (2008, Matteo Garrone). ©01
Distribution.

Instead, the NNC displays an increased emphasis on the periphery and the
urban hinterland, and in particular on locations like Bagnoli and Pozzuoli to
the east and Secondigliano and Scampia to the north, locations entirely absent
from earlier films.[7] Thus the films of the NNC reflect Cicelyn and Fofi's description of Naples as a 'metropolis' rather than a 'city' (Bassolino et al. 1996: 17).

This concentration on the periphery could not be further removed from
Bassolino's emphasis on 'sites of identity' that create a sense of community,
and hence citizenship, for the entire populace. The Vele in Scampia are huge,
pyramidal, concrete tower blocks surrounded by large open spaces, built in the
late 1970s in order to reduce congestion in the centre of Naples and to house
the working class (see Figs 3.1 and 5.1). The Vele soon became incredibly run
down, with people living in overcrowded conditions yet isolated by the vast
open spaces and lack of amenities surrounding them. Afflicted by unemployment, crime, drugs, vandalism and under-investment, they are emblematic of
the alienation and malaise that can characterise city life, an urban hell that
completely reverses the image of communal living provided by the *bassi* and
courtyards of the NF. Significantly, the Vele (see below) have become one of
the most frequented locations of the NNC, and the films that are set there all
revolve around a sense of alienation, emphasising a lack of cultural identity
and the idea that the Vele constitute a prison from which it is impossible
to escape. If the Vele constitute a metonym of urban alienation and social

marginalisation, then Pozzuoli and the eastern periphery signify decay and senescence. For example, both *Giro di lune tra terra e mare* and 'Sofialòren', Capuano's episode of *I vesuviani*, take place against the backdrop of the evacuation of the Rione Terra district of Pozzuoli following the impact of *bradisismo* (see p. 119). Significantly, Bassolino has criticised the media's use of such images of alienation and urban decay claiming that,

> This insistence on exposing a degraded and disheartening reality can actually have consequences different from those intended . . . The emphasis on decay has, deliberately or not, frequently led to an excessive dependence on State subsidy. It implicitly suggests that the State or somebody else should be the ones to help us . . . Furthermore it has also often led to what I call an 'ideology of ugliness'; in other words complacency and a masochistic pleasure in degradation. (Becchi and Bevilacqua 1996: 228)

It is not only the depiction of particular locations that interests us here, but also the construction of the Neapolitan subject. While Bassolino's emphasis on *napoletanità* may recall both Lauro and the films of the NF, his use of the concept also has a political dimension that is entirely new – it aims to create a sense of 'citizenship' that will involve the Neapolitan people in the socio-political life of the city. However, the NNC problematises both of these uses of *napoletanità*. Nick Dines observes how the articulation of Piazza del Plebiscito as a symbol of the Neapolitan renaissance was actually founded as much on a process of exclusion – denying access to 'undesirables' such as *scugnizzi* and drug users – as it was on the aforementioned creation of a sense of universal citizenship, thus contradicting Bassolino's claims for the project (Dines 2004). As we have seen, the NNC repeatedly focuses on precisely these 'undesirables' and furthermore creates a parallel with 'ordinary' Neapolitans to highlight a more general crisis in Neapolitan identity.

The discussion thus far has suggested that the films of NNC cannot be simply identified with the discourse or policies of Bassolino's government. This is another factor that helps explain the discomfort that critics have experienced in relation to the idea of the NNC. This discomfort does not derive, as is often claimed, solely from the fact that the term describes a heterogeneous body of films with little in common (a claim which the preceding chapters have hopefully demonstrated does not bear up to close scrutiny); rather it also derives from the fact that the pessimistic and critical content of the films complicates the idea that they constitute a straightforward expression of a Neapolitan social-cultural-political renaissance.[8] However, I would like to suggest that it is the films themselves, as cultural artefacts and commercial commodities, and the critical discourse that surrounds them, rather than their content, that has clear affinities with Bassolino's government and the evolution of the Neapolitan renaissance. The success of Bassolino's first term (1993–7) and his re-branding of the city thus finds its parallel in the way the first films of Capuano, Corsicato and Martone were celebrated for their rejection of traditional stereotypes in favour of new narrative and stylistic models and a new vision of the city. However, in Bassolino's second term (1997–2000) it became clear that the administration was not going to be able to achieve all of its promises in the short duration of its mandate and the limitations of his symbolic politics became evident. According to Goffredo Fofi, the emphasis placed on 'normalisation' and 'legality' during Bassolino's first term shifted to a restrictive emphasis on 'normality' and a process of 'homogenisation' in his second (see Palestino 2003: 72). Concurrently, the critical failure of *I vesuviani* cast doubts on the claims that had been made about the NNC, while a number of national productions jumped on the band-wagon, siphoning off some of the innovations of the NNC and 'homogenising' them to fit the demands of a national audience.[9] This model of evolution explains why the idea of an NNC took hold, why it subsequently became the target of criticism, and why some filmmakers were eager to distance themselves from it. The rapid conversion of an innovation into a codified movement exploited by the film industry and those eager to further a discourse of Neapolitan social, political and cultural renewal both favoured the expansion and development of this 'movement' and worked to limit and restrain it.

THE PERSONALISATION OF POLITICS: REPRESENTATIONS OF THE BASSOLINO COUNCIL

'La salita' [The Climb], Martone's contribution to the collective film *I vesuviani/The Vesuvians* (1997), is worth examining in some detail since it deals explicitly with Bassolino and evaluates the achievements and failures of his mandate. Made immediately prior to Bassolino's re-election,[10] *I vesuviani* was accused of being a piece of pre-electoral propaganda made by a group of left-leaning directors, an interpretation with which Martone took issue:

> *I vesuviani* was the expression of five very different directors' desire to make a series of fables. Good or bad, these fables deserved to be judged for what they are and not because they constitute a manifesto of the new Naples, something which was never the intention of the film's directors or producers. (Martone 2004: 130–1)

Perhaps the only person to recognise the film's complexity was Giorgio De Vincenti:

> It's natural that Neapolitan filmmakers and artists in general are sympathetic to the city's left-wing administration, which is playing an unusually

progressive role. But the use they make of it . . . should make us careful in judging the role and intentions of this film. If in the past Neapolitan artists could only say 'no' to previous administrations, today they cannot simply say 'yes'. Rather, in the name of the city's inhabitants they demand specific things from politicians. Furthermore . . . in tackling subjects which reflect 3,000 years of history they can only say 'yes, but'. And it is this 'but' that is interesting. It is this indomitable critical edge . . . that fundamentally motivates the Neapolitan cinema of today. (Argentieri 1998: 44–5)

'La salita' is a kind of fantastic political parable in which the Mayor of Naples attempts to climb Vesuvius. The reference to Bassolino is clear and unambiguous; Toni Servillo plays a Neapolitan mayor called Antonio, who comes from Afragola, who is a lifelong member of the Italian Communist Party and who has been responsible for a Neapolitan renaissance. That Martone should explore the socio-political changes in Naples in the 1990s through a fictional representation of the mayor himself is not surprising; it is merely a reflection of the 'personalisation of politics' that has characterised Bassolino's career (see Cappelli 2003: 17–18 and 35–7). During the course of his climb Antonio encounters a number of figures with whom he enters into dialogue; at one point he even meets the Marxist talking crow from Pasolini's *Uccellacci e uccellini/Hawks and Sparrows* (1966) (see Fig. 5.2). The metaphorical dimension is evident from the very start, with Antonio's struggle to climb Vesuvius representing his efforts to improve the city.[11] His first encounter is with a busload of Japanese tourists, instantly establishing the extent to which Bassolino's policies revolved around the promotion of Naples as a tourist destination. His subsequent encounters are with Neapolitans who criticise him for his failings, while he repeatedly tries to justify himself. He encounters a singer who wants to break his contract and leave Naples, and who complains, 'I have a girlfriend in Palermo. Who will inspire my songs if not her – your intellectual friends?' An implicit criticism of Nicolini's emphasis on high culture is thus placed in the mouth of someone who represents the culture of popular Neapolitan song. Antonio's inappropriate response is to substitute him with the Alban Berg Quartet. He is criticised by the still-buried victims of Secondigliano who accuse him of never having retrieved their bodies and of failing to resolve the situation there.[12] He is criticised by a priest for his absence from the periphery and failure to address its decay (a reference to the revolt of the parish priests discussed above), and he encounters a group of minors employed as labourers in the construction of illegal housing.

However, Bassolino is primarily criticised for selling out, for compromising his political beliefs. The crow, as in Pasolini's film the voice of Marxist ideology and a kind of political conscience, complains, 'You are also the expression of a miracle: the product of the Neapolitan hinterland who has

Figure 5.2 A Pasolinian political fable for Bassolino's new Naples: the Mayor (Toni Servillo) confronts a Marxist talking crow in *I vesuviani* (1997). ©Mikado.

always been communist but who now governs accepting the rules of capitalist society – free markets, privatisation and cultural tourism.' Towards the end he encounters Francesca Nobili Strada, a journalist for *L'Unità*, who committed suicide in 1961 and who similarly accuses him of the poverty of his aims and his abandonment of a revolutionary project.[13] During the course of his climb Antonio discovers some books dropped by another man climbing the mountain: Derrida's *Spectres of Marx*, Hegel's *Elements of the Philosophy of Right* and Lenin's *The State and Revolution*. He picks up the latter and puts it in his pocket. At the end of the episode he finally reaches the top of Vesuvius and, looking into the crater, asks, 'What should I do here?' He takes out Lenin's book and flicks through its pages, then puts it back in his pocket and wraps his coat around himself to protect himself from the cold. Whatever Bassolino achieves, Martone seems to be arguing, will be limited and meaningless if it is not underpinned by an ideological or political project; symbolic politics and protestations of change will not ultimately resolve Naples' ills. Earlier in the episode, the short-sightedness and inadequacy of his policies are further emphasised when the crow predicts that, 'Sooner or later this volcano will erupt, burying the surrounding area.' To which Antonio can only reply, while making two horns with his hand to ward off the ill omen, 'And I've already got so many problems . . .'[14]

While many critics saw *I vesuviani* as pre-election propaganda, what Martone actually presents us with is an ambivalent, if not downright negative, portrait of the Mayor. That Martone provides a stage for such harsh criticism of Bassolino is slightly surprising since Martone has himself been involved in a number of projects typical of the Neapolitan renaissance, such as the restoration of the Teatro Mercadante, and is undoubtedly largely sympathetic to Bassolino's project. Yet this approach is also typical of Martone's cinema, which performs a delicate balancing act between two extremes. *Morte di un matematico napoletano* portrays the intellectual, elite culture of Naples in the 1950s but does so ambiguously through the figure of the alienated and suicidal Renato Caccioppoli, while *Teatro di guerra* celebrates the work of an independent, avant-garde theatre explicitly aligned with Teatri Uniti but depicts them engaged in a project that will ultimately end in defeat (see below). Such a balance is extremely unusual in Neapolitan cinema, which generally occupies the extremes of celebration or of apocalyptic negativity, and this constitutes another important innovation by the NNC.

POLITICAL ACTIVISM AND THE ROLE OF THE ARTIST-INTELLECTUAL

'La salita' is an example of political filmmaking in the sense that it explores and comments on a contemporary political situation. However, it is not a self-reflexive film and does not raise the question of what role a film or artist-intellectual like Martone might play in relation to that situation. However, there are also a number of films that pose this question directly and this can also be seen as a response to the existential alienation of artist-intellectuals in the films discussed in Chapter 3.

Antonietta De Lillo's *Il resto di niente* [The Remains of Nothing] (2004) is an adaptation of the novel by Enzo Striano, which became an unexpected *cause célèbre* among Naples' literary circle and a local best-seller on publication in 1987, but only gained the attention of a wider, national audience when re-published by Rizzoli 10 years later. The novel bears certain parallels with Giuseppe Tomasi di Lampedusa's *Il gattopardo/The Leopard* – it is a fictionalised account of real events based on extensive historical research, it deals with a period of historical turmoil in Southern Italy, it is focalised through a member of the aristocracy, and it depicts a moment of failed revolution in which the populace is unable to grasp the full political implications of the movement and from which Southern Italy emerges with its traditional values and social structures intact. Whereas *Il gattopardo* deals with the Risorgimento, *Il resto di niente* covers the brief period of the Neapolitan Republic (1799) in which, on the back of the French Revolution, the Bourbon King Ferdinando I was ousted and the Neapolitan populace momentarily took control of their own city, only for the King to return when the French abandoned the city, executing those responsible and reinstating the monarchy. The novel's protagonist is Eleonora Pimentel Fonseca, a member of the Portuguese aristocracy resident in Naples, who embraces Jacobin ideals, participates in the revolution, edits and publishes the movement's newspaper, *Il monitore*, and is ultimately hanged when the revolution is crushed.

Antonietta De Lillo purchased the rights to the novel in 1995 but repeated attempts to film it, beginning in 1998, were aborted due to production difficulties. The film was finally completed and released in 2005. For De Lillo one of the attractions of the novel was certainly the idea of Eleonora as a proto-feminist; she separated from her boorish husband, who prevented her from following her intellectual and literary ambitions, then participated in a political movement as an equal with men, before becoming the only woman to be executed by the Bourbons. The attempts to introduce democratic and libertarian ideals to Neapolitan society and the efforts of an educated woman like Eleonora to affirm her place within a patriarchal society constitute two of the main themes of the film. A third concerns the difficulties in communication between an educated intelligentsia and an uneducated populace, and the part that this difficulty played in the failure of the Republic. As the Republic's mouthpiece, through *Il monitore*, Eleonora is obviously the ideal character to articulate such a theme and its centrality to the film is made clear from the outset; the very first image shows Eleonora's failure to engage in conversation a young serving girl who has brought her a cup of coffee as she awaits execution. Later, when *Il monitore* is instituted, she is told that it is only worth printing 400 copies – 'a family thing' – since virtually everyone in Naples is illiterate. She responds, 'But I need to reach the people, in Naples and the provinces. I'll send newspaper-readers into the streets.' The Republic begins to unravel when it is unable to respond to demands for food and essential services, and the film presents us with a debate between the governors in which they make it clear that, 'the populace only understands the language of needs.' It is Eleonora who restates *Il monitore*'s key role in making the populace understand what the revolution is trying to achieve for the people. In a key scene Eleonora witnesses the success of a puppet show amongst a group of poor Neapolitan children and attempts to engage the puppeteer's services in order to use Pulcinella – the quintessential embodiment of popular Neapolitan culture – to articulate a political message. There are numerous other examples of this theme in the film but its importance to De Lillo's version is made explicit in Eleonora's relationship with Graziella, whom she tries to educate. De Lillo claims: 'Just as Striano invented the character of Vincenzo Sanchez, a kind of alter-ego who dialogues with Eleonora, I inserted Graziella, a woman of the people who acts as her servant but is really her opposite, her mirror; she is the symbol of popular culture' (Pia Fusco 1998). It is the Republic's failure to communicate with the people of Naples – the *plebe* as Eleonora defines them – that, together with the

French army's betrayal, ultimately dooms its revolutionary project and seals Eleonora's fate.

In a significant addition to the novel, Eleonora, while awaiting death, repeatedly converses with the imagined figure of Gaetano Filangieri, philosophical spokesperson for Jacobin ideals. Filangieri is played by Enzo Moscato, one of the key exponents of the New Neapolitan Theatre of the 1980s, whose 1991 play *Rasoi* was adapted and filmed by Martone in 1994 and whose monologue *Pozzi d'amore* formed the basis of the first episode of De Lillo's reflection on death, *Racconti di Vittoria*. Moscato's plays represent a curious hybrid between 'high' and 'popular' culture, and use a difficult plurilingual mix of virtually impenetrable Neapolitan dialect, foreign languages and flamboyantly literary Italian.[15] It is a significant piece of casting that highlights the theme of communication so central to the novel. De Lillo has worked repeatedly with Moscato both because of a personal affinity and because, for her, 'Moscato is Naples' (Author's interview, Rome, 27 June 2003). He represents both the expression of a popular Neapolitan culture and the possibilities for a more innovative, high cultural tradition. Moscato also appears in numerous other films of the NNC and significantly has a small cameo as one of the people that Crescenzio visits in *Il verificatore*. Here Moscato plays an intellectual who delivers a lengthy poetic soliloquy, only to have his discourse deflated by the matter-of-fact statement by a young girl, who has clearly taken on the practical demands of running the house in his place: 'He talks and talks . . . but all he says is a load of crap!'

This theme of communication is also relevant to the NNC as a whole, given that it too is the product of educated middle-class filmmakers and has replaced the popular culture of the earlier NF without successfully capturing a broad, popular audience either in Naples or elsewhere. The NNC's radical reworking of Neapolitan culture and identity also serves a political purpose – in relation to debates about *Meridionalismo*, the need to institute a different relationship between individual and society and to bring about social change and progress within the city – and thus can be considered a 'revolutionary' movement. While Eleonora attempts to adopt the language of the *plebe* (Neapolitan dialect) and of popular culture (Pulcinella) as a vehicle for politically radical content but fails, the NNC has – for the most part – abandoned popular Neapolitan culture in favour of the language of 'art' cinema.

De Lillo's approach to adapting the source material is worth considering here. The demands of shooting an eighteenth-century costume drama set during a revolution generate a huge number of logistical and budgetary problems, and this is one of the causes behind the project's troubled gestation. Luchino Visconti's approach to *Il gattopardo/The Leopard* (1963) was to shoot it as a big-budget spectacle co-produced by 20th Century Fox and featuring international stars. The result was the virtual bankruptcy of Titanus and the dilution of Visconti's vision by the commercial demands of the market place, at least as far as the international version was concerned. De Lillo's approach is diametrically opposed, but entirely consistent with that of the NNC as a whole; independently produced by Factory Film and Film Corsari using Government funding as a film in the national cultural interest, the film was made for a (relatively) low budget, thus guaranteeing a degree of artistic freedom and authorial control. The film was shot on digital video and uses a number of digital post-production devices to enhance its historical reconstruction. It was shot largely on location in and around Naples, making judicious use of existing locations that could be passed off as belonging to the eighteenth century – as Martone and Dionisio had done for the 1950s in *Morte di un matematico napoletano* and *La volpe a tre zampe* – and using deliberately naïve animations in order to depict the major revolutionary battles (in sharp contrast with Visconti's spectacular battle for Palermo). Yet the absence of spectacle that such an approach demands puts the film in a difficult position in relation to the commercial demands of the market place; it risks relegating it to that portion of Italian production that struggles to obtain a market share, described in Chapter 1. Predictably, the film performed poorly at the box office (see Appendix 2) and De Lillo publicly spoke out against the State-owned distributor Istituto Luce's handling of the film, an action that landed her in court.

Il resto di niente, then, focuses on a strong-willed woman who attempts to reach out to the Neapolitan *plebe*, to speak their language and communicate a radical, libertarian political message. However, the fact that she is martyred by the traditional monarchic and patriarchal structures of Neapolitan society,[16] and that De Lillo chooses to frame the entire film around Eleonora's waiting for death, draws attention to a certain pessimism inherent in the film's politics – a characteristic neatly encapsulated in the Neapolitan phrase that lends both the book and film their title and which provides Eleonora with her final words: 'What can I do now? Nothing. The remains of nothing, as they say in Naples.'

The only other film of the NNC to attempt a true historical reconstruction of centuries past is Lamberto Lambertini's *Fuoco su di me* [Fire at My Heart] (2005), which takes place at the end of the reign of Gioacchino Murat (1808–15) and culminates with his execution and the restoration of the Bourbon Ferdinando I. Thus, like *Il resto di niente*, it too focuses on a moment of revolutionary fervour destined to end in failure. However, the film does not really centre on Murat but on Eugenio, a young soldier who, while recovering from a serious injury, rediscovers the city of Naples, turns his back on the military, dabbles in the world of literature and falls in love for the first time. In the film's final scenes, after the fall of Murat, Eugenio strips off his uniform and, pursued and cornered by enemy soldiers, launches himself into the Bay of Naples while in voice-over he announces that this is the happiest moment of his life. If Eugenio represents idealism, artistic-intellectual endeavour and the existential quest for meaning, then the narrative resolves itself with yet another affirmation of liberty at the moment of death (see pp. 104–6). Rather than being a straightforward reconstruction of historical events, the film is really about the role of the individual and the choices (s)he makes within a historical frame. Furthermore, given that this narrative also alternates with scenes synthesising Murat's reign, which are narrated by Eugenio's grandfather, Prince Nicola, who is writing a book on the subject and who fulfils a similar role to Filangieri in *Il resto di niente*, the film also addresses the role of history. At one point Prince Nicola asks, 'what is history if not a painted backdrop against which different actors perform the same roles?' Thus the film transfigures a mere reconstruction of history on to an almost philosophical plane in order to explore a moment of involution in which revolutionary idealism was replaced by pessimistic pragmatism. As in *Il resto di niente*, the budget necessitates an absence of spectacle (most notably in the elision of the battle against the Austrians and English, which ended Murat's reign) and a reliance on digital effects (as in the eruption of Vesuvius).[17] Instead, Lambertini pursues a deliberately anti-realist, emphatically pictorial aesthetic that is quite anomalous within the NNC.

The theme of the role played by the intellectual artist within the political process is also explored, this time in a contemporary setting, in Mario Martone's *Teatro di guerra/Rehearsals for War* (1998), which focuses on the process of artistic representation in the theatre. The film represents the latest of Martone's film–theatre hybrids after the filmed plays, *Foresta nera* (1980) and *Rasoi* (1993), and multimedia theatrical projects such as *Tango glaciale* (1982) and *Ritorno ad Alphaville* (1986). On one level the film is a documentary-style recording of the preparations for the staging of a low-budget, experimental theatrical production of Aeschylus' *The Seven Against Thebes*.[18] Although Martone had the idea for the film first, he realised that it would not work if the rehearsals were merely staged for the camera.[19] Thus he decided to stage a real play and film the rehearsals in 16mm. The play was performed once only at the Teatro Nuovo on 19 December 1996, and then again in June of the following year when the shooting of the rest of the film took place. Around this documentary element Martone shot a series of fictional scenes detailing the lives of the members of the troupe and the problems in staging such a show. These elements are seamlessly blended so that the distinction between these two narrative levels is hard to distinguish. Martone insisted that Andrea Renzi, who plays the director in the film, co-direct the real show, thus blurring the distinction between his filmic performance and his role in the theatrical production. He also chose to shoot the whole film in 16mm in order to unify these two levels visually (see Martone 1998: 20). Most of the troupe who appear in the film form part of the Teatri Uniti group and many of them play characters who share their own first names and some feature autobiographical traits (for example, real-life husband and wife Roberto De Francesco and Iaia Forte play lovers in the film). Various people who belong to the Neapolitan theatrical world have small cameos within the fictional sequences, further contributing to the impression that the diegetic world that the film depicts is closely related to the extra-filmic reality both of Neapolitan theatre and of the film's own production. The final party scene thus features NNC regular Renato Carpentieri, theatre actress Nadia Carlomagno, theatre director and the film's second unit director Alessandra Cutolo, camera operator Renaud Personnaz and many others. Of course, I am not suggesting that the majority of the film's audience would pick up on this. However, it reflects the kind of double address discussed in relation to *Morte di un matematico napoletano* by which the film acquires an extra level of significance for a small part of the Neapolitan audience.

The film depicts not just one theatrical environment, however, but two. On the one hand, we have the world of low-budget, avant-garde theatre in the Teatro Nuovo (the theatre in which Teatri Uniti have always rehearsed their shows). On the other, there is the expensive production of *The Taming of the Shrew* at the State-funded Teatro Comunale. It is interesting to read the original treatment's description of this second theatre, which makes explicit the extent to which the film depicts and explores the culture of the Neapolitan renaissance:

> The theatre in which Leo is working is a communal theatre recently restructured and returned to the city. Naples is enjoying a euphoric moment: after many years of bad government a new administration is working to improve the image of the city. The reopening of the Teatro Comunale is one of the successes of the new administration. Franco Turco, one of the new generation of directors who is trying to modernise Neapolitan traditions, has been called to direct it. On one occasion he will stage a European interpretation of a Neapolitan text, the next a Neapolitan reading of a European play. The critics applaud and the spectators sign up in droves. Turco is cunning, cynical and quick to exploit the chaotic economy of the Italian theatrical market, but he is not a bad actor . . . It is his direction that is redundant and irritating to Leo . . . who accuses him of slovenliness and approximation in his working methods, a disinterest in the actor's craft, an easy sentimentality and a reliance on kitsch and superficial effects. (Martone 1998: 24)

Martone was involved in the project to restore the Teatro Mercadante in 1995 and later also served as a director of a Teatro Stabile – in Rome not Naples – like the fictional Franco Turco. He has also been part of this process to 'modernise Neapolitan traditions', in particular through plays like Enzo Moscato's *Rasoi* (first staged in 1991 and filmed in 1993). While Turco does not, obviously, function as an alter ego in the way that Leo does, the character does represent an aspect of the theatrical process from which Martone is not entirely extraneous. Interestingly, one of the most obvious tropes seen on stage – a large mirror suspended above the stage and angled to permit the audience to see the action from above – was subsequently adopted by Martone himself for the third act of his 2005 Covent Garden production of *Un ballo in maschera*, which was the subject of similar criticism for its privileging of spectacle at the expense of the more traditionally dramatic (and musical) elements (see Canning 2005). I do not mean to suggest that Martone is presenting an explicit self-criticism, but rather that he is exploring the problems surrounding a particular aspect of theatrical production – the function of *mise-en-scène* and its relation to the work of the actors themselves. Martone has always been particularly aware of this aspect and many of his earlier theatrical productions (in particular the aforementioned *Ritorno ad Alphaville*) were notable precisely for employing innovative approaches to staging that owed little to traditional theatre.

The second level on which the film works is that of metaphor. The play that Leo stages in the film is Aeschylus' *The Seven Against Thebes*, 'which deals with a siege and a war between brothers' (Martone 1998: 19), and this choice is significant because of the parallels it establishes with the situation in Bosnia. This parallel is heightened by Leo's (and Martone's) decision to stage the play in modern dress. The film's use of a theatrical metaphor in order to illuminate a current historical-political situation was seen as problematic by a number of Bosnians whom Martone encountered during the preparation of the project. In his diary of his visit to Sarajevo during pre-production Martone notes, 'The main problem is that there is a certain suspicion of anyone who attempts to deal with the city through a fictional story' (Martone 1998: 46). There is a parallel with other films of the NNC here, and in particular with Capuano's use of Greek tragedy to address a social problem in *Luna rossa*. In 2000 Martone himself revisited this approach in *Un posto al mondo*, a programme made for Rai television, part of which revolves around the preparations for a theatrical performance of a Greek tragedy, this time Sophocles' *Oedipus Rex*, performed by immigrants at the Teatro Argentina in Rome. Once again, this documentary element is contrasted with other scenes that contextualise the drama and help establish a contemporary meaning for an archetypal text. Rather than a fictional back-story, however, here Martone uses found footage from the Rai archives depicting war, starvation, migration, and so on.[20] The fictional level of *Teatro di guerra* adds a second metaphorical dimension, however, linking the situation in which the troupe finds itself in Naples to that of the bellicose setting of the play and of Bosnia. Thus we witness the routine drive-by shooting of a small-time *camorrista* just outside the theatre. The theatre custodian warns the troupe to be careful because there are weapons on the streets, at which point Leo closes the back door to the theatre with a heavy iron bar, shutting the troupe inside the theatre and away from the dangers outside. During a rehearsal a number of actors waiting outside in the alley (which serves as the theatre's wings) are arrested by police, who mistake their patently fake guns for real weapons. In the scenes in which Rosario goes to visit his parents in Secondigliano the general state of urban decay and the wreckage caused by a gas explosion (an explicit reference to an event that generated much criticism of the Bassolino government's neglect of the periphery, as described above) give the area the appearance of a war-torn city.

This metaphorical dimension is important, as one of the themes of the film is the way in which the theatre is used to represent and reflect on reality and the ethical and moral implications of such a process. At one point Luisella, one of the actresses in the play, argues with Leo, suggesting that a Greek tragedy performed in Italian will be absolutely meaningless to the people of Sarajevo, who have much greater material needs.[21] She accuses him of indulging in an abstract intellectual operation simply to alleviate his own conscience. Of course, Martone's own impetus for making the film and staging the play was a concern over the situation in Bosnia and his own sense of guilt at Italy's, and his own, failure to do anything constructive to help (see Martone 1998: 17). As a man of the cinema and the theatre, his response was to produce a film to reflect on these issues. But someone as self-aware as Martone could not have been unaware of the limitations of such an approach. Indeed, during his trip to Sarajevo he encountered a well-known Bosnian theatre director, Havris Pasović:

> He accused me of having an intellectual vision and urged me to get emo-
> tionally involved 'as an Italian', narrating what has happened in Bosnia
> directly in accordance with the tradition of the great Italian cinema of the
> past. (Martone 1998: 47)

As in the criticisms addressed to Leo quoted above, Pasović objects to Martone's intellectual approach and sees a more productive and ethically jus-tifiable approach in the Neorealist model. This problem does not relate solely to the extreme situation of Bosnia, but to that of Naples too. When the actors are arrested for carrying false weapons, they justify themselves by saying that they are actors, to which the police superintendent responds: 'Do you know what the situation in the Quartieri Spagnoli is like? Don't you think it would be better to do a different job?' It is left to Vittorio to respond, not by present-ing an argument for the socially constructive role of the theatre, but rather by justifying himself: 'Superintendent, I work in the Quartieri Spagnoli – I'm a teacher.'

I have already suggested that not only does Martone essentially represent his own theatrical practice and experience in the film, but also that Leo effectively acts as an alter ego for the director, and it is perhaps worth examining this aspect of the film in greater detail. There are two significant differences between Leo and Martone. Firstly, whereas Leo's intention is to stage the play in Sarajevo as a 'sign of solidarity', Martone's is to stage the play in Naples in order to make the film. Thus whereas Leo is hoping to have an impact on the Bosnian people themselves, Martone is addressing himself primarily to Italians.[22] The second difference is that, whereas Leo fails in his operation – the death of the theatre owner in Sarajevo means that the play will not, at least for the time being, go to Sarajevo – Martone succeeds in making and releasing his film. The film thus explores the extent to which the theatre can fulfil a useful social purpose through a narrative in which it fails to do so. However, the film does not suggest that the theatre is incapable of performing such a function; it is not that the play goes to Sarajevo and then Luisella's fears about the inappropriateness of the operation are verified, but rather that the project is defeated by practical difficulties. Thus Francesca Piccolo has convincingly argued for a more positive interpretation of Martone's approach by examining the relationship between the two different ways of doing theatre depicted in the film, that of the Teatro Nuovo and that of the Teatro Comunale.[23]

> One could argue that the film narrates the impotence of one form of theatre against the power of the other. But it is not that simple. The viewer of *Teatro di guerra* sees the play that will never be staged but not the play that is, because the former serves a function, even though . . . [Franco Turco] claims that a play must be seen, 'otherwise why perform it?' Well, we perform it because it allows us to grow, to understand the world, to improve ourselves . . . we do so because it is useful, even if nobody sees it. On the contrary we never see *The Taming of the Shrew* because it is pointless to do so, because we already know the play. (Piccolo 1998)

Like De Lillo, then, Martone raises the question of the difficulties in communicating a political message and the questions relating to form and medium that such a problem presupposes. Despite Martone's obvious ambivalence about the difficulties inherent in political theatre (or cinema), there is no doubt that he still believes in the necessity of such a project – as the example of 'La salita' amply demonstrates.

Several of the ideas touched on in *Teatro di guerra* recur in the contemporaneous *Fondali notturni* [Neapolitan Backdrops] (1998), Nino Russo's film of his own stage play. Shot entirely on a theatrical stage set depicting a deserted *piazza* of the historic centre,[24] the film is constructed as a series of dialogues between Peppino, a seller of contraband cigarettes, and Vittoria, a newsagent. Like 'La salita', the film articulates a metaphor about the state of contemporary Naples; atypically, however, the crisis afflicting the city is not depicted in terms of overcrowding and urban decay but rather as a complete absence of people, as in the second episode of *Polvere di Napoli*. This metaphorical dimension is rendered explicit by the newspapers Vittoria is seen reading, which begin with a 1799 edition of *Il monitore* reporting the Jacobin Revolution depicted in *Il resto di niente* before passing through the Risorgimento, the post-war victories of the Christian Democrats, and ultimately concluding with Bassolino's triumph over Alessandra Mussolini. Thus the film traces the by-now familiar passage from revolutionary promise, through political involution and stagnation towards a cautious optimism for political renewal. However, like the inhabitants of via Marinella in *Nel regno di Napoli*, Peppino and Vittoria remain victims of the forces of history rather than protagonists. The film is not uncritical of their impotence, and the fact that they have never left the square and do not even know whether things are completely normal just around the corner highlights the insularity and introspection of Neapolitan society and culture. Moreover, their misunderstanding of a newspaper article about the State subsidies for the South provides a wonderfully pithy illustration of the Neapolitan reliance on fatalism and a patronage polity described in Chapter 2, when they misinterpret the meaning of 'provvidenze' as 'providence' rather than 'measures'. Nevertheless, the inadequacy of established politics in relation to the city's problems is also highlighted by the group of politicians who at one point wander through the square while debating; each reiterates exactly the same position before announcing that it is up to the voters to decide. This uniformity masquerading as freedom of choice stands as a stark condemnation of the failure of democracy.

Given their political impotence, all Peppino and Vittoria can do is to try to pass the time 'until night passes' and the 'revival' of the city finally takes place.[25] They repeatedly tell each other the same stories about life before the crowds disappeared, thus making explicit the way in which Neapolitan culture has traditionally relied on a recycling of the same consolatory myths about its past, as discussed in Chapter 2. The film develops this notion into a broader formal strategy as fragments of Neapolitan songs fill the soundtrack and clips of famous Neapolitan films interrupt the film, frequently summoned by lines of dialogue spoken by the characters. Within this process of narrative recycling the theatre comes to assume a privileged position with the unexpected appearance of a troupe of unemployed actors who adopt a disused stage in the corner of the square for their rehearsals. Judging by the political slogans that hang in tatters in the background, the stage was once used for left-wing political rallies and its disuse is just another indication of the abdication of responsibility by organised politics. The actors insist on the apolitical nature of their work, denying that the politicians were really just the actors performing a role, claiming instead that they only perform 'comic plays' and 'works of pure fantasy'. Nevertheless, despite the lack of an audience, they insist on carrying out rehearsals, utilising the same justification that Francesca Piccolo used for the play in *Teatro di guerra*: 'We want to do it, because we have to do something here.'

Thus *Fondali notturni* recycles fragments of traditional Neapolitan culture and reshuffles clichés about the social ills and political failings of the city in a highly sophisticated way typical of the NNC. While it never resolves itself into a coherent political statement in the way that the other films discussed in this chapter do, it none the less makes a compelling argument for the role of the theatre (and by extension, the cinema) as both a vehicle for escapism and a place for a meditation on social-political issues. Yet the film ends by deliberately prioritising reality over fiction. As day finally breaks, the actors invite Peppino and Vittoria to witness their play; unexpectedly, Peppino and Vittoria step on to the stage and join the actors looking down from an artificial balcony on to a presumably real street below as realistic street sounds fill the soundtrack.

EXEMPLARY CITIZENS?

The prioritising of the real enacted in *Fondali notturni*'s final scene becomes central to a couple of recent 'political' films based on the lives of real individuals. Maurizio Fiume's *E io ti seguo/I Will Follow* (2003) recounts the true story of 26-year-old journalist Giancarlo Siani, who reported from Torre Annunziata on the activities of *camorrista* Valentino Gionta and on the third *camorra* war between the Nuvoletta and Bardellino clans, only to be murdered in 1985 shortly after being transferred to *Il mattino*'s head office in Naples. Significantly, Siano came from Vomero and thus *E io ti seguo* depicts a middle-class intellectual who dares to venture into the alternate socio-geographic space of the Neapolitan periphery and to confront the *camorra* mentality so profoundly rooted in the territory with a more liberal and enlightened belief system. Indeed, in an early scene Siani admits he had never even heard of Torre Annunziata before accepting the job of correspondent for the Castellammare di Stabia branch of *Il mattino* and a colleague advises him to get out as soon as possible. However, Siani repeatedly insists that he came there 'to be a serious journalist' and thus he sets about learning everything he can about the town – not only the things that he should know in order to write with authority but also the things which he should not, as Tore, a sympathetic colleague who becomes his closest friend, puts it. Even when he accepts a career-advancing transfer to the newspaper's Neapolitan headquarters, he does not cease to write about Torre Annunziata and after he co-authors a book with Tore, which is seized by the *camorra*, his fate is sealed. With admirable ethical restraint, the film chooses not to depict his murder on screen; instead it elides the 12-year hiatus between his death and his killer's trial to conclude with their conviction, a series of still photos of the real Siani and a final caption stating the date of his death. Six years after Fiume's biopic, the Italian national film industry produced a second film on the same subject, *Fortapàsc* (2009, Marco Risi), which follows an identical narrative trajectory, beginning with Siani joining the staff of the Castellammare office, and concluding with shots of the killers' incarceration following their conviction, a series of captions, and a still image of the real Siani.[26]

On one level, these films constitute a logical progression of the focus on the role of politically engaged, middle-class intellectuals and artists evident in films like *Teatro di guerra* and *Il resto di niente*. Even the title of Fiume's film, which references the investigative magistrate's promise to follow through on his investigation if Siani first publishes the information he has gathered, draws attention to this theme. Moreover, the fact that both films conclude with the death of their protagonist locates them within a recent tradition of politically engaged anti-Mafia films that, as Millicent Marcus has suggested, memorialise martyrs to their cause. Like *I cento passi/The Hundred Steps* (2000, Marco Tullio Giordana), they both 'transmit the legacy of moral engagement and social justice for which their protagonists died . . . [and] end with written texts on screen, the postscripts of their respective narrations' (Marcus 2007: 292). The ending of *I cento passi* contradicts a *mafioso*'s suggestion that young anti-Mafia activist Peppino Impastato will soon be forgotten by depicting a huge demonstration of solidarity on the occasion of his funeral, orchestrated to Procul Harum's *A Whiter Shade of Pale* and followed by a montage of photos of the real Peppino. This sequence is undoubtedly dramatically effective and extremely moving; however, it is also rhetorical in the extreme. Moreover, *I cento passi*'s attempt to 'transmit the legacy of moral engagement and social justice' was greeted with some misgivings in Sicily, where its hagiography of a character who is, after all, martyred for his beliefs, was seen as counterproductive to a call for political engagement in the local youth. Thus it could be argued that the way the film's message is articulated, although emotive, betrays its origins in a national film industry far removed from the socio-geographic milieu it depicts and thus incapable of effectively communicating its political message to a (Sicilian) audience.

Although *E io ti seguo* concludes with a similar memorialist ending, it is less rhetorical and more fraught with ambiguity. The editor of *Il mattino*'s decision to run a very small article on Siani's murder provokes a dramatic revolt from the other journalists, who demand a full-size, front-page article alongside other exposés of *camorra* activities. Ironically, however, it is Tore who interrupts their fervour, interjecting that 'It would be nice to be able to change things but that's not how it works . . . It's those people out there who decide what we can do and what we can't. Isn't it about time you faced facts?' Although the film subsequently shows that the journalists got their way and that the killers were ultimately arrested and convicted, by placing this crucial line of dialogue in the mouth of the one character most closely aligned with the deceased Siani's mission, the film opens up an area of ambiguity largely absent from Giordana's film. Although *Fortapàsc* also refuses *I cento passi*'s triumphalist ending, elsewhere the film is closer to the conventional dramaturgy and rhetorical register of *I cento passi*, and this is indicative of the principal differences between the NNC's approach to such subject matter and that of the national film industry. For example, *Fortapàsc* escalates the depiction of both Siani's relationship with his girlfriend and his friendship with Tore by focusing on his neglect of the former in favour of his work and his consequent reluctance to have a child, and by substituting Tore with the character of Rico, a journalist struggling with heroin addiction. Both of these additions undoubtedly add to the film's pathos and make Siani a more dramatically rounded character. However, the reliance on neat character arcs and parallel plotlines reveals the influence of conventional scriptwriting techniques that contrast markedly with the functional approach to the facts of the case pursued by Fiume. Similarly, while *E io ti seguo* depicts a public protest against the *camorra* via archival footage and the massacre of eight people in the town centre via the actual newspaper report written by the real Siani, *Fortapàsc* chooses to dramatise these events via a dramatic speech in the rain (in which the equation between Torre Annunziata and Fort Apache, which gives the film its title, is first made) and a spectacular shoot-out complete with a chase through the streets. In short, *E io ti seguo* makes a virtue out of its budgetary restrictions; its restless hand-held camera, observational aesthetic, refusal of spectacle and reliance on archive footage and Siani's own words create a considerable sense of authenticity. *Fortapàsc* substitutes this approach with more conventional cinematic dramaturgy and an emphasis on spectacle. As such it can be considered, like *Certi bambini* (2004, Andrea and Antonio Frazzi), emblematic of the way in which the national film industry has been influenced by certain elements of the NNC, such as subject matter and setting, but has diluted them in an attempt to appeal to a wider audience.

Another film that provides a positive example of political engagement by focusing on a martyr is Antonio Capuano's *Pianese Nunzio: 14 anni a maggio/ Sacred Silence* (1996). With its articulation of a moral message and simultaneous rejection of the hypocrisy of moralism, *Pianese Nunzio* constitutes one of the authentic masterpieces of the NNC. It is based on the true story of a priest in the Sanità (named Lorenzo Borelli in the film), whom Capuano establishes as a heroic figure – the one point of reference that the local *scugnizzi* have and a courageous and vocal opponent of the *camorra*.[27] Like Vito in *Vito e gli altri*, 13-year-old Nunzio Pianese comes from a broken home that offers little support; his mother has abandoned the family, his father suffers from mental problems and his brother has already succumbed to heroin addiction and drifted into a life of crime. Thus far Nunzio remains untainted by such criminal associations and instead earns extra money singing Neapolitan neomelodic songs on local recordings; he lives in an overcrowded flat with his aunt and her family, and studies hard at school in order to become a priest. However, 25 minutes into the film Capuano suddenly and unexpectedly reveals to us that Borelli and Nunzio are engaged in a sexual relationship. Capuano does not refrain from showing the negative effects the relationship has on the adolescent Nunzio, particularly in the later part of the film, nor does he conceal Borelli's moments of self-doubt, remorse and confusion, which are delivered as a confessional monologue in voice-off. However, neither does he depict it as an explicitly abusive relationship, as one might expect. Indeed, when Borelli discovers that Nunzio has denounced him to the authorities he does not turn against the boy and promises that he will never do or say anything to harm him. Capuano has argued that, on the basis of research, which revealed that the priest really loved the boy and that the boy needed the priest because he had nobody else, the relationship was a legitimate one. Therefore, rather than the choice of theme *per se*, it is Capuano's decision to film 'a tender story about a great love' that makes the film dangerous and politically incorrect (Author's interview, Naples, 14 June 2003). And it was this approach that generated the controversy that similarly themed films like *Priest* (1994, Antonia Bird) largely escaped.[28] However, despite Capuano's comments, the film itself comes across as more ambiguous and complex; it does not unequivocally endorse Borelli's point-of-view, but nor does it condemn it. Furthermore, the film suggests that, despite Borelli's relationship with Nunzio, he remains a positive social force within a corrupt society and the only person truly willing and able to help and protect the *scugnizzi* from institutional neglect and the exploitation of organised crime. On the one hand, we are invited to identify with Borelli's humanitarian and political project to help the youth of the Sanità and combat the *camorra*; on the other, our allegiance to him is thrown radically into question by the ethical questions his relationship with Nunzio raises. It is the contradiction between these two elements that makes Father Borelli a truly radical figure, one with whom it is almost impossible for the viewer to identify fully.

Borelli's proclamations against the *camorra* are made during Church services that recall the 'revolt of the parish priests' discussed above, and Capuano deliberately emphasises the theatrical and performative nature of these occasions. Borelli generally dresses in civilian clothes – he is nicknamed 'the priest in blue jeans' – yet for these rites he first has to don the priest's robes. His statements are addressed to an assembled public and Capuano uses a shot-reverse-shot structure to emphasise the efficacy of his address as we witness *camorristi* looking ashamed and members of the congregation weeping. This theatricality is particularly evident in the highly moving scene following the accidental shooting of Ada, Nunzio's girlfriend. Images of

Nunzio singing *Nun te pozzo perdere* [I Can't Lose You] in a recording studio segue into Borelli's service for the girl; Borelli's speech is audible on the sound-track as Nunzio's song gradually fades out and the camera tracks above the heads of the congregation. This deliberate theatricality recurs in the final scene, in which Borelli leads a procession under the pouring rain through the Sanità to the Cimitero delle Fontanelle. The procession represents the Stations of the Cross and each time it stops, a member of the congregation speaks. Their statements reinterpret the biblical story in explicitly local terms, constructing Jesus as an ordinary inhabitant of the Sanità and his executioners as *camorristi* and corrupt politicians. The story of the Passion is thus used as a parable, a metaphor for oppression in contemporary Naples, and in this way the radical, political dimension of Christ's teachings is recuperated. One of the congre-gation reads, 'Nobody imagined that from this moment on a terrifying rite began – the condemnation of an innocent man.' Capuano immediately cuts to Nunzio giving his deposition to the district attorney. The rest of the sequence is constructed around a process of parallel montage, which gradually clarifies that the metaphor of the innocent man applies not primarily to Nunzio, as a more politically correct film might prefer, but rather to Borelli. The humanitar-ian Borelli (Christ) is martyred for the political, rather than ethical, implica-tions of his message; Nunzio (Judas) hands him over to the political forces that he threatens – the *camorra* (Pharisees) – who use the institution of the State legal system (the Romans) to condemn him. The film thus makes it clear that Borelli is condemned not by the State for his sexual liaison with Nunzio, but by the *camorra* for his political speeches.[29] Meanwhile, Nunzio also becomes a victim, not of Lorenzo's sexual exploitation but rather of the way in which he is manipulated in order to eliminate Borelli.

Through the use of these metaphorical parallels, the religious dimension that is so central to Neapolitan culture, but which is conspicuously largely absent from most of the NNC, resurfaces. However, it is not the trappings of Catholicism characteristic of the NF but rather the radical, political dimen-sion of Christ's message that Capuano emphasises, much like Pasolini in *Il Vangelo secondo Matteo/The Gospel According to Matthew* (1964). In Father Borelli, Capuano presents us with a politically radical figure who manages to cut through hypocrisy and orthodoxy in order to make a direct impact on Neapolitan society. The question of style also plays an important role in this process. In *Pianese Nunzio* Capuano makes radical use of elements of popular Neapolitan culture – in particular, Neapolitan song – by assigning them a function within the film's political project. Significant in this sense is Nunzio's singing of *Nun te pozzo perdere* after the killing of Ada. The song was originally performed by Nino D'Angelo and featured in *Fatalità* (1992, Ninì Grassia); however, rather than as a love song about exclusivity and the need to possess a loved one, in *Pianese Nunzio* the song is reinterpreted as the desperate cry of a person who has lost someone to *camorra* violence. The film also makes repeated use of Almamegretta, along with 99 Posse one of the principle exponents of the recent musical hybrid of rap, African beats and Neapolitan music. Formed in the new social centres of Naples, these groups use popular musical forms in order to articulate a political message about discrimination and social inequality in Italy, and in particular about the problems facing the South.[30]

Even more significant is Capuano's use of the direct address to camera. At various points in the film characters suddenly become aware of the camera, step out of the diegesis and address the camera directly, stating their name, age and relationship to Nunzio. Many critics invoked Brechtian distanciation in regard to this device; however, Capuano has rejected this interpretation, pointing out that these moments actually represent Borelli's trial, anticipated within the narrative in an extremely original fashion (Author's interview, Naples, 14 June 2003). Nunzio's deposition to the district attorney, cross-cut with the Stations of the Cross procession, is also delivered in such a fashion and, in the final shot of the film, Borelli himself finally faces the camera and speaks a line taken directly from the trial transcripts: 'Lorenzo Borelli, born to unknown parents in Piacenza on the 8th April 1960. Conscious of the moral and legal responsibilities that I assume with this deposition, I promise to tell the truth and not conceal anything.' This direct-to-camera address is a recurrent feature in Capuano's cinema. *Vito e gli altri* also contains a number of 'interviews' with *scugnizzi*, while *Luna rossa* is framed by Oreste's deposition to the DA. Capuano has explained his use of the device thus: 'Personally, I love this device . . . I am moved when I go to the cinema and the character speaks directly to me, something that happens all too rarely . . . It's a technique that generates emotion but also makes you responsible: it urges you to participate' (Author's interview, Naples, 14 June 2003). With this statement Capuano draws attention to two key characteristics of his approach in *Pianese Nunzio*: the desire to provoke an emotional response in the viewer but also to make him responsible, a participant in the action. The fact that the court is absent and the depositions are addressed directly to the audience invests the audience with the moral responsibility of judging the actions of the film, and it is on this level that Capuano's use of such a radical and problematic figure as Borelli becomes significant. Adelina Preziosi perceptively argues that, 'The film's thesis is that the two aspects of Borelli's personality are not mutually exclusive and nor do they produce a monster' (Preziosi 1996: 36). To suggest that Capuano is offering a justification for paedophilia in this film, as several critics have done, is, therefore, to miss the point.[31] Rather he is exposing a moral hypocrisy: how can a society that abandons a child like Nunzio and leaves him at the mercy of the *camorra* pass judgement on Borelli for abusing the boy? And how can a society that forces Nunzio to assume the responsibilities of an independent life then denounce Borelli on the grounds that Nunzio is not mature enough to give his consent to participate in a sexual relationship? The moral hypocrisy underpinning these dual standards is what allows the *camorra* to use the state legal system to further its own ends; rather than protecting Nunzio and boys like him, the courts merely remove an important social reformer who is opposing the *camorra* and offering the boys shelter and support.

A second Neapolitan film dealing with an almost identical theme was released two years later – *Per tutto il tempo che ci resta/Acts of Justice* (1998, Vincenzo Terracciano).[32] It tells of an investigative judge, Giorgio Nappi, who returns to his home town – an unidentified town on the Sorrento coast – in order to investigate the case of his childhood friend, a priest who has repeatedly and courageously denounced the local boss but has subsequently been accused, apparently on the boss's instigation, of abusing an underage girl in his congregation. Nappi is successful in clearing his friend's name only to discover subsequently that he was, in fact, guilty. However, he is aware that, should he reveal the truth, the accusations made by the priest against the boss, who has now been arrested, would be discredited and he would go free. Thus he confronts his friend and says that this knowledge will be their shared curse and that, in order to ensure that he never repeats his crime, he will continue to watch over him 'for the rest of our days' ('per tutto il tempo che ci resta'). Terracciano's film is interesting and dramatically effective, but less complex than Capuano's in the way in which it implicates the viewer in its ethical dilemma. Although it makes it clear that the priest's actions are to be considered criminal, in both moral and legal terms, it nevertheless contrasts his crime with that of the *camorra* boss and, like Capuano, finds the latter to be far more serious.

Pianese Nunzio provides an exciting example of the way in which the NNC's re-appropriation of traditional, popular Neapolitan culture (Catholic ritual, Neapolitan song) and its reconfiguring of stereotypes (the *scugnizzo*, the heroic priest) can be used to articulate a progressive socio-political message. It also shows how the stylistic devices of both popular and avant-garde culture can be fused to engage a mass audience radically. Yet the film was only moderately successful at the box office. Capuano interprets this in terms of the moral backlash against the film's complex treatment of such contentious issues, observing how, following a successful and controversial Venice premiere, the Catholic newspaper, *L'osservatore romano*, ran an article in which a cardinal said 'a veil of silence must fall on this film.' The film then opened with 25 rather than the expected 60 copies and was pulled from the Modernissimo in Naples while still playing to packed houses (Author's interview, Naples, 14 June 2003). Thus the film, like its protagonist, found itself martyred for the controversial implications of its ethical stance.

CONCLUSION

The NNC mirrors Bassolino's desire to provide an alternative vision of the city, but the kinds of image it offers are radically different from the one articulated by the media-driven Neapolitan renaissance. If anything, the NNC highlights the limitations of Bassolino's interventions in the city. While many of the films exhibit a profound pessimism about the state of the city and the possibilities for change, this has not stopped a number of filmmakers from directly addressing the question of political engagement. While the Bassolino government emphasised the importance of media, art and culture to the process of social and political change in the city, filmmakers like De Lillo, Capuano and, above all, Martone have raised questions about the socio-political role of artists and intellectuals and their function and efficacy. There is, then, a politically engaged dimension to the NNC. However, I would suggest that this political dimension extends beyond those films that explicitly address political questions discussed above and instead concerns the re-negotiation of Neapolitan identity that lies at the heart of the NNC as a whole. I will now address this question by way of drawing some conclusions about the innovations that the NNC has brought about.

NOTES

1. For a more detailed account of the 'Bassolino era' and public opinion, see Cappelli 2003: 15–70.
2. See Bassolino's comments in Becchi and Bevilacqua 1996: 209–10.
3. The reclaiming of Piazza del Plebiscito was engineered on the occasion of the G7 summit in July 1994, which also gave the city the opportunity to exploit the symbolic value of other historic locations; Palestino focuses on the wide dissemination of images of Bill Clinton jogging in via Caracciolo and of Hillary Clinton's visit to the cloisters of Santa Chiara (Palestino 2003: 90–1).
4. For maps of the 'symbolic sites' of the Bassolino council see Palestino 2003: 91, 96 and 99.
5. *Le montagne di sale, Offertorio, I colori della città celeste, Tarantantara*, all 1999.
6. The film is discussed at length in La Trecchia 2003: 268–78.
7. The first person to represent the northern periphery was Salvatore Piscicelli, who set all of his early works in his home town of Pomigliano d'Arco. See also the discussion of this shift to the periphery in Corsicato's films on pp. 152–3.
8. On the relationship between the mass media, Bassolino and the construction of the NNC, see also Castellano 1997a.
9. See, for example, *Certi bambini* (2004, Andrea and Antonio Frazzi), *Domenica* (2001, Wilma Labate), *Malefemmene* (2001, Fabio Conversi), *Rosa Funzeca* (2002, Aurelio Grimaldi) and the discussion of *Fortapàsc* on p. 181.
10. It was released in September 1997 shortly before Bassolino's re-election in November.
11. Such symbolism also appears in Mimmo Paladino's art installation in Piazza del Plebiscito, an enormous mountain of salt with several artificial horses sticking out of it. The installation was filmed by Pappi Corsicato as *La montagna di sale* (1999).

12. A number of buildings collapsed as a result of earlier building speculation, causing several deaths.
13. The portrayal of this historical figure establishes an interesting parallel with *Morte di un matematico napoletano*; the two frequented the same circle, were friends, and committed suicide only 2 years apart.
14. The city councils of recent years have all been accused of lacking an adequate evacuation procedure in the event of the large-scale eruption that volcanologists predict is already overdue. This theme is also touched upon in *La vita degli altri* (see pp. 130–1).
15. On Moscato's theatrical work see Fiore 2002: 71–119.
16. The fact that Eleonora is found guilty as much for her transgression of traditional gender roles as for her political beliefs is made clear in the final trial: 'You are a member of the nobility. You left your husband and went into the streets to make speeches . . . in front of the people . . . this is the behaviour of a shameless and immoral woman.'
17. In the audio commentary on the Cecchi Gori DVD, Lambertini has described how he wanted to create digital effects that looked like the artificial backdrops of eighteenth-century puppet theatre or the *sceneggiata*.
18. There are interesting parallels with Jacques Rivette's rarely seen 12½ hour opus *Out 1, noli me tangere* (1971), which also deals with an attempt to stage Aeschylus, features two separate theatrical troupes, and interweaves the lives of the troupe with the events of the production itself.
19. See Martone's comments in Salvi 1998.
20. Alessandra Orsini provides an interesting account of Martone's use of Greek tragedy in his theatrical works, including *Teatro di guerra* (see Orsini 2005).
21. One is reminded of the theme of the 'language of needs' in *Il resto di niente*.
22. The film is set in 1994. Thus Leo's project takes place during the war, whereas Martone's (begun in 1996 and completed 2 years later) takes place after the war.
23. Laura Rascaroli claims that the film 'also make[s] the point that avant-garde theatre is a "theatre of war" – a war against the establishment, represented in the film by the prosperous company of the Teatro Stabile' (Rascaroli 2003: 69).
24. A strategy that cleverly turns economic limitations into an aesthetic virtue and which is also employed by other film–theatre hybrids like *Rasoi* and *Tatuaggi* [Tattoos] (1997, Laura Angiulli). The latter is a stage adaptation of Jean Genet's play *Haute Surveillance*, translated by playwright Enrico Fiore into thick Neapolitan dialect. (A similar process of adaptation is employed by Capuano in his play, *Medea*, discussed on p. 129.) It was staged in 1995 at the Teatro Stabile d'Innovazione Galleria Toledo in Naples and then filmed on 35mm in 1997. Although it screened at the Venice Film Festival that year and subsequently picked up several prizes for its use of an 'innovative cinematic language', it never received a regular theatrical release.
25. The film expresses this waiting for change with what is arguably the most famous line from Neapolitan theatre: 'ha da' passà 'a nuttata', from Eduardo De Filippo's *Napoli milionaria*.
26. There is also an earlier Neapolitan short, *Mehari* (1994, Gianfranco De Rosa), written by Siani's colleague, Maurizio Cerino, and starring Alessandro Ajello and Nello Mascia.
27. The credits end with a conventional disclaimer about the fictional nature of the film, presumably to safeguard artistic licence, protect those involved and avoid potential legal repercussions.
28. On the reception of the film, see Chiacchiari 1996: 74.
29. Throughout the narrative we have been party to a series of scenes in which

members of the *camorra* contact those around Lorenzo and Nunzio in order to gain information to incriminate Borelli; it is only then that the social services and police become involved.

30. On these groups and, in particular, the political dimension to their work, see La Trecchia 2003: 164–222. La Trecchia also discusses *Pianese Nunzio* as an example of socially and politically engaged cinema, although her characterisation of the film in terms of 'New-Neorealism' does not seem to me the most useful or appropriate way of approaching to the film (see La Trecchia 2009).

31. For example, ACEC (the Catholic Association of Cinema Exhibitors) defines the film as 'a programmatic, demagogic, misleading and squalid attempt to legitimise the repulsive figure of a homosexual paedophile' (www.db.acec.it).

32. The project was actually conceived several years earlier and entirely independently of Capuano's film.

CONCLUSION

The Evolution of Neapolitan Cinema

In the introduction I suggested that the NF, with its fixed narrative conventions and stereotypical use of readily identifiable locations, was largely responsible for the creation of the idea of a 'Neapolitan cinema' within popular consciousness. Subsequent chapters have explored how in recent years Neapolitan films have drawn on this tradition but also challenged and reconfigured its conventions. In order to understand better the reasons behind this change, it is useful to review briefly the notion of genre and generic evolution. In *Questions of Genre*, Steve Neale observes that:

> Genres do not consist only of films: they consist also, and equally, of specific systems of expectation and hypothesis which spectators bring with them to the cinema, and which interact with films themselves during the course of the viewing process . . . these systems of expectation and hypothesis involve a knowledge of . . . various regimes of verisimilitude, various systems of plausibility, motivation, justification and belief . . . As Tzvetan Todorov, in particular, has insisted, there are two broad types of verisimilitude applicable to representations: generic verisimilitude on the one hand, and, on the other, a broader social or cultural verisimilitude. Neither equates in any direct sense to 'reality' or 'truth'. (Neale 1990: 46–7)

Neale's comments are helpful in explaining the shift in conventions underpinning the construction of Neapolitan cinema. Chapter 2 suggested that the NF depended on both a set of generic conventions, deriving from melodrama, and particular cultural beliefs, which I termed a 'Neapolitan world view', and that these two were inextricably linked. Another way to describe this would be to say that cultural verisimilitude was translated into a particular regime of generic verisimilitude. The conventions of the NF, 'its regimes of verisimilitude, systems of plausibility, motivation, justification and belief', while rooted in the pre-existing conventions of melodrama, also constituted the perfect expression of a specific, regional culture and thus the NF was able to address an audience that shared this same belief system successfully. Such an interpretation is important for two reasons. Firstly, it allows us to reconfigure conventional analyses of Neapolitan cinema; rather than denigrating the films for being formulaic and stereotypical, we are now able to interpret them in terms of their conventions and the functions they served within a specific cultural context. This is the approach taken in Chapter 2. Secondly, it provides us with an additional framework for understanding the reasons behind the evolution from the NF to the NNC.

Chapter 1 explained how the industrial context of which Neapolitan cinema is a product has changed in recent years. Rather than arising from the kind of commercial-based production industry typical of Italy in the 1950s, it is now heavily reliant on State funding and based around director–producer figures concerned with ideas of authorial expression; rather than being addressed primarily to a local audience based around the second- and third-run sector, it is now aimed at a national (and occasionally international) audience based around first-run cinemas with particular emphasis on film festivals and cultural spaces of exhibition (art-house cinemas, film clubs, and so on). This shift in terms of the addresser and addressee has also implied a shift in the nature of the text itself, since neither the producers nor the consumers of the NNC share the same cultural beliefs as the producers and consumers of the NF.[1] A shift in cultural verisimilitude has led to a change in generic verisimilitude. A parallel can be made here with the so-called 'revisionist westerns' that emerged in the late 1960s and early 1970s, such as *Little Big Man* (1970, Arthur Penn), *McCabe and Mrs Miller* (1971, Robert Altman) and *The Hired Hand* (1971, Peter Fonda). These films sought to reconcile the western and its mythic narrative of the origins of American civilisation with the counter-cultural values that questioned the very fundamentals of that civilisation through a subversion of generic convention.

One of the standard interpretations of the NNC is that it has rejected the stereotypes of traditional Neapolitan cinema in favour of a greater realism. However, such an interpretation is potentially misleading. Todorov (drawing on Aristotle) observes that 'the verisimilar is not a relation between discourse and referent (the relation of truth) but between discourse and what readers believe is true' (quoted in Neale 1990: 47). Thus the images of Naples depicted and the kinds of discursive structure articulated by the NNC are not necessarily more authentic or real than those of earlier Neapolitan cinema, but they do correspond more closely to the beliefs held by filmmakers, national Italian audiences and the critical establishment. Significantly, the films of the NNC have been well received critically but have not found favour with popular Neapolitan audiences (see pp. 34–5) – a complete reversal of the way the NF was received. This explanation of the evolution of Neapolitan cinema invites an ideological reading of the films, exploring their relation to wider socio-political currents.

Chapter 3 demonstrated how the NNC has undercut the traditional, positive images of Naples and *napoletanità* with a newfound pessimism, while Chapter 4 showed how the traditional forms of narrating the city have been problematised or subjected to playful, postmodern pastiche. If, as Todorov's ideas would suggest, these approaches are not necessarily in the interest of greater realism, then what purpose do they serve? One could argue that they have aesthetic value in their own right. Let us consider again those three debuts that launched the NNC. Certainly, *Vito e gli altri* is characterised by a highly stylised, almost experimental aesthetic, which betrays the presence of a first-time director eager to try the expressive capabilities of a new medium – like a boy with the world's greatest train set, as Orson Welles once remarked – and this desire to experiment is undoubtedly one of the most striking differences from earlier Neapolitan cinema. Many critics commented on the style of *Morte di un matematico napoletano*, too, expressing surprise that a director associated with experimental theatre had produced such a classical work and commenting on Martone's mature stylistic assurance. Yet here too we see a first-time director keen to display his control of the medium and to avoid falling into the trap of clichéd rhetoric, and stylistic choices are paramount to this desire. Similarly, in *Libera*, Corsicato's postmodernism depends entirely on a firm grasp of prior cinematic styles and the ability to quote these playfully and upset their conventional connotations for comic effect. The experimental drive of *Vito e gli altri* can also be found in Gaudino's *Giro di lune tra terra e mare* and Marrazzo's *Malemare*, Martone's classical assurance and avoidance of cliché returns in Di Majo's *Autunno* and De Rinaldo's *Il manoscritto di Van Hecken*, and Corsicato's postmodernism resurfaces in De Bernardi's *Appassionate*.

This is not to suggest that there is not an element of greater 'realism' in some of the films of the NNC (Marra in particular springs to mind), but rather to suggest that it does not apply to the NNC as a whole. Rather than a pursuit of heightened realism, what the NNC is primarily concerned with is an escape from cliché and stereotype, a rejection of outmoded forms of representation. And I would suggest that this escape from stereotype fulfils an important role in relation to the position occupied by Naples and the South in current political discourse.

THE SOUTHERN QUESTION

In the previous chapters, we touched on the concept of the 'Southern Question' (*questione meridionale*) and its relationship to Neapolitan narrative tradition. The rise in the late 1980s of the Northern League (Lega Nord) with its federalist/separatist agenda has placed the Southern Question firmly back on the national agenda. In particular, the use of stereotypes in the frequently virulent attacks on the South by Umberto Bossi, the leader of the Northern League, has made the need for a more balanced depiction of Southern culture as pressing now as it was in the early parts of the nineteenth century. Concurrently, historiography has responded by re-addressing the Southern Question, approaching Southern culture through a range of different frameworks rather than solely through a binary opposition with the North and interpreting it simply as a 'problem'. In particular, there has been an emphasis on the plurality of political, social and cultural realities in the South and thus on studying these realities at a local level. For example, the problems inherent in the adoption of Edward Banfield's concept of amoral familism – originally applied to a very specific context in Lucania – as a descriptive term to cover the South as a whole have been highlighted. Thus writers such as Marta Petrusewicz, Paolo Macry, Nelson Moe and others have applied different models of analysis to a particular area or culture within the South, contributing to a portrait of Southern culture that resembles a detailed mosaic rather than the impressionist painting created by the work of earlier *meridionalisti*.[2] This paradigm shift is also evident in approaches to film history, which displays a newfound emphasis on studying the geographical complexity of Italian cinema and the history of the cinema of individual towns or regions.[3] This book is entirely consistent with such a methodology. It attempts to (re-)interpret Neapolitan filmmaking, traditionally viewed in relation to national cinema and judged pejoratively, on its own terms, making reference to specifically Neapolitan cultural traditions and social and political history.

In order to highlight the implications of the Southern Question for contemporary cinema, let us briefly examine two recent films that have taken Naples and the South not simply as their setting but also as their theme. Significantly, neither can be considered an expression of the NNC since they are both products of the national film industry made by non-Neapolitan filmmakers and are constrained by conventional approaches to the representation of Naples. *Incantesimo napoletano* [A Neapolitan Spell] (2002, Paolo Genovese and Luca Miniero) is a comic fable about two ultra-traditional Neapolitans who are shocked when their daughter Assuntina's first words are 'Mamy' rather than

'Mammà'.[4] The girl grows up speaking only Milanese dialect, prefers *risotto* and *panettone* to *spaghetti alle vongole* and *sfogliatelle*, and spends her spare time sketching the Duomo in Milan. Her father, Gianni, says he could understand if she spoke standard Italian, but why Milanese? And so he does his best to teach her to be Neapolitan, hiring a linguist to teach her dialect and even baptising her in the Bay of Naples. What we are presented with is a parable of inverse racism; rather than the Northern distrust of the South typical of the Northern League, we are presented with the South's attachment to its own traditions and rejection of the North. What is significant is the extent to which the innocent Assuntina becomes a victim of this process, confined to her home and forbidden to meet anyone for fear of the shame she will bring her parents. As a last resort she is sent to Torre del Greco, where they 'speak such a thick dialect that they cannot even understand one another!'[5] But Assuntina takes advantage of this newfound freedom and, on discovering that sexuality does not know racist prejudice, sleeps with every young man she can find. She returns pregnant and ignorant of the father's identity, provoking Gianni's final, complete breakdown. He emerges when his grandchild is born, only for the process to begin anew as he immediately attempts to teach the newborn baby his first words in Neapolitan dialect.

Incantesimo napoletano is an extremely effective and amusing comedy. However, it remains firmly rooted in an established comic tradition that plays on the opposition between Northern and Southern stereotypes. A perfect example of this tradition is *Milanesi a Napoli* [Milanese in Naples] (1954, Enzo Di Gianni), in which a Northern industrialist descends on Naples with the intention of industrially producing and mass-marketing the pizza.[6] A string of comic plays on cultural stereotypes eventually leads to a finale that attempts to reconcile these two conflicting traditions through a literal double marriage between Northerners and Southerners. However, in the closing scenes, Ugo Tognazzi's Northern industrialist rejects his new wife's suggestion that 'the rhythm of your machines will fuse with the sweetness of our melodies,' claiming that 'our machines are made in Switzerland and, in any case, we want to listen to your melodies here [in Naples].' The film ends on the motto that 'one moment of Naples . . . is enough to become Neapolitan,' reflecting the idea that the two different cultures can never be reconciled and suggesting that one must necessarily absorb and replace the other. The negative implications of such a tradition are more evident in a recent comedy far less sophisticated than *Incantesimo napoletano*, *La Repubblica di San Gennaro* [The Republic of San Gennaro] (2003, Massimo Costa). The film takes place in 2013, after Italy has voted in favour of the secession of the North from the South that the Northern League has been fighting for, and is set in a walled ghetto for Southern migrants on the outskirts of Milan. Its protagonist is Gennaro Strummolo, an inmate in the camp who nevertheless is desperate to affirm his Northern European status, calling himself Genny Strumm. The film thus presents us with a Neapolitan who has absorbed the negative criticisms of the Northern League and attempts to erase his own identity as a result. Whereas in *Incantesimo napoletano* Gianni reaffirms his own cultural identity and in so doing refuses to accept or enter into dialogue with anything that lies outside that tradition, Gennaro Strummolo attempts to deny and erase his cultural heritage. Both, however, remain mired in the binary thinking of the Southern Question from which recent approaches to the South, such as those described above, have attempted to escape.

Beyond Stereotype: a New Gaze on Naples

The films described above stress Naples' and the South's estrangement from the rest of Italy and construct its otherness in terms of a problem, like the earliest *meridionalisti*. Although they are both comedies intended as light entertainment, they nevertheless embody a series of deep-rooted political questions, since the construction of Naples as an other perpetuates its alienation from the political process, something Bassolino attempted to reverse by creating Neapolitan 'citizens' (see p. 160). Their narratives suggest that an Italian national politics cannot encompass the realities of both North and South. Ever since the earliest *meridionalisti*, the idea of a Southern Question has implied a process of State intervention in which the South must be supported and changed by national political policy in order to overcome its internal difficulties. However, such a project has not been successful in solving the South's problems, and in many cases has merely exacerbated them. For example, attempts to foster economic growth through industrialisation have resulted in urban decay and internal migration, which have further damaged the fabric of Southern society. The South has responded either by internalising such negative stereotypes (as in the case of Gennaro Strummolo) or by attempting to counter them through an affirmation of its own culture (as in the case of Gianni). These approaches can be considered two sides of the same coin, and neither is without its problems.

The films of the NF mirror Gianni's position, presenting us with an ossified image of traditional Neapolitan culture in the face of change and emphasising the local and the familial at the expense of the social. This works against political engagement and, in some cases, even leads to the perpetuation and glorification of anti-social and criminal structures such as the *camorra*. The films starring Mario Merola and Pino Mauro provide a good example of this. Stefano Masi has argued that these films represent a fusion between the NF and the urban crime films (*polizieschi*) popular in Italy in the 1970s (Masi 1982). However, it could also be argued that they represent a natural extension of the ideology of the NF: the need for the individual to protect himself and his family from an external threat in the absence of a State or institution capable of structuring society and aiding the individual. In these films the figure of the *guappo* dear to earlier Neapolitan films naturally evolves into the *camorrista* and it is significant that the film which effectively launched Merola's career was titled *L'ultimo guappo* [The Last Guappo] (1978, Alfonso Brescia).[7] Within the NNC Antonio Capuano, in particular, seems to be acutely aware of this danger. The speech of a reformed *camorrista* during a mass for a victim of *camorra* violence in *Pianese Nunzio*, for example, emphasises the extent to which popular Neapolitan narratives can provide a justification for such criminal practices:

> When I was little I used to go to see *sceneggiate* and I believed that people could be divided into two categories: those that command respect and everybody else. It took me a long time to realise I was mistaken, that things are not like this, and that *camorristi* are all sad and deluded individuals who believe they are somebody when in reality they are nobody.

With *Luna rossa*, Capuano suggests that the *Gemeinschaft* philosophy lies at the root of the *camorra*, while in *Pianese Nunzio* he reappropriates elements of this popular culture but uses them to very different 'political' ends.

The questioning of stereotypical depictions of Naples and Neapolitan culture and the re-interpretation of its narrative conventions thus fulfil an important, political function.[8] In the NNC the family and localised community is either shown to exist no longer or to be the site of internal conflict and repression; the archetype of the joyous and liberated *scugnizzo* is replaced by a marginalised and alienated figure who is no longer absorbed back into the family but instead recruited into organised crime; the divine and the miraculous are no longer seen as a means of resolving social and personal problems but are presented as an absurd mystification; the notions of honour, exclusivity and sexual purity underpinning gender relations are shown to conceal misogyny, patriarchal repression, exclusion and domestic violence; and the subservience of the individual to the family or the localised community is revealed as the basis of the *camorra* and of political stasis.

On one level, therefore, the NNC can be considered as very much a political cinema. Francesco Rosi's *Le mani sulla città/Hands over the City* (1963) is arguably the first film to engage with Naples and its problems in an explicitly critical, political fashion, revealing the political corruption that lay behind the building speculation of the Lauro era. Its approach is completely different from that of earlier Neapolitan films, but it is also an approach that has not significantly influenced later Neapolitan filmmaking; it is an isolated case, an extraordinary film, but one that is closer to the Italian political cinema of the period (of which Rosi was the principal exponent) than to Neapolitan cinema before or since. Rosi is interested in revealing a socio-political truth concealed by the corrupt institutions of big business and party politics; the NNC, on the other hand, is concerned with reconfiguring the way in which the city is depicted and narrated. In a sense, this is also what Bassolino's political project was all about – reconfiguring the image of Naples in order to bring about political change – although, as Chapter 5 demonstrated, the ways in which the NNC and Bassolino have set about doing this are radically different, as are the images of Naples they have articulated.

As stated in the introduction to this book, Antonio Capuano has asserted that the films of the NNC are defined by the presence of a 'new gaze' on Naples (Author's interview, Naples, 14 June 2003). But what are the characteristics of this gaze and to whom does it belong? Capuano's own films are characterised by the unmistakeable presence of an other, an external gaze on the diegetic reality; thus, while *Vito e gli altri* attempts to narrate the *scugnizzo*'s experience from within (Capuano's stated goal), there is also both a sociological and an anthropological dimension to his analysis and a deliberate use of radical stylistic devices that serve to defamiliarise the material.[9] The presence of such an external perspective is characteristic of many of the films of the NNC. It is present in the postmodern irony that Corsicato brings to 'trash' culture, to the *sceneggiata*, to neomelodic Neapolitan song and to the 'baser' elements of popular Catholicism (in particular the Neapolitan belief in miracles, also parodied by De Lillo in *Matilda*). It is present in the way in which Stefano Incerti fuses the narrative conventions of the *sceneggiata* with an analysis of urban alienation borrowed from the New Hollywood in *Il verificatore*. And it is present in the sociological and political investigation of the marginalised urban poor in the films of Vincenzo Marra. All of the films of the NNC testify to the unmistakeable presence of an authorial gaze.

The Future of Neapolitan Cinema

To conclude, then, there is a clear line of continuity throughout the history of Neapolitan cinema and the NNC does share the same cultural roots as the NF. However, there is also something decidedly new about these films in terms of the position that they choose to take in relation to these roots. Central to this shift is the authorial presence within the films. Whereas the films of the NF are mostly homogenous (be they produced by Amoroso, Montillo or Di Gianni, or directed by Fizzarotti, Montero or Furlan), the films of Capuano, Corsicato, Martone et al. all present significant differences from one another, and it is these differences that critics have found difficult to reconcile with the idea of a coherent 'school' or 'movement'. Critics who are reluctant to use such loaded terminology and substitute it with vague and largely meaningless terms like 'Neapolitan laboratory' are hedging their bets; they sense the need to associate these films, but are hesitant to do so because they have failed to identify clearly what it is that they have in common. All of the films of the NNC – regardless of their generic, thematic or stylistic differences – reflect a desire to engage critically with Neapolitan society and culture, to problematise existing forms of representation, and to propose new ways of depicting the city and its culture. It is precisely this critical engagement that distinguishes the NNC both from earlier Neapolitan filmmaking and from the majority of Italian films produced in recent years, and that makes these films so richly rewarding.

Where does this leave the NNC on its twentieth anniversary? The number of films that can be ascribed to the NNC has dwindled from 20 between 1995 and 1999 and 17 between 2000 and 2004 to just 6 between 2005 and 2009. Several filmmakers have moved on and joined the national film industry; indeed, since his relocation to Rome, Sorrentino has, with films like *Il divo* (2008), become arguably the most high-profile and critically successful Italian director to emerge since the new millennium.[10] Megaris closed its doors in 2003 and Indigo Film relocated to Rome, where, in collaboration with Fandango, it has become one of the most innovative of independent producers; only Teatri Uniti, Artimagiche/Thule Film and Figli del Bronx continue production in the city. These facts would suggest that the unique cultural and industrial moment that opened up with Bassolino's government and the New Cinema Law in the early 1990s and allowed the NNC to flourish has possibly passed. So has the NNC left us with anything other than a uniquely interesting body of films to be consigned to history? I would suggest that it has and perhaps the best evidence can be found, paradoxically, in a product of the national film industry: the internationally celebrated *Gomorra* (2008, Matteo Garrone).[11]

Numerous critics have drawn attention to the fact that *Gomorra* undercuts all the stereotypes of the gangster genre, deglamorising its subject in order to 'give organised crime back its everyday ordinariness' (Masoni et al. 2008: 9). Yet surprisingly few – particularly in Italy – have commented on its rejection of a stereotypical image of Naples and this omission alone betrays the quantum shift in the cinematic conception of the city that has taken place in just under two decades. As in so much of the NNC, in *Gomorra* the setting is the post-industrial hinterland to the North of the city: the area around Caserta, Casal de Principe and, above all, the omnipresent Scampia with its Vele. As in *Luna rossa*, the focus is exclusively on the brutal and devastating effect of the *camorra* and here, too, we can interpret this analysis in terms of the collapse of the *Gemeinschaft* society. The failed architectural project of Scampia, which prevents any possibility of the formation of a sense of community, the absence of any social or economic prospects for its inhabitants and their consequent rejection of the socio-political beliefs of the *Gesellschaft* and the institutions of the State create an enormous and desperate void. The only thing capable of filling that void is the *camorra*, which, significantly, is only ever referred to as 'the System'. This System constitutes 'the connective tissue of the community', a 'para-welfare state' (ibid.: 10 and 14), and the film focuses exclusively on the way this System infiltrates every facet of life in the city: from an innocent housewife who ends up murdered because of a clan war to which she was entirely extraneous, to a master tailor whose talent will only be exploited and never recognised, a gifted and educated young man whose only employment prospects lie within the morally and legally compromised waste disposal business, and two young *scugnizzi* whose lack of cultural horizons lead them to tragically misinterpret their place in society and the inevitability of their destiny. The analysis of a concrete, resolutely local reality offered by Garrone is characteristic of the work of the post-*Meridionalisti* historians described above, of which Roberto Saviano's 2006 book on which the film is based is a good example. The world of *Gomorra* is never seen in opposition to the North;[12] it is analysed in its concrete specificity, much like the *scugnizzi* problem is in *Vito e gli altri*. This approach generated consternation amongst some critics, who regretted the absence of any analysis of the role of the State, the legal system and international business in the perpetuation of this System (for example, see Angrisani 2008). However, this absence is precisely the point of the film; these institutions are entirely lacking from the socio-cultural horizons of the inhabitants of the world depicted, and it is this lack that permits the System to exist. Garrone's choice to restrict his focus to these four of the ten narratives contained in Saviano's book is thus a significant one. Despite this fact, the film concludes with four brief captions revealing that Scampia is the biggest open drug market in the world, that the *camorra* has killed more people than any other criminal organisation in Europe, and that it has even invested in the reconstruction of the Twin Towers in New York. It is a simple but brilliant move that suddenly shifts the audience's focus from the micro-histories in which they have been immersed for two hours to the macro-history of the *camorra*'s role in a global context.[13]

There are numerous affinities, then, between *Gomorra* and the NNC: the focus on the new heart of Naples centred on Scampia,[14] the micro-analysis of a particular social reality, the interpretation of the *camorra* as the product of the collapse of traditional social structures, and the focus on the flip-side of the Neapolitan renaissance.[15] Furthermore, just as Piscicelli, Capuano and Incerti brought a new gaze to a traditional Neapolitan generic matrix by adopting a stylistic register borrowed from extraneous cultural traditions, so Garrone builds his unconventional gangster film through stylistic devices characteristic of modern European art cinema. Shot on location with a constantly moving hand-held camera in thick dialect necessitating subtitles even for its Italian release, the film is stylistically perched somewhere between the uncompromising realism of *Tornando a casa* and the baroque stylisation of *Pianese Nunzio*.[16] In short, the film embodies elements of all three of the tendencies discussed in Chapters

3 to 5: a shift to a negative conception of *napoletanità*, the reconfiguration of conventional narrative and stylistic models, and the addition of a 'political' interpretation of Neapolitan reality. Garrone appears to have recognised, understood and digested the innovations of the NNC and reconfigured them into something relevant and dramatically engaging not just for a national audience, but for an international one too.[17] Although the fact that it took a Roman director and the Rome-based Fandango to realise a film based on a book that is very much a product of a specific regional analysis should give us pause for thought about the current health of the Neapolitan production industry, the fact that the Italian national film industry has assimilated the lessons of the NNC so well should also give us hope that the cinema will no longer be able to recycle the same images and narrative clichés of Naples with complete naïveté.

Thus it looks as if the 'new gaze' of the NNC will continue to make its presence felt, providing much needed creative impetus to Italian national cinema for years to come through the work of directors like Sorrentino, whose approach to cinema was formed within this context, and those, like Garrone, that it influenced. And we can hope that directors like Martone, Capuano and Corsicato will continue to plough their individual authorial furrows both in Naples and beyond. We need only wait for industrial and political conditions in Naples to become ripe once more, allowing independent production to flourish in the city again, as it has with periodic regularity throughout the first century of cinema history.[18]

NOTES

1. See the discussion of exhibition statistics on pp. 32–5.
2. On the development of this new approach to the South, see Lumley and Morris 1997 and in particular Jonathan Morris's overview, 'Challenging Meridionalismo: Constructing a New History for Southern Italy' on pp. 1–19.
3. On the regional variations of Italian cinema as a whole, see Martini 1997 and Martini and Morelli 1997. There is an extensive and ever-expanding bibliography on the cinemas of individual regions, of which I will cite only a couple of the most significant examples dealing with the South: Gesù 1993, Morreale 1996 and Scarfò 1990. As far as individual cities are concerned, see the series of volumes published by Marsilio under the collective title *Luci sulla città*.
4. Thus the film revolves around 'Neapolitan fundamentalism', which Medusa's DVD helpfully defines as 'a misguided civic pride . . . a dangerous illness that leads one to confuse [the city's] vices with its virtues'.
5. The film subtitles the ludicrously unintelligible conversation between the aunt and uncle from Torre del Greco until even the subtitles lose track of the conversation and comically admit defeat.
6. The film is a product of the Neapolitan firm Eva Film, which specialised in the NF, and is directed by the Neapolitan Enzo Di Gianni.
7. Merola actually made his debut in *Sgarro alla camorra* (1973, Ettore Maria Fizzarotti) but it was this title, made five years later, that launched a whole series of films starring the popular singer.

8. Interestingly, Capuano has stated: 'I'm not afraid of representing anything that exists. You can even represent a picture-postcard Naples. It depends on what you want to narrate . . . I do things in complete freedom. I tell a certain type of story in the way that I want to, but not in order to escape from stereotypes. It's not a problem for me' (Author's interview, Naples, 14 June 2003). Regardless of his intentions, by telling 'a certain type of story in the way that he wants to', Capuano undoubtedly does challenge existing stereotypes as, I hope, has been amply demonstrated in previous chapters.

9. See Marlow-Mann, forthcoming 2012.

10. Other directors to film outside Naples include Incerti, Martone and Marra. Even Capuano has recently completed a film set in Turin (*Giallo?*, 2009), although his next (provisionally titled *L'amore buio*) is once again set in Naples.

11. The Rome-born Matteo Garrone also made the fascinating *L'imbalsamatore/The Embalmer* (2002), which is set in the hinterland between Naples and Caserta and also offers a decidedly unconventional take on the region and its culture.

12. Significantly, the only time such an opposition is raised in the film it is by Franco (Toni Servillo), who uses it to abdicate all moral responsibility and justify the toxic waste disposal business he represents, thus undermining the validity of such a position.

13. Admittedly, Garrone's film never goes as far as Saviano, who clearly shows that the *camorra* is not an aberration but rather a logical consequence of global capitalism.

14. A recent literary-sociological account of the area is significantly entitled 'Naples Begins in Scampia' (Braucci and Zoppoli 2005).

15. It is interesting to compare *Gomorra* to *Vedi Napoli e poi muori* (2007), a feature documentary by Neapolitan director Enrico Caria. This self-reflexive work depicts Caria's return to Naples (after heeding De Filippo's advice and fleeing to Rome in the early 1980s) with the intention of participating in the Neapolitan renaissance and producing a documentary on such an important cultural moment. However, the reality he finds there is very different from the media's image and when the *camorra* wars erupt in the periphery, he chooses to make a very different documentary, focusing instead on Scampia.

16. See, for example, the contrast between the sequences detailing Don Ciro's rounds delivering money and the stylised, almost surreal opening sequence in the tanning salon.

17. It took all of the major prizes at the David di Donatello and European Film Awards, as well as the Grand Prize at the Cannes Film Festival. It was also nominated for the Cannes Palme d'Or and the Bafta for best foreign language film. It has been widely distributed and critically well received internationally and has done excellent box office.

18. The construction of a large complex of film and television studios in Bagnoli, which is currently in the planning stages, could, potentially, favour the next renewal.

APPENDICES

Appendix 1: Location of Production Companies in Italy (1930–2009)

Date	Number in Italy	Number in Rome	Number in the regions	Number in Naples	Percentage in Rome	Percentage in the regions	Percentage in Naples
1930–4	43	37	6	0	86.0	14.0	0.0
1935–9	121	105	16	0	86.8	13.2	0.0
1940–4	126	107	19	0	84.9	15.1	0.0
1945–9	217	158	59	7	72.8	27.2	3.2
1950–4	381	295	86	11	77.4	22.6	2.9
1955–9	366	303	63	7	82.8	17.2	1.9
1960–4	473	408	65	5	86.3	13.7	1.1
1965–9	508	447	61	7	88.0	12.0	1.4
1970–4	586	507	79	7	86.5	13.5	1.2
1975–9	512	443	69	6	86.5	13.5	1.2
1980–4	429	343	86	10	80.0	20.0	2.3
1985–9	411	336	75	3	81.8	18.2	0.7
1990–4	444	344	100	10	77.5	22.5	2.3
1995–9	378	323	49	7	85.4	13.0	1.9
2000–4	275	208	59	9	75.6	21.5	3.3
2005–9	345	251	86	10	72.8	24.9	2.9

Figures for 1930–94 are based on an elaboration of the list of production companies in Bernardini (2000).
Figures for 1995–99 are based on the lists in the *Annuario del cinema italiano & audiovisivi* and the *Cinema italiano annuario* for those years. Figures for 2000–9 are based on the list in www.filmitalia.org.
It was not possible to identify all of the companies in operation in the period 1995–2009 (and this explains the drop in the total number of companies operating in Italy during this period). The totals for this period should therefore be considered less accurate; however, the percentages should still be indicative.

Appendix 2: Exhibition Statistics for the New Neapolitan Cinema

Title (date of production)	Release date	City of release	No. of cities	Naples as % of capozona	Naples as % of total	Milan as % of capozona	Milan as % of total	Spectators (total)
Matilda (1990)	19/10/1990	Naples	12	20.6	20.1	0.0	0.0	10478
Vito e gli altri (1991)	12/09/1991	Naples	13	49.4	47.8	6.4	6.2	4642
Morte di un matematico napoletano (1992)	08/09/1992	Naples	60	16.6	12.3	15.2	11.2	131225
Baby Gang (1992)	03/12/1992	Naples	1	100.0	100.0	0.0	0.0	554
Libera (1993)	16/04/1993	Naples	43	12.8	11.5	17.6	15.8	82993
Rasoi (1993)	16/03/1994	Rome	8	48.9	42.1	0.0	0.0	3014
L'amore molesto (1995)	12/04/1995	Naples	95	17.6	12.2	15.8	11.0	342788
Il verificatore (1995)	01/09/1995	Wide	23	31.4	24.7	16.6	13.1	9743
I buchi neri (1995)	04/10/1995	Naples	63	16.0	9.8	24.0	14.7	101683
Racconti di Vittoria (1995)	03/05/1996	Naples	2	100.0	66.3	0.0	0.0	89
Pianese Nunzio: 14 anni a Maggio (1996)	05/09/1996	Wide	57	36.0	26.4	18.7	13.7	46656
Isotta (1996)	30/04/1997	Rome	3	0.0	0.0	0.0	0.0	539
I vesuviani (1997)	04/09/1997	Wide	39	43.1	27.0	10.9	6.8	19272
Per tutto il tempo che ci resta (1998)	24/04/1998	Rome/Bari	10	10.4	10.2	9.2	9.0	3651
Teatro di guerra (1998)	30/04/1998	Wide	53	19.1	15.1	19.9	15.7	55313
Polvere di Napoli (1998)	08/05/1998	Wide	17	27.4	26.4	8.3	8.0	20841
Giro di lune tra terra e mare (1997)	24/09/1998	Rome	10	25.5	21.5	13.3	11.2	7042
Prima del tramonto (1999)	03/09/1999	Wide	30	24.1	17.6	14.5	10.5	9241
Autunno (1999)	03/09/1999	Wide	31	26.7	20.6	9.0	6.9	25205
Appassionate (1999)	19/11/1999	Wide	16	41.6	24.9	6.2	3.7	6399
Rose e pistole (1998)	03/12/1999	Naples	6	20.9	20.9	12.4	12.4	3462
Il manoscritto di van Hecken (1998)	17/12/1999	Naples	2	100.0	71.6	0.0	0.0	222

Film	Date	Location						
Lontano in fondo agli occhi (2000)	02/03/2001	Rome	5	0.0	0.0	0.0	0.0	3871
Chimera (2001)	06/04/2001	Wide	16	16.9	15.9	39.3	36.8	21343
Non con un bang (1999)	25/05/2001	Rome	1	0.0	0.0	0.0	0.0	1606
L'uomo in più (2001)	01/09/2001	Wide	49	29.4	22.8	5.3	4.1	17306
Tornando a casa (2001)	07/09/2001	Wide	44	13.6	9.5	23.3	16.2	19556
Luna rossa (2001)	12/10/2001	Rome/Naples	33	42.7	35.8	5.1	4.3	14415
Ribelli per caso (2000)	14/12/2001	Rome	20	36.8	28.1	8.0	6.1	9050
Non è giusto (2001)	05/04/2002	Wide	13	28.0	25.9	27.3	25.1	4092
La vita degli altri (2001)	24/04/2002	Rome	4	27.4	16.7	0.0	0.0	3670
Fondali notturni (1998)	27/09/2002	Wide	3	0.0	0.0	2.9	2.9	1549
Capo Nord (2002)	07/03/2003	Wide	7	26.6	17.1	2.8	1.8	3849
Pater Familias (2003)	14/03/2003	Wide	28	43.1	35.2	5.1	4.2	8963
E io ti seguo (2003)	11/06/2004	Naples	3	100.0	71.8	0.0	0.0	655
Te lo leggo negli occhi (2004)	03/09/2004	Wide	79	10.9	6.7	8.3	5.1	36593
Vento di terra (2003)	17/09/2004	Wide	42	8.6	6.4	18.1	13.4	11951
Le conseguenze dell'amore (2004)	24/09/2004	Wide	165	11.4	7.5	18.7	12.3	171918
Il resto di niente (2004)	25/03/2005	Wide	55	42.8	33.4	13.8	10.8	47008
La guerra di Mario (2005)	03/03/2006	Wide	138	15.2	9.3	14.8	9.1	66914
Fuoco su di me (2006)	31/03/2006	Wide	64	47.7	31.0	5.9	3.9	24350
Mater Natura (2005)	21/04/2006	Wide	60	29.7	21.5	16.7	12.0	20512
I cinghiali di Portici (2003)	07/07/2006	–	–	–	–	–	–	–
Il seme della discordia (2008)	05/09/2008	–	–	–	–	–	–	–
Ossidiana (2007)	13/11/2008	–	–	–	–	–	–	–
Tris di donne & abiti nuziali (2009)	18/09/2009	–	–	–	–	–	–	–
Malemare (1997)	N/A	–	–	–	–	–	–	–

Appendix 2: (continued)

Title (date of production)	Release date	City of release	No. of cities	Naples as % of *capozona*	Naples as % of total	Milan as % of *capozona*	Milan as % of total	Spectators (total)
Tatuaggi (1997)	N/A	–	–	–	–	–	–	–
La volpe a tre zampe (2002)	N/A	–	–	–	–	–	–	–
Sotto la stessa luna (2006)	N/A	–	–	–	–	–	–	–
Average				20.3	14.7	15.9	11.5	32 720

Source: Data compiled from the end-of-season reports published in *Il giornale dello spettacolo: Borsa Film*. They ceased to publish a regional breakdown of statistics in 2007, so data for more recent films are not available. Percentages are based on the number of spectators in the first-run cinemas of the principal Italian cities.

Appendix 3: Exhibition Statistics for a Selection of Popular Neapolitan Films

Title (date of production)	Release date	City of release	No. of cities	Naples as % of *capozona*	Naples as % of total	Milan as % of *capozona*	Milan as % of total	Spectators (total)
Neapolitan Formula								
Fatalità (1991)	04/10/1991	Naples	5	83.4	55.4	0.0	0.0	10995
Attenti a noi due (1994)	21/01/1994	Naples	3	91.3	84.1	0.0	0.0	1423
Annarè (1998)	30/04/1998	Naples	15	98.5	66.4	1.0	0.7	33418
Cient'anne (1999)	12/02/1999	Naples	9	100.0	61.7	0.0	0.0	25922
Aitanic (2000)	27/10/2000	Wide	56	90.3	25.4	0.0	0.0	129869
Il latitante (2003)	17/01/2003	Naples	11	100.0	21.5	0.0	0.0	18815
Average (Neapolitan Formula)				94.0	37.4	0.2	0.1	36740
Neapolitan comics								
Pensavo fosse amore . . . (1992)	20/12/1991	Naples	91	11.8	6.6	15.9	8.9	1049589
Il postino (1994)	22/09/1994	Wide	97	17.3	9.0	15.4	8.0	1287802
L'amico del cuore (1998)	16/12/1998	Naples	116	53.7	30.9	5.4	3.1	690194
Amore a prima vista (1999)	29/10/1999	Wide	166	45.0	20.0	5.0	2.2	748282
Volesse il cielo (2002)	25/01/2002	Wide	163	56.5	18.4	4.6	1.5	313646
Cose da pazzi (2005)	25/03/2005	Wide	167	56.7	14.6	3.4	0.9	338603
Average (Neapolitan comics)				30.1	14.8	11.1	5.5	738019
Other (Wertmüller, Loy etc.)								
Pacco, doppio pacco e contropaccotto (1993)	22/01/1993	Wide	32	44.0	32.2	5.8	4.2	90252
Ninfa Plebea (1996)	12/04/1996	Wide	100	32.3	15.9	5.4	2.7	162786
N'gopp (2002)	17/05/2002	Naples/Bari	30	81.8	28.6	2.1	0.7	20824
Incantesimo napoletano (2002)	08/02/2002	Wide	97	27.5	15.5	14.1	7.9	154951
La repubblica di San Gennaro (2003)	06/06/2003	Wide	6	11.4	10.8	0.0	0.0	4046
Totò Sapore e la storia magica della pizza (2003)	19/12/2003	Wide	214	24.2	10.8	10.5	4.7	106046
Average (other Neapolitan films)				33.2	18.0	8.8	4.7	89818
Overall								
Average (overall)				32.7	16.1	10.5	5.2	

Source: Data compiled from the end-of-season reports published in *Il giornale dello spettacolo: Borsa Film*. Percentages are based on the number of spectators in the first-run cinemas of the principal Italian cities.

Appendix 4: Percentage of the Audience for the New Neapolitan Cinema Located in Naples

Legend: □ Naples as a Percentage of Capozona   ■ Naples as a Percentage of Total   □ Naples as a Percentage of Total

Categories (top to bottom): Average, Mater Natura, Fuoco su di me, La guerra di Mario, Il resto di niente, Le conseguenze dell'amore, Vento di terra, Te lo leggo negli occhi, E io ti o segno, Pater Familias, Capo Nord, Fondali notturni, La vita degli altri, Non è giusto, Ribelli per caso, Luna rossa, Tornando a casa, L'uomo in più, Non con un bang, Chimera, Lontano in fondo agli occhi, Il manoscritto di van Hecken, Rose e pistole, Appassionate, Autunno, Prima del tramonto, Giro di lune tra terra e mare, Polvere di Napoli, Teatro di guerra, Per tutto il tempo che ci resta, I vesuviani, Isotta, Pianese Nunzio: 14 anni a Maggio, Raccolti di Vittoria, I buchi neri, Il verificatore, L'amore molesto, Rasoi, Libera, Baby Gang, Morte di un matematico napoletano, Vito e gli altri, Matilda

Axis: 0, 10, 20, 30, 40, 50, 60, 70, 80, 90, 100

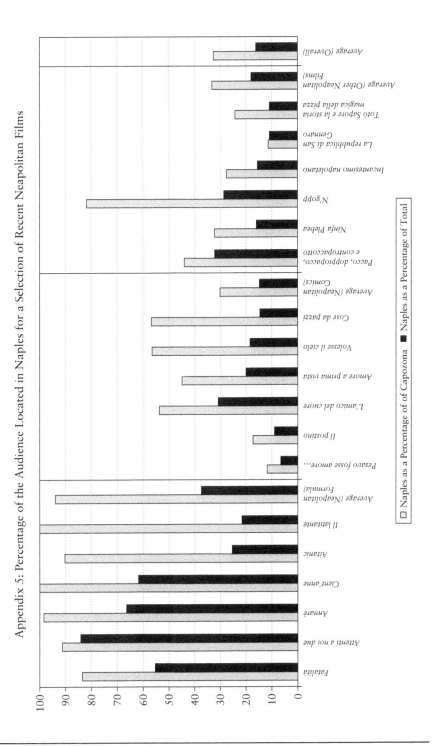

Appendix 5: Percentage of the Audience Located in Naples for a Selection of Recent Neapolitan Films

□ Naples as a Percentage of of Capozona   ■ Naples as a Percentage of Total
□ Naples as a Percentage of Total

Appendix 6: Locations of the New Neapolitan Cinema: the City of Naples

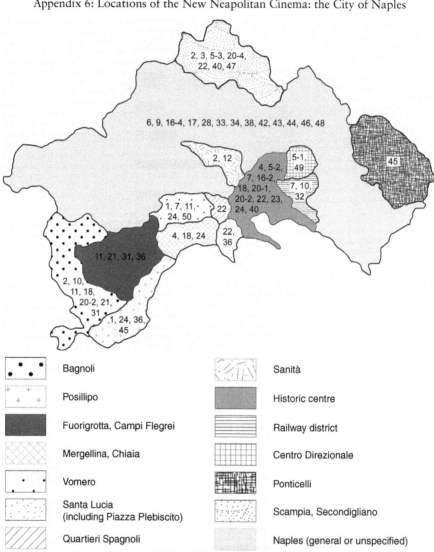

Bagnoli		Sanità	
Posillipo		Historic centre	
Fuorigrotta, Campi Flegrei		Railway district	
Mergellina, Chiaia		Centro Direzionale	
Vomero		Ponticelli	
Santa Lucia (including Piazza Plebiscito)		Scampia, Secondigliano	
Quartieri Spagnoli		Naples (general or unspecified)	

Note: The numbers refer to the films included in the Filmography; a hyphen followed by an additional number indicates the episode within an anthology feature.

Appendix 7: Locations of the New Neapolitan Cinema: the Province of Naples

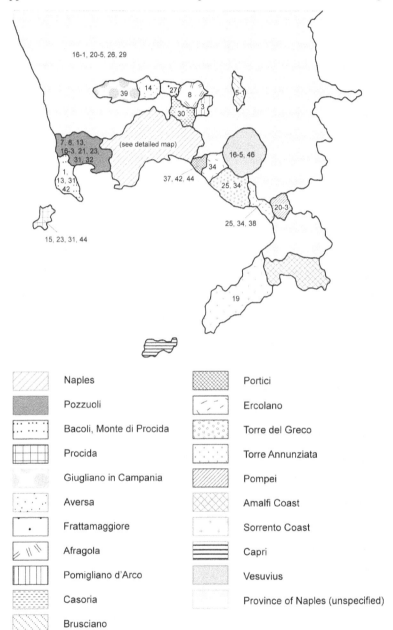

Naples		Portici	
Pozzuoli		Ercolano	
Bacoli, Monte di Procida		Torre del Greco	
Procida		Torre Annunziata	
Giugliano in Campania		Pompei	
Aversa		Amalfi Coast	
Frattamaggiore		Sorrento Coast	
Afragola		Capri	
Pomigliano d'Arco		Vesuvius	
Casoria		Province of Naples (unspecified)	
Brusciano			

Note: The numbers refer to the films included in the Filmography; a hyphen followed by an additional number indicates the episode within an anthology feature.

Appendix 8: Key Figures of the New Neapolitan Cinema

One of the most frequently made arguments in favour of the existence of a NNC is the fact that the filmmakers all draw on a common pool of Neapolitan actors and technicians to make their films. In order to demonstrate this empirically, this appendix lists those people who have made a significant contribution to the NNC. The numbers following each entry refer to the Filmography and indicate the films on which they worked. The capacities in which they served are also indicated, with the earliest role(s) played listed first. All are believed to be of Neapolitan origin unless otherwise indicated. At the foot of the filmography is a short list of the most significant production companies, followed by their location and the name of the associated producer(s).

PEOPLE

1. **Accetta, Cesare** (1,4,6,7,9,15,16–2,24,29,31,36,37,42)
   Still photographer then cinematographer. Member of Teatri Uniti.
2. **Apuzzo, Carla** (3,21)
   Writer, producer and director. Founding member of Falco Film.
3. **Avitabile, Anna** (5,8,16)
   Actress. See Figure 4.2.
4. **Bigazzi, Luca** (4,7,16,41,45)
   Milanese cinematographer.
5. **Bonaiuto, Anna** (4,7,16,22,23)
   Actress born in Udine.
6. **Boscaino, Luigi** (4,5,6,7,8,10,11,16,21,22,26,29,49)
   Production assistant.
7. **Bruschetta, Antonino** (5,8,10,26,33,37,38)
   Sicilian actor, a.k.a. Ninni Bruschetta.
8. **Bufi Landi, Aldo** (13,19,36)
   Historic Neapolitan actor of stage, screen and *sceneggiata*; star of *Malaspina* (1947).
9. **Calzone, Maria Pia** (19,28,39,46)
   Actress.
10. **Cantalupo, Salvatore** (21,22,23,50)
    Actor.
11. **Capodanno, Paola** (1,9,16,31)
    Production assistant, assistant director and producer. Assistant to Antonietta De Lillo and partner in Megaris.
12. **Capuano, Antonio** 2,12,16–3,20,30,45
    Writer, director and producer.

13. **Carpentieri, Renato** (4,9,10,16,18,22,34,48)
     Actor born in Avellino.
14. **Catalano, Pasquale** (8,16,33,41,45)
     Composer.
15. **Cecchi, Carlo** (4,23,30)
     Actor born in Florence.
16. **Cecere, Emanuele** (10,11,18,25,27,29,30,36,37,41,45)
     Sound recordist.
17. **Celoro, Italo** (7,30,33,39)
     Actor.
18. **Cima, Francesca** (9,26,33,36,41,45)
     Production assistant, then producer.
19. **Corsicato, Pappi** (5,8,16,29,49)
     Director, writer and producer. Also musician and art director on his own films.
20. **Curti, Angelo** (4,6,7,10,22,26,33,36,38,41)
     Producer. Member of Teatri Uniti.
21. **De Cicco, Rosaria** (2,12,33,45)
     Actress.
22. **De Francesco, Roberto** (4,10,22,23,33,38)
     Actor. Member of Teatri Uniti.
23. **De Lillo, Antonietta** (1,4,9,16,31,42)
     Director, writer and producer. Partner in An.Gio Film and Megaris.
24. **De Rinaldo, Nicola** (18,34)
     Writer and director.
25. **Di Majo, Nina** (7,10,16,22,24,36)
     Assistant director, script supervisor, casting director, then writer, director, actress and art director.
26. **Di Marino, Vincenzo** (13,27,34,35,48)
     Producer. Founding member of Artimagiche.
27. **Di Pace, Mario** (12,16–3,20,24)
     Production designer.
28. **Di Terlizzi, Enzo** (7,10,11,24,26,30,33)
     Assistant director.
29. **Dionisio, Sandro** (4,7,16,22,36)
     Assistant director, casting director, then writer and director.
30. **Donadio, Cristina** (5,8,14,16,21,29)
     Actress.
31. **Fiorito, Lino** (1,23,33,41,45)
     Still photographer, then art director.
32. **Fiume, Maurizio** (11,38)
     Writer, director and producer.

33. **Formisano, Gennaro** (11,16,18,22,23,26,29,31,33,36,41)
    Production assistant.
34. **Forte, Iaia** (3,5,6,8,16–1,22,23,29,49,50)
    Actress. Member of Teatri Uniti. See Figure 4.3.
35. **Franchini, Giogiò** (9,12,16–2,16–3,20,24,30,31,33,37,41,42,45,48,49)
    Editor. Partner in Megaris.
36. **Gaudino, Giuseppe** (13,27)
    Writer, director, editor and art director.
37. **Giuliano, Nicola** (7,9,10,12,16,22,26,33,36,41,45)
    Production assistant, then producer. Former member of Teatri Uniti and
    founder of Indigo Film.
38. **Iaquone, Mario** (7,10,16,22,28,36,50)
    Sound recordist.
39. **Iavarone, Franco** (4,16,28,36,46)
    Actor.
40. **Incerti, Stefano** (4,5,6,8,10,16,26)
    Production assistant and assistant director, then scriptwriter and director.
41. **Iuorio, Antonino** (4,10,20,30)
    Actor. See Figure 3.3.
42. **Lanzetta, Peppe** (7,22,33)
    Novelist, playwright, songwriter and actor.
43. **Leonardi, Silvana** (13,27,34,35,48)
    Producer. Founding member of Artimagiche.
44. **Lori, Renato** (10,16,18,26)
    Art director.
45. **Luce, Angela** (7,36)
    Actress.
46. **Luglio, Carlo** (35,47)
    Writer and director.
47. **Maglietta, Licia** (4,6,7,30)
    Actress. Member of Teatri Uniti.
48. **Magliulo, Giorgio** (1,4,11,16,20,23,24,37)
    Writer, director, production designer, assistant producer and producer.
    Former partner in An.Gio Film and Megaris.
49. **Marchitelli, Gennaro** (3,26,29,31,33,37,40,45)
    Production assistant.
50. **Mari, Pasquale** (1,4,6,7,10,11,16,22,26,33)
    Camera operator, then cinematographer. Member of Teatri Uniti.
51. **Marra, Vincenzo** (22,32,40)
    Assistant director, then writer and director.
52. **Martone, Mario** (4,6,7,16–5,22)
    Writer and director. Founding member of Teatri Uniti.

53. **Massa, Umberto** (1,19,28,39,46,50)
    Production assistant, then producer. Founder of Kubla Khan.
54. **Memoli, Bruno** (5,7,10,12,16,20,23,24,30,33,41,43,45)
    Production assistant, assistant director and casting director.
55. **Minervini, Gianni** (12,20)
    Producer. Founder of A.M.A. Film.
56. **Moraes, Silvia** (5,7,10,16,22,23,29,31,41,45,49)
    Sound editor.
57. **Moscato, Enzo** (4,5,6,9,10,14,16,42,46)
    Actor, playwright, author and singer.
58. **Muselli, Giancarlo** (4,7,11,22,31,36)
    Art director.
59. **Peluso, Vincenzo** (5–2,8,16–5,19,26)
    Actor.
60. **Pennarella, Antonio** (8,10,13,15,16,27,30,39,45)
    Actor.
61. **Personnaz, Renaud** (7,9,10,13,16,22,24,26,29,36)
    Camera operator.
62. **Piscicelli, Salvatore** (3,21)
    Writer, director, editor and producer. Founding member of Falco Film.
63. **Quadri, Jacopo** (4,6,7,10,16,22,36)
    Editor.
64. **Raboni, Metella** (4,6,7,10,16,26,30)
    Costume designer.
65. **Ragni, Lucia** (3,22,30,31,39,42,45)
    Actress.
66. **Ramondino, Fabrizia** (4,16)
    Novelist and writer.
67. **Renzi, Andrea** (4,22,33,45,48)
    Actor. Member of Teatri Uniti.
68. **Rocca, Giuseppe** (27,42)
    Writer and director.
69. **Rondanini, Daghi** (4,6,7,10,16–1,16–3,16–5,22,33,36,41,45)
    Sound recordist and music consultant. Member of Teatri Uniti.
70. **Russo, Rosa** (13,25,27,34,35)
    Assistant director, casting director and producer. Founder of Thule Film.
71. **Sabatino, Laura** (11,16,19,28,42,50)
    Scriptwriter.
72. **Santella, Valia** (1,3,4,6,7,8,9,11,12,16,22,23,29,43)
    Assistant director and script supervisor, then writer and director.
73. **Saponangelo, Teresa** (10,11,12,16–4,20–2,34,43,48)
    Actress.

74. **Serao, Lello** (4,15,16–5,19,21,22,34)
    Actor.
75. **Servillo, Toni** (4,6,16,22,30,33,41)
    Actor and theatrical director. Founding member of Teatri Uniti. See Fig. 5.2.
76. **Sorrentino, Paolo** (10,20,33,41)
    Production assistant, then writer and director.
77. **Taiuti, Tonino** (4,6,12,16,20,43)
    Actor and writer.
78. **Terracciano, Vincenzo** (19,28,50)
    Writer and director.
79. **Triola, Nando** (2,12,39)
    Actor.

Production Companies

80. **A.M.A. Film** (12,20)
    Rome; Gianni Minervini.
81. **An.Gio Film** (1,4,9)
    Rome; Antonietta De Lillo and Giorgio Magliulo.
82. **Artimagiche** (34,35,48)
    Naples; Vincenzo Di Marino and Silvana Leonardi.
83. **Falco Film** (3,21)
    Rome; Salvatore Piscicelli and Carla Apuzzo.
84. **Figli del Bronx** (47)
    Naples; Gaetano Di Vaio.
85. **Hathor Film** (5,29)
    Naples; Pappi Corsicato.
86. **Indigo Film** (33,41,45)
    Naples then Rome; Nicola Giuliano.
87. **Kubla Khan** (28,39,46,50)
    Rome; Umberto Massa.
88. **Megaris** (16,31; and as a post-production facility 9,20,23,24,31,37)
    Naples; Antonietta De Lillo and Giorgio Magliulo.
89. **Teatri Uniti** (4,6,7,10,22,36)
    Naples; Angelo Curti.
90. **Thule Film** (34,35; and as a distributor 25,27,34,35,48)
    Naples; Rosa Russo.

FILMOGRAPHY

This filmography contains those films that fulfil the criteria used in the definition of the NNC throughout this book: films that are produced by a Neapolitan company or have a predominantly Neapolitan cast and crew, which are set in Naples or deal with Neapolitan characters, and which depart significantly from conventional depictions of the city. It includes several marginal works that received little or no distribution and a number of films rarely discussed in existing accounts of the NNC. Non-fiction films, shorts and television films are not included.

The films are ordered chronologically according to copyright (where given) or censorship visa; in some cases release dates are much later and these can be found in Appendix 2. Where a film received an international theatrical or festival release, the most common English language title(s) are given in parentheses; otherwise a literal translation is provided in square brackets. The director is also listed. Films that received State funding are indicated with the letters SF.

1. **Matilda**
    1990, Antonietta De Lillo and Giorgio Magliulo, SF
2. **Vito e gli altri** (Vito and the Others)
    1991, Antonio Capuano, SF
3. **Baby Gang**
    1992, Salvatore Piscicelli, SF

4. **Morte di un matematico napoletano** (Death of a Neapolitan Mathematician)
   1992, Mario Martone, SF
5. **Libera** [Free]
   1993, Pappi Corsicato
   Episodes: 1. Aurora, 2. Carmela, 3. Libera
6. **Rasoi** [Razors]
   1993, Mario Martone
7. **L'amore molesto** (Nasty Love)
   1995, Mario Martone, SF
8. **I buchi neri** (Black Holes)
   1995, Pappi Corsicato, SF
9. **Racconti di Vittoria** [Tales of Victory/Victoria's Tales]
   1995, Antonietta De Lillo
   Episodes: 1. Pozzi d'amore, 2. In alto a sinistra, 3. Racconti di Vittoria
10. **Il verificatore** (The Meter Reader)
    1995, Stefano Incerti, SF
11. **Isotta**
    1996, Maurizio Fiume, SF
12. **Pianese Nunzio: 14 anni a maggio** (Sacred Silence/Pianese Nunzio 14 in May)
    1996, Antonio Capuano, SF (The film was unable to take advantage of the funding awarded; see p. 25 for more details.)
13. **Giro di lune tra terra e mare** [Moon Orbits Between Land and Sea]
    1997, Giuseppe Gaudino, SF
14. **Malemare**
    1997, Pasquale Marrazzo
15. **Tatuaggi** [Tattoos]
    1997, Laura Angiulli
16. **I vesuviani** (The Vesuvians)
    1997, Pappi Corsicato, Antonietta De Lillo, Antonio Capuano, Stefano Incerti and Mario Martone, SF
    Episodes: 1. La stirpe di Iana, 2. Maruzzella, 3. Sofialòren, 4. Il diavolo in bottiglia, 5. La salita
17. **Fondali notturni** [Neapolitan Backdrops]
    1998, Nino Russo, SF
18. **Il manoscritto di van Hecken** [Van Hecken's Manuscript]
    1998, Nicola De Rinaldo, SF
19. **Per tutto il tempo che ci resta** (Acts of Justice)
    1998, Vincenzo Terracciano, SF
20. **Polvere di Napoli** [The Dust of Naples]
    1998, Antonio Capuano, SF

21. **Rose e pistole** (Guns and Roses)
    1998, Carla Apuzzo, SF
22. **Teatro di guerra** (Rehearsals for War)
    1998, Mario Martone, SF
23. **Appassionate** [The Passionate Ones]
    1999, Tonino De Bernardi, SF
24. **Autunno** [Autumn]
    1999, Nina Di Majo
25. **Non con un bang** (Not with a Bang)
    1999, Mariano Lamberti, SF
26. **Prima del tramonto** [Before Sunset]
    1999, Stefano Incerti
27. **Lontano in fondo agli occhi** (Pictures Deep in One's Eyes)
    2000, Giuseppe Rocca, SF
28. **Ribelli per caso** [Rebels by Chance]
    2000, Vincenzo Terracciano
29. **Chimera**
    2001, Pappi Corsicato
30. **Luna rossa** (Red Moon)
    2001, Antonio Capuano, SF
31. **Non è giusto** (It's Not Fair)
    2001, Antonietta De Lillo, SF
32. **Tornando a casa** (Sailing Home)
    2001, Vincenzo Marra, SF
33. **L'uomo in più** (One Man Up)
    2001, Paolo Sorrentino, SF
34. **La vita degli altri** (Other People's Lives)
    2001, Nicola De Rinaldo, SF
35. **Capo Nord** (Cape North)
    2002, Carlo Luglio, SF
36. **La volpe a tre zampe** (The Three-Legged Fox)
    2002, Sandro Dionisio, SF
37. **I cinghiali di Portici** [The Wild Boars of Portici]
    2003, Diego Olivares, SF
38. **E io ti seguo** (I Will Follow)
    2003, Maurizio Fiume
39. **Pater familias** [Head of the Family]
    2003, Francesco Patierno
40. **Vento di terra** [Land Breeze]
    2003, Vincenzo Marra, SF
41. **Le conseguenze dell'amore** (The Consequences of Love)
    2004, Paolo Sorrentino

42. **Il resto di niente** [The Remains of Nothing]
    2004, Antonietta De Lillo, SF
43. **Te lo leggo negli occhi** (I Can See It in Your Eyes)
    2004, Valia Santella
44. **Fuoco su di me** [Fire at My Heart]
    2005, Lamberto Lambertini, SF
45. **La guerra di Mario** (Mario's War)
    2005, Antonio Capuano
46. **Mater natura** [Mother Nature]
    2005, Massimo Andrei
47. **Sotto la stessa luna** a.k.a. Sotto la luna di Scampia [Under the Same Moon]
    2006, Carlo Luglio
48. **Ossidiana** [Obsidian]
    2007, Silvana Maja, SF
49. **Il seme della discordia** [The Seed of Discord]
    2008, Pappi Corsicato, SF
50. **Tris di donne & abiti nuziali** (Bets and Wedding Dresses)
    2009, Vincenzo Terracciano, SF

SELECT BIBLIOGRAPHY

Addonizio, Antonio, Geremia Carrara, Roberto Chiesi, Ernesto De Simone, Roberto Lippi, Eugenia Premuda and Gianluca Roncaglia (eds) (1997), *Loro di Napoli. Il nuovo cinema napoletano 1986–1997*, Palermo: Edizioni della Battaglia.

Allum, Felia and Marco Cilento (2001a), 'Parties and Personalities: The Case of Antonio Bassolino, Former Mayor of Naples', *Regional and Federal Studies*, 11:1, Spring, pp. 1–26.

Allum, Felia and Marco Cilento (2001b), 'Antonio Bassolino: From Mayor of Naples to President of Campania', in Mario Caciagli and Alan S. Zuckerman (eds), *Italian Politics: Emerging Themes and Institutional Responses*, Oxford/New York: Berghahn, pp. 119–32.

Allum, Percy (1973), *Politics and Society in Post-War Naples*, London/New York: Cambridge University Press.

— (2001), *Il potere a Napoli: fine di un lungo dopoguerra*, Naples: L'ancora.

— (2003), *Napoli punto e a capo: partiti, politica e clientelismo. Un consuntivo*, Naples: L'ancora.

Angrisani, Silvia (2008), 'That's Camorra', *Sight and Sound*, 18:11, November, pp. 18–22.

Aprà, Adriano (ed.) (1994), *Napoletana: Images of a City*, New York/Milan: Museum of Modern Art/Fabbri.

Aprà, Adriano and Claudio Carabba (eds) (1976), *Neorealismo d'appendice: per un dibattito sul cinema popolare: il caso Matarazzo*, Rimini/Florence: Guaraldi.

Aprà, Adriano and Jean A. Gili (eds) (1994), *Naples et le cinéma*, Milan/Paris: Fabbri/Centre Georges Pompidou.

Arcagni, Simone (2006), *Dopo Carosello: il musical cinematografico italiano*, Alessandria: Falsopiano.

Archibugi, Albertina, Bruno Roberti and Francesco Suriano (1996), 'Molteplici segni: conversazione con Antonio Capuano', *Filmcritica*, 470, December, pp. 516–22.

Argentieri, Mino (ed.) (1998), *Panoramica napoletana*, Naples: Associazione Culturale G. Barattolo.

Argentieri, Mino and Dario Minutolo (2002), 'Alla riscoperta della visualità a Napoli e dintorni. Incontro con Antonio Capuano', *Cinemasessanta*, 265, pp. 28–36.

Aristarco, Guido (ed.) (1981), *Sciolti dal Giuramento: il dibattito critico-ideologico sul cinema negli anni Cinquanta*, Bari: Dedalo.

Aristofane (2005), 'Fatti e misfatti: quel impunito di Bassolino', http://www.forza-italia.it/notizie/pol_6247.htm, last accessed 4 June 2005.

Armiero, Mirella (1996), 'Antonio e gli altri', *Duel*, 33, January, pp. 33–4.

Assessorato alla cultura del comune di Roma (1979), *La città del cinema: produzione e lavoro nel cinema italiano 1930/1970*, Rome: Napoleone.

Avondola, Carlo (2002), 'Non è giusto', *Segnocinema*, 114, March–April, pp. 42–3.

Bassolino, Antonio (1996), *La repubblica delle città*, Rome: Donzelli.

Bassolino, Antonio, Francesco Ceci, Eduardo Cicelyn, Goffredo Fofi and Daniela Lepore (1996), *Verso un rinascimento napoletano. Spunti per una discussione della città*, Naples: Liguori.

Baudrillard, Jean (1983), *Simulations*, New York: Semiotext(e).

Becchi, Ada and Piero Bevilacqua (1996), 'Napoli, il Sud e la "rivoluzione comunale": conversazione con Antonio Bassolino', *Meridiana*, 26–27, pp. 203–46.

Behan, Tom (2002), *See Naples and Die: the Camorra and Organized Crime*, London/New York: I.B. Tauris.

Bello, Marisa and Stefano De Matteis (1977), 'La sceneggiata', *Scena*, 2:1, February, pp. 38–43.

Bernardini, Aldo (ed.) (1991–3), *Archivio del cinema italiano: il cinema sonoro* [3 vols], Rome: ANICA.

— (ed.) (2000), *Il cinema italiano 1930–1995: le imprese di produzione*, Rome: ANICA.

Bernardini, Aldo and Vittorio Martinelli (eds) (1986), *Titanus: la storia e tutti i film di una grande casa di produzione*, Milan: Coliseum.

Bertetto, Paolo (1981), 'Salvatore Piscicelli: l'altra faccia della sceneggiata', in *Il cinema più brutto del mondo*, Milan: Bompiani, pp. 141–5.

Bo, Fabio (1988), 'Salvatore Piscicelli: corpi e luoghi', in Franco Montini (ed.), *Una generazione in cinema: esordi ed esordienti italiani 1978–1988*, Venice: Marsilio, pp. 115–20.

Bo, Fabio and Silvana Cielo (1985), 'Venti chilometri di cinema. Conversazione con Salvatore Piscicelli', *Filmcritica*, 353, March, pp. 171–80.

Bolzoni, Francesco (1993), 'Esordio anomalo, ma non è Almodovar', *Rivista del cinematografo e delle comunicazioni sociali*, 63:6, June, p. 14.

Bondanella, Peter (1999), *Italian Cinema from Neorealism to the Present*, Northam: Roundhouse.

Braucci, Maurizio and Giovanni Zoppoli (eds) (2005), *Napoli comincia a Scampia*, Naples/Rome: L'ancora del mediterraneo.

Brunetta, Gian Piero (1993), *Storia del cinema italiano. Volume terzo: Dal neorealismo al miracolo economico 1945–1959*, Rome: Editori Riuniti.

Bruno, Giuliana (1993), *Streetwalking on a Ruined Map: Cultural Theory and the City Films of Elvira Notari*, Princeton/Oxford: Princeton University Press.

— (1997), 'City Views: The Voyage of Film Images', in David B. Clarke (ed.), *The Cinematic City*, London/New York: Routledge, pp. 46–58.

— (2005), 'Naples', in Thierry Jousse and Thierry Paquot (eds), *La Ville au cinéma: encyclopédie*, Paris: Cahiers du Cinéma, pp. 492–9.

Caldiron, Orio and Stefano Della Casa (eds) (1999), *Appassionatamente. Il mélo nel cinema italiano*, Turin: Lindau.

Caldwell, Lesley (2000), 'Imagining Naples: The Senses of the City', in Gary Bridge and Sophie Watson (eds), *A Companion to the City*, Oxford: Blackwell, pp. 55–64.

Canning, Hugh (2005), 'This Ball Lacks Bounce', *The Sunday Times*, 17 April 2005.

Capizzi, Gaetano, Aurora Fornuto and Gianni Volpi (1992), 'Il segno di un percorso', in *Isole: cinema indipendente italiano*, Turin: Pervisione, pp. 91–101.

Cappelli, Ottorino (ed.) (2003), *Potere e società a Napoli a cavallo del secolo: omaggio a Percy Allum*, Naples: Edizioni Scientifiche Italiane.

Caprara, Valerio (1985), 'I comici sotto il vulcano', in Sandro Bernardi (ed.), *Si fa per ridere, ma è una cosa seria*, Florence: La Casa Usher, pp. 51–8.

— (ed.) (1998), *Spettabile pubblico: Carosello napoletano di Ettore Giannini*, Naples: Guida.

— (2006), 'La formula Amoroso' and 'Il filone napoletano da Piscicelli al rinascimento', in *Il buono, il brutto, il cattivo: storie della storia del cinema italiano*, Naples: Guida, pp. 73–88 and 213–22.

Capuano, Antonio (1993), 'Vito e gli altri', *Dove sta Zazà*, 1, February, pp. 44–52.

— (1994), *Medea*, Sorrento: Franco Di Mauro.

Cardoni, Giovanni (1998), 'Istituito il Ministero per i beni e le attività culturali', *Cinema d'oggi*, 32:20–1, 20 November, p. 9.

Castellano, Alberto (1993), 'Benessere spaccone e kitsch', *Panoramiche*, 11–12, July-December, pp. 105–9.

— (1997a), 'Il cinema vesuviano', in Giuseppe Ghigi (ed.), *12ª settimana internazionale della critica di Venezia*, Venice/Rome/Milan: La Biennale di Venezia/Il castoro/SNCCI, pp. 95–102.

— (1997b), 'L'altro cinema napoletano. Marrazzo a Venezia con un film costato 80 milioni', in *Il mattino*, 17 August.

Catelli, Daniela (1993), 'Libera', *Panoramiche*, 6, Autumn, p. 13.

Catelli, Daniela and Luigi Boscaino (1993), 'Napoli visionaria: conversazione con Pappi Corsicato', *Panoramiche*, 6, Autumn, pp. 10–11.

Cauli, Franco (1993), 'Gli obiettivi dei giovani produttori: Colloquio con Maurizio Tini e Agnese Fontana', *Cinema d'oggi*, 27:12, 24 June, p. 8.

— (1996), 'Intervista con Gianni Minervini: due assi nella manica', *Cinema d'oggi*, 30:4, 7 March, p. 3.

Causo, Massimo (1995), 'Il verificatore', *Cineforum*, 348, October, pp. 64–8.

Cawelti, John G. (1975), *The Six-Gun Mystique*, Bowling Green, OH: Bowling Green University Popular Press.

— (1976), *Adventure, Mystery and Romance: Formula Stories as Art and Popular Culture*, Chicago, IL/London: University of Chicago Press.

Chambers, Iain (1994), 'Under Vesuvius', in *Migrancy, Culture, Identity*, London/New York: Routledge, pp. 104–7.

Chiacchiari, Federico (1996), 'Pianese Nunzio 14 anni a Maggio', *Cineforum*, 357, August, pp. 74–75.

Chiacchiari, Federico, Dora Mellone, Demetrio Salvi, Giuseppe Gariazzo, Giacomo Caruso, Giona A. Nazzaro, Lella Tricarico and Anna Pellegrini (1995), 'Ricomincio da Napoli [Sentieri Selvaggi n.8]', *Cineforum*, 344, May, pp. 30–48.

Chiti, Roberto and Roberto Poppi (1991), *Dizionario del cinema italiano. Vol. 2. I film dal 1945 al 1959*, Rome: Gremese.

Cianfarani, Carmine (1997), 'Ripresa condizionata', *Cinema d'oggi*, 31:1, 16 January, p. 1

Comer, Brooke (1997), 'Antonio Capuano's Pianese Nunzio: 14 in May', *American Cinematographer*, 78:2, February, pp. 123–4.

'Conferenza stampa: le cifre della stagione', *Cinema d'oggi*, 32:13, 30 June 1998, p. 3.

'Considerazioni del Ministro Tognoli sulla situazione del cinema italiano', *Cinema d'oggi*, 25:9, 23 May 1991, p. 3.

Corsi, Barbara (2001), *Con qualche dollaro in meno. Storia economica del cinema italiano*, Rome: Editori Riuniti.

Corsi, Barbara and Claudio Zanchi (2000), 'Attrazione fatale tra film e città', *Il giornale dello spettacolo*, 56:2, 21 January, p. 12.

Cozzi, Emilio (2004), 'Gente che tiene poche parole', *Cineforum*, 436, July, pp. 11–14.

Crespi, Alberto (2004), 'Soffia un duro Vento di terra nell'ottimo film di Marra', *L'Unità*, 22 September.

Curcio, Alessandra and Valeria Bonamassa (2004), 'Una "luna rossa" per "Due soldi di felicità": Il film popolare napoletano degli anni cinquanta', *Cinemasessanta*, 279, September-October, pp. 65–81.

Curti, Roberto (2006), 'Tutti figli di Mammasantissima', in *Italia odia. Il cinema poliziesco italiano*, Turin: Lindau, pp. 255–84.

Daney, Serge (1980), 'Schroeter et Naples', *Cahiers du cinéma*, 307, January, pp. 28–9.

De Crescenzo, Maria Cristina (ed.) (1995), *Napoli, una città nel cinema*, Naples: Ministero per i beni culturali ed ambientali/Biblioteca universitaria di Napoli.

De Matteis, Stefano (1991), *Lo specchio della vita. Napoli: antropologia della città del teatro*, Bologna: Il Mulino.

De Sanctis, Pierpaolo, Domenico Monetti and Luca Pallanch (eds) (2008), *Non solo Gomorra. Tutto il cinema di Matteo Garrone*, Cantalupo in Sabina: Edizioni Sabinae.

Detassis, Piera (1987), 'Piscicelli e l'articolo 28', *Cineforum*, 263, April, pp. 51–3.

Dines, Nick (2004), 'Contested Claims to Public Space: the Re-imaging of Naples and the Case of Piazza del Plebiscito', in Robert Lumley and John Foot (eds), *Italian Cityscapes: Culture and Urban Change in Contemporary Italy*, Exeter: Exeter University Press, pp. 114–26.

Eco, Umberto (1983), 'Postmodernism, Irony, the Enjoyable', in *Reflections on The Name of the Rose*, London: Secker & Warburg, pp. 65–72.

Edelman, Murray Jacob (1985), *The Symbolic Uses of Politics*, Urbana/Chicago, IL: University of Illinois Press.

Emiliani, Simone (2003), 'Pater familias', *Cineforum*, 425, May, pp. 76–7.

Faldini, Franca and Goffredo Fofi (eds) (1979), *L'avventurosa storia del cinema italiano raccontata dai suoi protagonisti 1935–1959*, Milan: Feltrinelli.

Ferzetti, Fabio (1983), 'Conversazione con Salvatore Piscicelli', *Filmcritica*, 331, January, pp. 34–46.

'Film Commission anche in Toscana', *Cinema d'oggi*, 34:5, 15 March 2000, p. 7.

Fiore, Enrico (2002), *Il rito, l'esilio e la peste: percorsi nel nuovo teatro napoletano: Manlio Santanelli, Annibale Ruccello, Enzo Moscato*, Milan: Ubulibri.

Fofi, Goffredo (1977), 'La sceneggiata uccisa dalla storia e dai neofiti', *Scena*, 2:1, February, pp. 44–8.

— (1990), *La grande recita*, Naples: Colonnese.

Foglia, Paolo, Ernesto Mazzetti and Nicola Tranfaglia (1995), *Napoli ciak: le origini del cinema a Napoli*, Naples: Colonnese.

Francia di Celle, Stefano and Sergio Toffetti (1995), *Dalle lontane province: il cinema di Tonino De Bernardi*, Turin: Lindau.

Frezza, Gino (2005), 'Contrabbandieri, guappi e caschetti: i film napoletani', in Vito Zagarrio (ed.), *Storia del cinema italiano vol. XIII: 1977/1985*, Venice/Rome: Marsilio/Centro sperimentale di cinematografia, pp. 444–54.

Fusco, Gaetano (2006), *Le mani sullo schermo. Il cinema secondo Achille Lauro*, Naples: Liguori.

Garofalo, Marcello (1993), 'Libera', *Segnocinema*, 62, July-August, pp. 35–6.

— (1995), 'I buchi neri', *Segnocinema*, 75, September-October, pp. 92–3.

Gendrault, Camille (2007a), 'Naples: aux détours d'un cliché', in Hélène Menegaldo and Gilles Menegaldo (eds), *Les Imaginaires de la ville: regards croisés*, Rennes: Presses Universitaires de Rennes, pp. 277–90.

— (2007b), 'La Ville métisse. Naples, l'ailleurs du cinéma italien', in Laurent Creton and Kristian Feigelson (eds), *Théorème 10: Villes cinématographiques, ciné-lieux*, Paris: Presses Sorbonnes Nouvelle.

— (2009), 'Naples: repenser la ville à partir de la qualité des frontières internes', *Espaces et sociétés*, 138, 2009/3, pp. 85–97.

Genette, Gérard (1980), *Narrative Discourse: an Essay in Method*, Ithaca, NY: Cornell University Press

Gesù, Sebastiano (ed.) (1993), *La Sicilia e il cinema*, Catania: Giuseppe Maimone.

Gledhill, Christine (2007), 'Melodrama', in Pam Cook (ed.), *The Cinema Book [3rd edition]*, London: BFI, pp. 316–25.

Goddard, Victoria A. (1997), *Gender, Family and Work in Naples*, London: Berg.

Grano, Enzo (1976), *La sceneggiata*, Naples: Attività bibliografica editoriale.

— (1996), *Cent'anni di cinema napoletano e dintorni*, Naples: Bellini.

Grano, Enzo and Vittorio Paliotti (1969), *Napoli nel cinema*, Naples: Azienda Autonoma Soggiorno e Turismo.

Gribaudi, Gabriella (1999), *Donne, uomini, famiglie: Napoli nel novecento*, Naples: L'ancora.

Higson, Andrew (1989), 'The Concept of National Cinema', *Screen*, 30:4, Autumn, pp. 36–46.

Hutcheon, Linda (1989), *The Politics of Postmodernism*, London/New York: Routledge.

Iaccio, Pasquale (1991), 'Cinema e mezzogiorno', in *Storia del mezzogiorno vol. 14: la cultura contemporanea*, Naples: Edizioni del sole, pp. 323–56.

— (1998), 'Guerra e dopoguerra nella Napoli cinematografica', in *Cinema e storia: percorsi, immagini, testimonianze*, Naples: Liguori, pp. 87–127.

— (1999), 'Anni difficili: la riscoperta del Sud nel cinema del secondo dopoguerra', *Nord e Sud*, 45:6, November-December, pp. 131–46.

— (ed.) (2000), *Nord e Sud, 47:4: Napoli e cinema (1896–2000)*, Naples: Edizioni scientifiche italiane.

— (2002), *Il mezzogiorno tra cinema e storia: ricordi e testimonianze*, Naples: Liguori.

La Penna, Daniela (2005), 'The Cinema of Giuseppe M. Gaudino and Edoardo Winspeare: Between Tradition and Experiment', in William Hope (ed.), *Italian Cinema: New Directions*, Bern: Peter Lang, pp. 175–97.

La Trecchia, Patrizia (2003), *Art Under Vesuvius: Cultural Practices in Contemporary Naples*, PhD thesis, Philadelphia, PA: University of Pennsylvania.

— (2009), 'Sites of "Glocal" Representations and Artistic Resistance: the Neapolitan Urban Imaginary in Antonio Capuano's *Sacred Silence*', *Studies in European Cinema*, 6:1, pp. 31–45.

Landy, Marcia (ed.) (1991), *Imitations of Life: a Reader on Film and Television Melodrama*, Detroit, MI: Wayne State University Press.

Liggeri, Domenico (1996), 'Gli altri siamo noi', *Duel*, 33, January, p. 35.

London Film Festival Catalogue (1995), p. 82.

Lori, Sergio (1996), *Da Totò a Troisi*, Rome: Newton & Compton.

Lucente, Giovanna Corrias (1997), 'Articolo 28, assolto il Comitato Credito perché il fatto non sussiste', *Cinema d'oggi*, 31:17–18, 15 October, p. 3.

Lucisano, Fulvio (1998), 'Considerazioni sui dati dell'industria cinematografica italiana per il 1999', *Cinema d'oggi*, 32:13, 30 June, p. 1.

— (2001), 'Sei proposte per il cinema italiano', *Cinema d'oggi*, 35:3–4, 25 February, pp. 4–5.

Lumley, Robert and Jonathan Morris (eds) (1997), *The New History of the Italian South: The Mezzogiorno Revisited*, Exeter: University of Exeter Press.

Lyotard, Jean-François (1984), *The Postmodern Condition: A Report on Knowledge*, Manchester: Manchester University Press.

McIntyre, Steve (1985), 'National Film Cultures: Politics and Peripheries', *Screen*, 26:1, January-February, pp. 66–78.

Mancino, Anton Giulio (1992), 'Antonio Capuano: i margini della commedia', *Cinecritica*, 15:24–5, January-June, pp. 41–9.

— (2000), 'Lontano in fondo agli occhi', *Cineforum*, 399, November, p. 49.

Marangi, Michele (2000), 'Rose e pistole', *Cineforum*, 397, August-September, pp. 50–1.

Marcus, Millicent (2007), 'In Memoriam: The Neorealist Legacy in the Contemporary Sicilian Anti-Mafia Film', in Laura E. Ruberto and Kristi M. Wilson (eds), *Italian Neorealism and Global Cinema*, Detroit, MI: Wayne State University Press, pp. 290–30.

Marlow-Mann, Alex (2009), 'The Tears of Naples' Daughters: Re-Interpreting the *Sceneggiata* in Mario Martone's *L'amore molesto*', *The Italianist*, 29, pp. 199–213.

— (forthcoming 2010), 'Character Engagement and Alienation in the Cinema of Paolo Sorrentino', in William Hope (ed.), *Italian Film Directors in the New Millennium*, Cambridge: Cambridge Scholars, pp. 161–73.

— (forthcoming 2011), 'The Italian Musical: a Nonexistent Genre?', in Corey Creekmur and Linda Mokdad (eds), *The International Film Musical*, Edinburgh: Edinburgh University Press.

— (forthcoming 2012), 'Subjectivity and the Ethnographic Gaze in Antonio Capuano's *Vito e gli altri*', in Roger Pitt and Danielle Hipkins (eds), *The Child in Italian Film*, Bern: Peter Lang.

Martinelli, Vittorio (1986), 'Sotto il sole di Napoli', in Gian Piero Brunetta and Davide Turconi (eds), *Cinema e film: la meravigliosa storia dell'arte contemporanea (vol. 2)*, Rome: Armando Curcio, pp. 366–70.

Martini, Giulio (1997), *Patchwork: 100 anni di cinema in Italia. Un viaggio attraverso le regioni*, Milan: Finzioni/Soley Gruppo Editoriale Informatico.

Martini, Giulio and Guglielmina Morelli (eds) (1997), *Patchwork due. Geografia del nuovo cinema italiano*, Milan: Il Castoro.

Martone, Mario (1996), *L'amore molesto: sceneggiatura dall'omonimo romanzo di Elena Ferrante*, Mantova: Circolo del Cinema di Mantova/Comune di Mantova.

— (1998), *Teatro di guerra: un diario*, Milan: Bompiani.

— (2004), *Chiaroscuri. Scritti tra cinema e teatro*, Milan: Bompiani.

Masi, Stefano (1979a), 'Il cinema regionale della sceneggiata fra marginalità e autodistruzione', *Cineforum*, 184, May, pp. 266–81.

— (1979b), 'Nel regno di Napoli', *Cineforum*, 188, October, pp. 622–9.

— (1982), 'Come ti nazionalizzo la Napoli verace dei film di Merola', *Cineforum*, 203, April, pp. 21–9.

Masi, Stefano and Mario Franco (1988), *Il mare, la luna, i coltelli: per una storia del cinema muto napoletano*, Naples: Tullio Pironti.

Masoni, Tullio (1992), 'Morte di un matematico napoletano', *Cineforum*, 318, October, pp. 62–5.

Masoni, Tullio, Francesco Cattaneo, Anton Giulio Mancino and Emilio Cozzi (2008), 'Tracce di pietà nel regno del male', *Cineforum*, 475, June, pp. 6–17.

Mauro, Sandro (2003), 'Pater familias', *Segnocinema*, 121, May-June, pp. 63–4.

Melanco, Mirco (2005), 'Paesaggi, passaggi e passioni. Le trasformazioni del paesaggio sotto il Vesuvio nello scrigno del cinema (dal 1930 a oggi)', in *Paesaggi, passaggi e passioni. Come il cinema italiano ha raccontato le trasformazioni del paesaggio dal sonoro ad oggi*, Naples: Liguori, pp. 107–67.

Migliaccio, Gianni (1985), 'Intervista ad Amoroso', *Il nuovo spettatore*, 6:10, December, pp. 49–70.

Morreale, Emiliano (1996), *Lampi sull'isola: Il nuovo cinema siciliano (1988–1996)*, Palermo: Battaglia.

— (2001), 'Il limbo dei desideri', *Cineforum*, 404, May, pp. 30–3.

— (2006), 'Giocatori tenaci in uno stadio vuoto', *Cineforum*, 457, August-September, pp. 23–4.

— (2008), 'Mondo Camp e famiglie di plastica', *Cineforum*, 478, October, pp. 32–4.

Morreale, Emiliano and Dario Zonta (2009), 'Nina Di Majo: i borghesi, gli intellettuali', in *Cinema vivo: quindici registi a confronto*, Rome: Edizioni dell'Asino, pp. 55–64.

Neale, Steve (1990), 'Questions of Genre', *Screen*, 31:1, Spring, pp. 45–66.

O'Healy, Áine (1999a), 'Revisiting the Belly of Naples: the Body and the City in the Films of Mario Martone', *Screen*, 40:3, Autumn, pp. 239–56.

— (1999b), 'Violence and the Erotic in Salvatore Piscicelli's *Immacolata e Concetta*', *Romance Languages Annual*, 11, pp. 292–6.

Ornanni, Roberto (1995), *Napoli nel cinema*, Rome: Newton Compton.

Orsini, Alessandra (2005), *Città e conflitto: Mario Martone regista della tragedia greca*, Rome: Bulzoni.

Padovan, Igor Molino (1996), 'Intervista a Pappi Corsicato', *Amarcord*, 1:1, February-March, pp. 59–63.

Palestino, Maria Federica (2003), *MiraNapoli. La costruzione dell'immagine urbana negli anni '90*, Naples: Clean.

Pandolfi, Vito (ed.) (1958), *Copioni da quattro soldi*, Firenze: Luciano Landi.

Papa, Armando (1976), 'Gli equivoci di un dibattito', *Cinemasessanta*, 112, November, pp. 6–8.

Pasolini, Pier Paolo (1999), '[La Napoletanità]', in *Saggi sulla politica e sulla società*, Milan: Mondadori, pp. 230–1.

Pasquale, Alberto (1997), 'Una stagione in crescita "sconvolta" dal ciclone', *Il giornale dello spettacolo: Borsa Film*, 53:22, 18 July, p. 16.

Pellegrini, Valerio, Dario Minutolo, Gianfranco Cercone, Angelo Pizzuto, Sergio Minutolo, Pasquale Iaccio, Quirino Di Paolo, Daniele Villa and Pappi Corsicato (1996), 'Laboratorio partenopeo', *Cinemasessanta*, 228, March-April, pp. 19–53.

Petitti, Giovanni (1998), 'Un film stratificato', *Cineforum*, 378: October, pp. 33–4.

Pezzotta, Alberto (2001), 'Chimera', *Segnocinema*, 109, May-June, pp. 36–7.

Pia Fusco, Maria (1998), 'Il mio film su Eleonora la rivoluzionaria di Napoli', *La Repubblica*, 19 July.

Piccolo, Francesco (1998), 'La Napoli amara di Martone', *Il corriere del Mezzogiorno*, 23 April.

Preziosi, Adelina (1996), 'Pianese Nunzio: 14 anni a Maggio', *Segnocinema*, 82, November-December, pp. 35–6.

Ramondino, Fabrizia and Andreas Friedrich Müller (eds) (1989), *Dadapolis: caleidoscopio napoletano*, Turin: Einaudi.

Ramondino, Fabrizia and Mario Martone (1992), *Morte di un matematico napoletano*, Milan: Ubulibri.

Ranucci, Georgette and Stefanella Ughi (eds) (1995), *Mario Martone*, Rome: Dino Audino.

Rappaport, Roy A. (1999), *Ritual and Religion in the Making of Humanity*, Cambridge: Cambridge University Press.

Rascaroli, Laura (2003), 'A Present and True City? Naples in Mario Martone's Cinema', in Ewa Mazierska and Laura Rascaroli (eds), *From Moscow to Madrid: Postmodern Cities, European Cinema*, London/New York: I. B. Tauris, pp. 51–72.

Ravveduto, Marcello (2007), *Napoli . . . Serenata calibro 9. Storia e immagini della camorra tra cinema, sceneggiata e neomelodici*, Naples: Liguori.

Repetto, Monica and Carlo Tagliabue (eds) (2000), *La vita è bella? Il cinema italiano alla fine degli anni novanta e il suo pubblico*, Milan: Il Castoro.

Ritzer, George (2000), *The McDonaldization of Society*, Thousand Oaks, CA: Pine Forge.

Roberti, Bruno (1992a), 'Rovine circolari', *Filmcritica*, 424, April, pp. 169–71.

— (1992b), 'Conversazione con Mario Martone', *Filmcritica*, 424, April, pp. 172–81.

Robertson, Roland (1995), 'Glocalisation: Time-Space and Homogeneity-Heterogeneity', in Mike Featherstone, Scott Lash and Roland Robertson (eds), *Global Modernities*, London: Sage, pp. 25–44.

Runcini, Romolo (1989), 'Tempo libero e cultura popolare a Napoli: il caso della sceneggiata', in Giovanni Bechelloni (ed.), *Il mutamento culturale in Italia (1945–1985)*, Naples: Liguori, pp. 207–25.

Salvi, Demetrio (1993), 'Intervista a Pappi Corsicato', *Cineforum*, 324, May, pp. 59–60.

— (1997), 'La stirpe di Antonio', *Cineforum*, 367, August, pp. 9–10.

— (1998), 'Teatri di guerra napoletani', *Cineforum*, 374, May, p. 20.

Scarfò, Giovanni (1990), *Calabria nel cinema*, Cosenza: Periferia.

— (1999), *Cinema e mezzogiorno*, Cosenza: Periferia.

Scarlini, Luca (1996), 'Geografie del desiderio: note a margine del cinema di Pappi Corsicato', *Amarcord*, 1:1, February-March, p. 58.

Schneider, Jane (ed.) (1998), *Italy's 'Southern Question': Orientalism in One Country*, Oxford/New York: Berg.

Scialò, Pasquale (1995), *La canzone napoletana dalle origini ai giorni nostri*, Rome: Newton Compton.

— (ed.) (2002), *Sceneggiata: rappresentazioni di un genere popolare*, Naples: Guida.

Sesti, Mario (1991), 'Vito e gli altri', *Cinecritica*, 14, September, pp. 46–52.

Sklan, Carole (1996), 'Peripheral Visions: Regionalism, Nationalism, Internationalism', in Albert Moran (ed.), *Film Policy: International, National and Regional Perspectives*, London/New York: Routledge, pp. 234–48.

Small, Pauline (1999), 'Mario Martone's *L'amore molesto*: Desperately Seeking Delia', *The Italianist*, 19, pp. 298–317.

— (2000), 'Constructing Identity in Neapolitan Cinema', *Journal of the Institute of Romance Studies*, 8, pp. 195–210.

Sorlin, Pierre (1996), *Italian National Cinema 1896–1996*, London/New York: Routledge.

Spinazzola, Vittorio (1974), 'Il filone napoletano', in *Cinema e pubblico: lo spettacolo filmico in Italia 1945–1965*, Milan: Bompiani, pp. 176–89.

Tassi, Fabrizio (1998), 'Il mito e la storia s'incrociano col reale', *Cineforum*, 378, October, pp. 30–33.

— (2006), 'Un bambino in trincea', *Cineforum*, 453, April, pp. 23–4.

Tönnies, Ferdinand (1955), *Community and Association*, London: Routledge & Kegan Paul.

Troianelli, Enza (1989), *Elvira Notari: pioniera del cinema napoletano (1875–1946)*, Rome: Euroma.

Vecchi, Paolo (2002), 'Panorami familiari in minore', *Cineforum*, 415, June, pp. 37–40.

Verdicchio, Pasquale (2007), '*'O cuorp' 'e Napule*: Naples and the Cinematographic Body of Culture' in Laura E. Ruberto and Kristi M. Wilson (eds), *Italian Neorealism and Global Cinema*, Detroit, MI: Wayne State University Press, pp. 259–89.

Villari, Pasquale (1887), *Le lettere meridionali*, Florence: Le Monnier.

Wagstaff, Christopher (1992), 'A Forkful of Westerns: Industry, Audiences and the Italian Western', in Richard Dyer and Ginette Vincendeau (eds), *Popular European Cinema*, New York/London: Routledge, pp. 245–61.

Wood, Mary P. (2003), '"Clandestini": the "Other" Hiding in the Italian Body Politic', in Guido Rings and Rikki Morgan-Tamosunas (eds), *European Cinema: Inside Out. Images of the Self and the Other in Postcolonial European Film*, Heidelberg: Universitätsverlag Winter, pp. 95–106.

Zagarrio, Vito (1997), 'Immacolata e Concetta di Salvatore Piscicelli. Sceneggiate e scene madri', in Lino Micciché (ed.), *Il cinema del riflusso. Film e cineasti italiani degli anni '70*, Venice: Marsilio, pp. 444–52.

— (1998a), *Cinema italiano anni novanta*, Venice: Marsilio.

— (1998b), 'Il riferimento di base è l'emozione: incontro con Giuseppe Gaudino', *Cinemasessanta*, 240, March-April, pp. 27–32.

— (1999), '"Giro di lune" come un portoghese sull'autobus', in Vito Zagarrio (ed.), *In nome del cinema*, Milan: Il Ponte, pp. 188–95.

— (ed.) (2000), *Il cinema della transizione. Scenari italiani degli anni Novanta*, Venice: Marsilio.

— (ed.) (2006), *La meglio gioventù: nuovo cinema italiano 2000–2006*, Venice: Marsilio.

Zambetti, Sandro (1966), 'Il mezzogiorno d'Italia nel cinema', *Cineforum*, 57, September, pp. 539–64.

Zanetti, Alberto (2001), 'La doppia vita di Antonio', *Cineforum*, 409, November, pp. 63–5.

Zocaro, Ettore (2001), 'Venezia e il "nuovo cinema napoletano"', *Cinema d'oggi*, 35:14–15, 30 August, pp. 15–16.

229

INDEX